SO-AXO-178

Praise for
Alan Haft and *You Can Never Be Too Rich*

"Wildly imaginative, completely original, and extraordinarily effective: That's how I'd summarize my experience with Alan and his book."

—Mike S., CA

"This guy is for real and his book is a must read. We're living a very comfortable life, and our principal seems to increase every month. Now, that's what we call retirement!"

—Mark and Lees F., MA

"Forget the traditional financial advisors out there who all seem to preach the same thing. One meeting with Alan and his team is all it took for me to re-direct my lifelong investment strategies and I'm confident after reading his book you'll do the same for yourself."

—Barbara G., CA

"I've had several advisors before Alan, and thanks to him and his group, my eyes have been opened to a long list of highly innovative strategies I never knew existed."

—Brad H., NJ

"Honest to a fault, sharp, dedicated, and extraordinarily caring, we've known Alan for years, have followed the advice in his book, and, as a result, we're experiencing more success with our investments than we ever have before."

—Robert and Pauline L., CA

"A+ guy, A+ book. This entire package is a complete winner!"

—Michael and Lynn H., FL

"Alan is our fifth financial advisor, and we have finally struck gold. *You Can Never Be Too Rich* is a bible for investors and we happily recommend it to friends and family."

—Peter and Diane M., VT

"Having found someone like Alan we can trust implicitly, we couldn't be happier in our retirement."

—Lou and Nan Z., FL

"Alan and his company saved my financial life, and I'm sure the book will save yours."

—Brad G., CA

"This is great! Now I have a handy, entertaining, and informative book from Alan to supplement his excellent personalized advice and guidance."

—*Irene S., FL*

"We made a brilliant decision in choosing Alan as our financial advisor because he is accessible, professional, knowledgeable, dedicated to our success, and we are eternally grateful for it."

—*Anthony and Natasha K., FL*

"We have always felt that the advice and ideas Alan has implemented for us are totally focused on what is in our best interest. Such a thing is very hard to find in a financial advisor and now you can have it as well by reading his book."

—*Frank and Betty B., FL*

"With so many products on the market and no shortage of advisors to choose from, we're fortunate we were pointed in Alan's direction and that we now have his book to remind us of all the creative things he has done for us."

—*Ray and Donna L., FL*

"We are very happy to have Alan and his company as our financial advisors, and this book will share with you all their unique investment ideas that have fared quite well for us over the years."

—*Henry and Judy L., CA*

"Looking to get rich quick? This book is not for you. But if you are looking for smart, creative, and highly efficient investment advice, this book is definitely what you're looking for."

—*Greg and Ellen S., CA*

"Alan tells it like it is. His advice has made a huge impact on my portfolio. *You Can Never Be Too Rich* is a must read."

—*Leslie G., GA*

"Alan turned my financial life around. His advice is spectacular. I trust him immensely and so will you after reading *You Can Never Be Too Rich.*"

—*Jim O., NC*

"Alan treats us as if we're his only clients, putting our interests before his own. He is truly not just a financial advisor but also a friend, and we highly recommend his book."

—*Sonia S. and Beverly R., NY*

You Can Never
Be Too Rich

ESSENTIAL INVESTING ADVICE YOU
CANNOT AFFORD TO OVERLOOK

Alan Haft

John Wiley & Sons, Inc.

Copyright © 2008 by Alan Haft. All rights reserved.

Published by John Wiley & Sons, Inc., Hoboken, New Jersey.
Published simultaneously in Canada.

Wiley Bicentennial Logo: Richard J. Pacifico.

No part of this publication may be reproduced, stored in a retrieval system, or
transmitted in any form or by any means, electronic, mechanical, photocopying,
recording, scanning, or otherwise, except as permitted under Section 107 or 108
of the 1976 United States Copyright Act, without either the prior written
permission of the Publisher, or authorization through payment of the appropriate
per-copy fee to the Copyright Clearance Center, Inc., 222 Rosewood Drive, Danvers,
MA 01923, (978) 750-8400, fax (978) 646-8600, or on the Web at www.copyright.com.
Requests to the Publisher for permission should be addressed to the Permissions
Department, John Wiley & Sons, Inc., 111 River Street, Hoboken, NJ 07030, (201)
748-6011, fax (201) 748-6008, or online at http://www.wiley.com/go/permissions.

Limit of Liability/Disclaimer of Warranty: While the publisher and author have
used their best efforts in preparing this book, they make no representations
or warranties with respect to the accuracy or completeness of the contents of
this book and specifically disclaim any implied warranties of merchantability
or fitness for a particular purpose. No warranty may be created or extended
by sales representatives or written sales materials. The advice and strategies
contained herein may not be suitable for your situation. You should consult with
a professional where appropriate. Neither the publisher nor author shall be liable
for any loss of profit or any other commercial damages, including but not limited
to special, incidental, consequential, or other damages.

For general information on our other products and services or for technical support,
please contact our Customer Care Department within the United States at
(800) 762-2974, outside the United States at (317) 572-3993 or fax (317) 572-4002.

Wiley also publishes its books in a variety of electronic formats. Some content that
appears in print may not be available in electronic formats. For more information
about Wiley products, visit our Web site at www.wiley.com.

Library of Congress Cataloging-in-Publication Data:

Haft, Alan, 1966-
    You can never be too rich : essential investing advice you cannot afford to
overlook / Alan Haft.
        p.   cm.
    Includes bibliographical references and indexes.
    ISBN 978-0-470-13978-3 (cloth)
        1. Investments.   2. Retirement income—Planning.   I. Title.
HG4521.H2228   2008
332.6—dc22

                                                                    2007018532

Printed in the United States of America.
10   9   8   7   6   5   4   3   2   1

Contents

Preface

> **Rich,** *adjective:* having wealth or great possessions; abundantly supplied with resources, means, or funds; wealthy: *a rich man; a rich nation.*

That's Webster's definition of the word. What's yours?

To many people, the word immediately brings up thoughts of people such as Bill Gates, Donald Trump, Steven Spielberg, and Oprah Winfrey. On the other end of the spectrum, to someone like the mountainous client of mine I'll refer to as "Chicago Hank," the word has nothing to do with money but everything to do with moments spent cradling his tiny granddaughter in one hand while reading *Green Eggs and Ham* from the other.

Given that everyone will have his or her own definition of the word, I believe it is most efficient to define *rich* as: having an abundance of whatever it takes to provide one with inner peace. "Whatever it takes" could mean lots of money or, in Chicago Hank's mind, it could have virtually nothing to do with the subject of money.

However, given my role as an investment advisor, the title of this book, and my sacred oath to the publisher, I'd certainly disappoint many if I spent the next several hundred pages discussing the richness of spending time with those you adore, early-morning walks, or any of life's other simplistic pleasures that no amount of money could ever buy.

Keeping this in mind, you'll have to excuse me while for the remainder of this book I turn my attention to Webster's more capitalistic and materialistic definition of the word. After all, enjoying life's most simplistic, no-cost pleasures would be a bit challenging if one was dirt broke.

With our journey about to begin, it's also important to understand that I hardly place the value of my life, or any one else's for that matter, on the amount of money they have. In fact, of the seemingly thousands of people I have spoken to about their finances, I can honestly say the ones I've met who seem to enjoy life the most rarely, if ever, find deep inner peace, happiness, and fulfillment from the amount of money they have in their checking accounts.

I hope the pages that follow will in one form or another assist you in realizing *both* Webster and Chicago Hank's view of the word: acquiring whatever amount of money it takes for you to feel true inner peace so that you can best enjoy special moments reading *Green Eggs and Ham* or whatever else one's peaceful heart desires.

ALAN HAFT

Newport Coast, California
September 2007

Acknowledgments

The fingerprints of endless friends, family, clients, and business associates are on every page of this book, and I sincerely thank them all for their feedback, wisdom, and support.

Very special thanks to my agent Jackie Meyer at Whimsy for making this happen; Debra Englander and my friends over at John Wiley & Sons; Rick Frishman, Jared Sharpe, and everyone else at Planned TV Arts; 10e20 for their wisdom of the Web; IRA guru Denise Appleby; estate planning whiz Mark McWilliams; and, of course, my partners and the entire gang back at the office for their fearless support and hard work.

Many thanks to Mom and Dad for their boundless love, support, and friendship and to my big sister Sheryl, who I'll spend the rest of my life looking up to.

And last, but never least, many thanks to my three beauties—Stace, Lou, and Ray for their endless love and patience, especially while I wrote this book.

A. H.

Disclaimer

Everyone's personal situation is uniquely different. Investment, insurance, tax, and estate planning concepts addressed during the course of the book are complex subjects and should therefore be construed as examples only. With this in mind, please be sure to consult with a qualified tax, estate, and/or investment advisor before any action is taken.

In addition, case studies mentioned in this book are for example only, and for confidentiality purposes, names have been modified and may be a composite of several actual individuals.

INTRODUCTION

Hollywood and the
Art of Investing

As an investment advisor, speaker, and columnist, I share one fundamental goal with my many clients, audiences, and readers: the goal of creating simple, efficient, and powerful investment strategies. Everyone wants them. Everyone needs them. But where does one start?

For me, after spending years as a child helping family in an investment advisory business, my official start was surprisingly in none other than the world of Hollywood. It was within the powerhouse studios of Disney, Universal, and Warner Brothers that I played an integral role in some of the largest movie productions around, working alongside actors, directors, and producers such as Tom Cruise, Tom Hanks, Oliver Stone, Dolly Parton, Barry Levinson, Michael J. Fox, and many others.

What I clearly found was that beneath the power of creativity there was a strong foundation of highly efficient financial strategies. Nowhere was this more apparent than when I later partnered with my lifelong close friend, the indomitable Oscar-nominated actor James Woods, to launch a successful production company at Universal Studios.

Those were transformative years, the years where I sharply honed a wide variety of highly efficient financial strategies.

Like a great movie with powerful legs, the financial experience I had in Hollywood propelled me to launch a multinational corporation, which I helped take public on the international stock exchanges.

The experience in Hollywood also taught me the importance of not only making financial strategies as efficient and riskless as possible, but also making them understandable and simple. Having preached investing strategies in front of thousands of people all across the country in places such as Donald Trump's Mara Largo and countless other venues, thanks to Hollywood, my message remains concise, to the point, understandable, and—I'm confident—quite effective.

Hollywood taught me not only about the absolute critical importance of meticulous and hard-core planning, but also quite a bit about the power of the written word. My work has frequently attracted the attention of the national media, with requests for interviews by media outlets including *BusinessWeek, Forbes, Money Magazine,* the *Chicago Tribune,* the *Los Angeles Times,* the *Miami Herald,* and many others.

The more interviews I did, the more questions I answered, and the more investment engines I tuned up, the more I realized one thing remained constant: Many people were in need of assistance, and I passionately and genuinely enjoyed helping them out.

Now, more than ever before, I find people are on their own, swimming against a vicious tide where nasty creatures often lurk in the murky sea of investments. No longer is big business or the government taking care of us. If you're like most people, swimming in these unfamiliar, uncharted waters can be a frightening experience, bringing up such questions as: "Is there an easier way?" "Will I ever have enough to retire?" "Will I outlive my money?" "How can I understand all this complicated stuff?" "How can I possibly find the time to make it all work?" And one of the most common questions, "Who can I trust to keep my money safe while making sure it's growing?"

Whether it is baby boomers with several hundred thousand dollars, movie stars with a king's ransom, top executives of large corporations, members of a professional sports team, people with only a few thousand dollars to their names, or dedicated parents working real hard to make ends meet, the many people I've met may be from different walks of life, but the questions they ask and the concerns they share are often very much the same.

Not only do people need assistance, but those needing help frequently turn to advisors, and quite frankly, many of those advisors need help as well. I often find that many people, self-starters and professionals alike, make things just so darn *overcomplicated.*

In fact, as I'll show you during the course of this book, it really doesn't have to be that way. When it comes to making money in the markets and ensuring *consistent* and *sustainable* success, with rare exception, I find it does not have to be complicated for it to be efficient.

And when I remind myself of how Wall Street wants you to think of it, I often hear Kevin Spacey's voice whispering in my mind the classic line from *The Usual Suspects,* "The greatest trick the devil ever pulled off was convincing the world he doesn't exist."

When it comes to Wall Street, here's the greatest trick *that* place ever pulled off: making you believe that not only does it need to be complicated for it to be effective, but the professionals can do it far better than you.

The truth, however, is that with rare exception, very few can ever *consistently* outperform the market. What does beating the market mean? It means trying to pick individual stocks that will outperform *the market,* which is typically defined as an index, or basket, of untraded stocks representing various industries bundled together in a neat little package such as the Standard & Poor's 500, the Dow Jones Industrial Average, or the NASDAQ-100.

Have you ever heard of Leonard the Monkey? He's an orangutan that randomly picks individual stocks, and a web site out there compares his stock-picking performance to that of Jim Cramer, host of CNBC's *Mad Money.* "Who's winning?," you may ask. Not surprisingly, the orangutan is.

I'm not saying Cramer is not a sharp guy. Quite the contrary. When it comes to picking individual stocks, hands down he's one of the smartest guys around. But even that guy, who seemingly has stocks in his blood, has trouble beating the monkey, let alone the market.

Then there's a reporter from the *Wall Street Journal* who randomly throws darts at pages of stocks and compares the returns to picks from various professionals around the country. Guess who wins that game? You guessed it—the darts.

See a pattern? As far as I'm concerned, there is only one way to consistently beat the market, and that's to *be* the market. But how can you do that? How can you possibly *be* the market whereby you'll end up outperforming most professionals at their own game and at the same time make things so much easier and rewarding for yourself? It's much simpler than you may think, and you'll soon find out exactly how to do it.

In this book, you'll also find out things such as:

- A simple investment strategy that is statistically proven to outperform most of Wall Street's top fund managers.
- The insider's secret to buying low and selling high.

- All about what we refer to as the Private Pension—a simple strategy that can likely better than double your income at retirement, with a guarantee that you won't outlive it.
- An effortless way to automatically lock in your highest stock market value and later draw income from it *for the rest of your life.*
- How to identify and sell valuable hidden assets in your estate— assets that most people don't even know exist.
- How your parent(s) can potentially leave you "a free million dollars" at no cost to you or them.
- Five key secrets of investing that Wall Street, brokers, and many advisors would prefer you didn't know about.
- Hard-to-find resources that reveal hidden fees on the most popular investments.
- Certificates of deposit (CDs) that can potentially provide *double-digit* returns.
- How to potentially leave the value of your *taxable* individual retirement account (IRA) *tax-free* to heirs.
- How to invest in real estate without any of the headaches (and use your IRA money to do it).
- The biggest mistake most estate plans fail to include.
- And many other simple and effective tips that many people can use right away, including how shopping at Bloomingdale's can teach us valuable lessons about successful investing.

Bloomingdale's?

Precisely. Investment concepts can often be a tedious read, so I'm certainly going to try to put an interesting twist on all of this. One of the biggest problems many people have about trying to understand successful investing is that many of the books out there are either far too simplistic or just plain complicated, difficult, or downright boring. I've read scores of them, and if they're too simplistic, complicated, confusing, or boring to me, then presumably they're even more painful for you.

Recognizing this, I'm going to try and make otherwise complicated or boring concepts a bit more interesting. After all, has there ever been a book on investing that finds a connection between IRAs and your first kiss? Or what the neighborhood bully and his foul balls can teach us about diversification? Has there ever been a book on investing that shows us why the New York Yankees are similar to some of the biggest blunders many people make with their money?

And what about the valuable lessons television shows such as *Grey's Anatomy* can teach us?

If I can make it interesting, then maybe this book will have a chance at being one of the few investment books someone actually reads cover to cover. If I can achieve my goal of making things somewhat interesting, then maybe we'll both get lucky—you'll finish my book, and along the way, if there's just one idea that makes your life a bit more successful, then at least I'll have earned an honest day's pay.

Besides, when it comes to trying to make otherwise difficult concepts interesting and easy to understand, remember: I have a little Hollywood left in me. After all, I still spend time in that place quite often, creating and tuning up all sorts of investment engines for many people out there. And while I'm there, I'm constantly reminded of how my experience in that town taught me many things about successful and efficient investing.

Having helped raise money, plan productions, and obsess over every last detail to ensure profitability, I found that the road to success in Hollywood in many ways mirrors the prudent principles of successful investing.

The programs and movies we watch on TV and in theaters are examples of either prudent decisions based on proven principles or short-lived failures hastily born of poor planning. Ironically, all it takes is a little creative insight to realize that the movies, studio executives, and high-profile actors can teach the public an awful lot about the universal laws of successful investing.

So, as a little warm-up to the concepts I'll be covering throughout the rest of the book, I figure I'll have a little fun and use a few Hollywood anecdotes as a preview of what's to come.

Turn down the lights.

Grab a box of Junior Mints.

Turn off those cell phones.

And make one last trip to the rest room.

Still with me?

Good. Then let the previews begin.

CHAPTER 1

The Top 10 Lessons Hollywood Teaches Us about Investing

As you're now likely seated in the comfort of your own private theater awaiting the feature presentation, I bring to you "The Top 10 Lessons Hollywood Teaches Us about Investing" with an extra bonus thrown in at the end.

So, raise the curtain and start the projector, because here we go.

Lesson 1: Diversification Is the Key to Success

Hollywood. The typical Hollywood studio releases somewhere around 20 films per year. Does Paramount release 20 horror films each year? Not quite; the studios are much smarter than that. Most studios cover all genres—romantic comedy, science fiction, drama, action, teenage comedy, and so on. Why? They know it's impossible to predict which genre will be hot at any given time. Some will win and some will lose, but only one thing remains certain: Reducing risk through diversification always provides the best recipe for success.

Investors. Forget the line Oliver Stone wrote for Michael Douglas in *Wall Street*. Greed is *not* good. Greed can kill you. If you need proof, ask anyone who was too heavily invested in technology during the late 1990s.

Lesson Learned. Whether it's the lineup for this year's releases or a decision on where to invest, diversification among the standard asset classes is the first rule of consistent and successful investing.

Lesson 2: It Doesn't Have to Be Complicated for It to Be Effective

Hollywood. Years ago, I pitched many film projects to studios and learned the hard way that if you can't tell your story in a few minutes or less, you'll never make it through the pitch, let alone get a movie made. Every classic movie can be summarized in a single, simple sentence. If you make it any more complicated than that, forget it; you'll never get the film made. Learn from *E.T. the Extra-Terrestrial*: "It's a story about a bunch of kids who help a stranded alien get back home." One sentence, $756 million . . . just the way Hollywood likes it.

Investors. Here's a simple sentence: The S&P 500 index typically outperforms most managed mutual funds. Period. Statistically, those who invest in the S&P 500 and nowhere else have a better chance of *consistently* making more money than those who invest in a phone book of individual stocks, which are typically complicated and quite difficult to keep track of. For those who think trading individual stocks by themselves or through professionals earns more dollars, I offer a humbling fact: There are over ten thousand mutual funds in the country. Each fund has one or more professional money managers who trade stocks all day long, trying to pick the winners. Of those managers, guess how many have successfully outperformed the static, untraded, mindless S&P 500 more than 10 years in a row? Answer: just one—the legendary Bill Miller from fund company Legg Mason.

Lesson Learned. While it makes little sense to put all of your money in one place such as the S&P 500, the concept prevails: You don't need a complicated portfolio for it to be effective. Some of the most successful and rewarding investment engines I have ever witnessed, built or tuned up are extremely simple to understand, easy to monitor, and more rewarding than most people can possibly imagine.

Lesson 3: It's the Details That Count

Hollywood. James Woods once told me that while shooting the epic *Once Upon a Time in America*, legendary director Sergio Leone shot a few dozen takes of a dinner scene just to get a spoon in the right place. Screenwriter Peter Shaffer wrote a few dozen full-length drafts of his masterpiece *Amadeus*, then another dozen or so to refine it. Writer/director Cameron Crowe once said he spent well over a year doing absolutely nothing but writing one of the truly great screenplays in modern years—*Jerry Maguire*.

Investors. A financial advisor touts an appealing investment. It sounds decent, so without checking the facts, you agree to move money in, only to realize a month later that it's an illiquid limited partnership managed out of Estonia that can't be sold for another 18 years.

Lesson Learned. The fine print of any investment is more important than the window dressing itself. Ask questions and be sure to read the details; and if the spoon isn't in the right place, take your time to get it right.

Lesson 4: Costs Are Critical

Hollywood. An actor's most recent movie made more than the gross domestic product of Norway. He pitches his pet project and the studio green-lights it. While everyone works hard for it to be a hit, the budget skyrockets out of control and the movie is $250 million in the hole before anyone ever lays eyes on it.

Investors. A star money manager with a fantastic track record takes over the reins at a popular mutual fund. The offices are filled with expensive furniture, great food, a couple of espresso machines, fine art, and a magnificent pool table. Who is paying for all this stuff? You are—whether you realize it or not, the fund is taking it right out of your pocket. It doesn't matter whether the money manager makes or loses you money; it's you who's funding salaries and overhead, and that's not very efficient.

Lesson Learned. Fees kill returns. The less they take, the more you make—a simple, yet extremely important rule for investment success. Take, for example, an investor I recently met who couldn't understand why he wasn't making much money. A review of his holdings revealed he was paying a whopping 6 percent in annual fees and taxes on an investment portfolio worth just over $600,000. Over the seven years he's been in it, that's over $250,000 in fees and taxes alone. Ouch.

Lesson 5: Planning Is Key

Hollywood. Once green-lit into production, a screenplay is broken down into extremely precise, line-item moviemaking elements: costs, schedules, camera shots, makeup, hair, costumes, props, scenery, stunts, transportation, and a thousand other things. On the set, minutes can cost tens of thousands of dollars, if not more. Regardless of how good or bad the script is, a well-planned production is an incredible, well-oiled machine of intelligent efficiency, with thousands of people who often know exactly what they are doing every moment of the day all building toward one definitive, concrete goal—the date of release.

Investors. A few years from retirement, you suddenly wake up wondering how you are going to generate enough income off your savings to support the lifestyle you always wanted. After a few last minute calculations, your advisor realizes you're not going to make it. In a last ditch effort to save you, the advisor moves your money into the risky stuff and starts rolling the dice. Throwing for a high return, unlucky 7 comes up and you unfortunately find yourself crapped out. Dejected, you realize that your working life is going to drag on a few years longer than you anticipated.

Lesson Learned. Most movies take many years to plan. The smart guys realize that success rarely has shortcuts and can't be rushed; it has to be nurtured. If your investments are to end up with an Oscar, hard-core planning provides the greatest chance for success. Remember, this is *your life* we're talking about, not some trashy two-hour drive-in movie.

Lesson 6: Cut the Losers, Ride the Winners

Hollywood. By 7 P.M. on opening night, movie studios can predict with incredible accuracy the revenue a film will likely generate. Even more startling is the DVD market. Due to sales tracking systems at Wal-Mart, it's possible for the studio to accurately predict how much revenue it will earn by 3 P.M. the day of release. What will the studio do if the film is looking like a loser? Do executives pour endless money into advertising, hoping everyone will start loving it as much as they once did? No way. Advertising and marketing expenses are immediately cut, and in some cases, they are completely eliminated.

Investors. You buy a stock because you just love the company. For a while, it climbs. But then the downward spiral begins and it dips, and dips, and dips even more. You sit back and watch the stock do nothing but drop some more. You just love that company, though. Your broker reinforces your emotions and keeps telling you it will come back, but it rarely does.

Lesson Learned. As much as the studio execs might love a film, they rarely let emotions get the best of them. If something isn't working, they just cut their losses and move on. When it comes to your investments, you need to do the same. A stock doesn't know who you are; it couldn't care less about you, and it certainly has no emotional bond with you. Only you do. And as soon as you let your own emotions get in the way, bad things typically happen.

Lesson 7: Experts Focus on Reducing Risk; Novices Focus on Return

Hollywood. Many films have nearly bankrupted their creators. *Hudson Hawk, The Last Action Hero,* and *Cutthroat Island* are just a few examples that come to mind. As a result, partnerships on expensive features are now the norm. Take *Titanic,* for example. James Cameron wakes up one day with an idea to make a film about two people that fall in love on a sinking ship. One short sentence, over $200 million to produce. So what does Fox do? It partners with Paramount to reduce the risk. It's easy to look back and say Fox should have taken *all* the risk so it could have received *all* the return, but who would have thought *Titanic* would go on to become the most successful film ever made?

Investors. A few years back, the *New York Times* ran a feature article reporting where retired Federal Reserve chairman Alan Greenspan invests his money. He stated that he invests 95 percent of his money in U.S. Treasuries. In another interview, Suze Orman said most of her money is tucked away in AAA-rated insured government municipal bonds. Both are focused on only one thing: keeping their money, not losing it.

Lesson Learned. It's simple: If you don't need the *potential* return, why take the risk? Don't ever forget that. It could be one of the most important lessons you'll ever learn.

Lesson 8: Don't Reinvent the Wheel

Hollywood. In 1949, writer and scholar Joseph Campbell wrote a legendary thesis entitled *The Hero with a Thousand Faces* (Princeton University Press). His exhaustive study concluded that regardless of plot, all great stories throughout history share a very distinct and common structural foundation: The hero is introduced in his ordinary world; he receives a call to action; he refuses the call; a mentor convinces him to cross over the first threshold into the unknown; and so forth. Whether the story is out of the Bible, *Star Wars, Beverly Hills Cop,* or *The Lion King,* Campbell's handful of common elements can be found in virtually every timeless story.

Investors. Warren Buffett, along with many others, including myself, considers Benjamin Graham's timeless, early 20th century book *The Intelligent Investor* to be the bible of investing. In it, Graham teaches us to invest not to maximize profit but rather to minimize loss; to use discipline, research, and analytics to make unpopular but sound investments in undervalued stocks. These principles have stood the test of time and created significant wealth for Buffett and many others who avoid the frenzy and stick to Graham's most basic, timeless fundamentals.

Lesson Learned. The foundations of movie magic and intelligent investing were developed a very long time ago. Whether it's your next screenplay or stock pick, following the tried-and-true principles while avoiding the get-rich-quick schemes hands down gives you the best chance for consistent and efficient investment success.

Lesson 9: Complacency Is the Mother of All Disasters

Hollywood. The studio and production team can easily take a year just to plan the shoot. However, when it comes to filming on location, anything can happen. My personal experience on a film I once produced included: stolen cameras, violent weather, an actor nearly overdosing on diet pills, an angry mob wielding machetes, a generator falling off a cliff, food poisoning, stray horses, and a misplaced wardrobe truck a light-year from civilization. Some of the sharpest people I've ever worked with have saved entire productions by anticipating, thinking ahead, taking action, and making rapid-fire decisions.

Investors. Check out Morningstar's fund rankings at www.morning star.com. Take a look at the list of last year's top-performing funds; then where they are today. With some exceptions, yesterday's top performers are often this year's *Reservoir Dogs*. Like a good film crew, the sharp investor understands that monitoring, rebalancing, and updating a portfolio is essential for continued and rewarding success.

Lesson Learned. Stray horses and misplaced wardrobe trucks won't kill you, but complacency will. Whether it's producing a movie or investing to make money, anticipation, quick decisions, and action are the golden keys to anyone's success.

Lesson 10: Defy Conventional Wisdom and Take Smart Risks

Hollywood. Many of the most critically or commercially successful films ever made have been the ones that crack the mold of conformity, think outside the box, and go against the grain of conventional wisdom. *Pulp Fiction* turned the standard three-act narrative structure inside out; *Memento* ingeniously told the story backwards; and *Unforgiven* was one of the few films to successfully pull off making the villain the hero. Time and again, Hollywood has taught us that to stand out from the rest, you sometimes have to defy conventional wisdom, follow your gut, and have the courage to stop thinking like everyone else.

Investors. Emotions typically get the best of us. When the market is crashing, many people sell their stocks, but guess what? For every stock that gets sold, there has to be someone on the other side to buy it. Who are those beings buying your stock when the market is crashing? Aliens from another planet? Not quite. They are investors clearly going against the grain of popular wisdom, defying the masses, and, for better or worse, thinking outside the box. Likewise, there are many alternative investments that fly high above mainstream thought and could be a tremendous addition to a diversified portfolio; yet many people shy away from them simply because they are not traditional; the guy at the pool never heard of the investment, the accountant laughed at it, or a bunch of people over at the club said bad things about it.

Lesson Learned. If you enjoyed unconventional films such as *Unforgiven, Pulp Fiction,* and *Memento,* then you have a distinct appreciation for a willingness to take educated and intelligent risks. When it comes to investing, some of the very best opportunities out there defy mainstream thinking. Often, riches are made when thinking outside the box and educating yourself on ideas that are not otherwise in the mass mind-set of conformity. Having guts is not about taking unnecessary risk; it's about educating yourself and occasionally investing in things that sometimes your neighbor doesn't care about.

And One More for the Road: If There's a Will, There's a Way

Hollywood. While making *Apocalypse Now,* Francis Ford Coppola overcame a civil war, Martin Sheen's heart attack, personal bankruptcy, unimaginable shooting conditions, and a potentially distracting thing called death. He defied mass adversity and somehow managed to get his classic film done. Then there's Spike Lee, who was literally dirt broke when he made his breakout film, *She's Gotta Have It.* Lee's book on the making of that film is a lifelong lesson in intense perseverance, fearless courage, and laser focus. With only a few pennies in his pocket, Lee's intrepid tenacity amazingly found a way to get actors, a crew, film, cameras, locations, costumes, sets, music, editing, and a truly fantastic finished product. End result: a stellar career filled with an extremely impressive body of work.

Investors. Some of the most successful investors I've ever met started out with nothing. I'm not talking about Trump the billionaire; I'm talking about some truly incredible people such as Henry the electrician, Kyle the cop, Debbie the single mom, Lou the barber, Stan the piano teacher, and countless others. Although they basically started with nothing, year in and year out they somehow found a way to stash a little money away, taking one tiny baby step at a time by investing in smart, tax-efficient, and low-cost investments. End result: a fantastic retirement overflowing with an impressive standard of living most people would be extremely satisfied with.

Lesson Learned. Like most great film directors, Spike Lee envisioned his completed film long before it was finished, and nothing stopped him from getting it done. Likewise, envision your movie the way you want it to play out. Recognize there are no shortcuts. With the lessons in this chapter and the knowledge you'll get from this book, do whatever it takes to make sure your road toward or through retirement leads to a happy ending.

Fade lights . . .

With the previews over, it's now time to sit back and enjoy the feature presentation of this book. In the next handful of chapters, together we'll explore the above concepts in greater detail so that you, too, can end up with a few Oscars of your very own.

So, let's get going here. There's no time to waste and lots of money to make.

Close doors!

Lock set!

Roll sound!

Lights! Camera! Action!

. . . And let the show begin.

CHAPTER

2

To *Beat* the Market, *Be* the Market

I n this chapter, we explore some of the most important concepts this book covers:

- How can we consistently ensure that we make money in the markets?
- Is there a way to make investing less chaotic, more peaceful, and highly rewarding?
- What does "buy and hold" truly mean, and how can we make it effective?
- What is the best way to build an investment portfolio?
- How can we give ourselves the best possible chance to "buy low and sell high?"

By the end of this very important chapter, I am quite confident you'll be amazed at how effortless and simple all these concepts really are.

As we'll soon find out, what prevents us from achieving success is typically our very own emotions *and* the fact that many folks on Wall Street would rather you didn't know the timeless concepts I'm about to discuss even exist.

To start with, when it comes to trying to make money in the markets, we'll take our first step forward by taking a step back to the Introduction, where I mentioned that with rare exceptions, very few people out there can *consistently* beat the market.

One of the best fund managers in the country openly admits it. For 15 years Jack Meyer ran the Harvard University fund, the country's largest endowment fund that has literally over $30 billion in assets. Here's a guy who chalked up an incredible 15 percent average rate of return for over 15 years. A recent *New York Times* article stated Jack "was fond of saying that he had no clue which way the stock market would go, and generally did not change Harvard's asset mix to try to time the market" (Geraldine Fabrikant, "Playing Hunches at Harvard," March 15, 2007).

Think Main Street financial advisors or Wall Street market timers fare any better? Think again. Back in the Introduction I mentioned there's a web site out there that compares CNBC's *Mad Money* host Jim Cramer's stock picks with those from an orangutan named Leonard. As of this writing, Leonard's random, aimless picks have outperformed Cramer's picks. Many people see Cramer's picks as gospel, and although I deeply admire the guy for a variety of reasons, I see them as nothing but entertainment.

And then there's the *Wall Street Journal*'s dartboard that I also mentioned. Since 1988, reporters at the *Journal* have been throwing darts at a board filled with stocks and comparing their results against those of some of the best stock pickers around the country. For the latest contest held, the darts have been once again kicking the pants off the stock pickers, scoring returns greater than 10 percent above the professionals.

Would you trust your stock picks to a monkey? Or how about some randomly thrown darts? I certainly wouldn't, but knowing these "methods" have generally outperformed Cramer and some of the smartest professionals around the country, the million-dollar question is . . . "Why *wouldn't* you?"

Silly question, right? But it certainly has some validity to it. So, knowing you wouldn't trust Leonard or a bunch of randomly thrown darts with your money, where *do* you turn to make your stock picks more predictable, less risky, and more rewarding?

That's what this chapter is about, and that's why we'll spend considerable time making sure you don't leave this book feeling like you should entrust your money to a monkey or randomly thrown darts to get the best returns on your investment.

As much as I admire guys like Cramer and, quite frankly, some of the best stock pickers I've met around the country, most of these brilliant minds are at a distinct disadvantage. Because so much of the market's activity is based on *news* that no one can predict—not just local or national news, but global news as seen through the eyes of giants such as CNN—unless a mutual fund manager or financial advisor is psychic, trying to guess what's going to happen next in the markets is downright impossible.

Am I much better? Am I the "smartest guy in the room" when it comes to picking stocks? Not a chance. But here's where I *am* smart: I have enough confidence in myself and the many timeless ideas that have been around for ages to openly admit what many Wall Street professionals wouldn't dare do: With very rare exceptions, picking individual stocks to *consistently* outperform the market is most often a loser's game. And anyone who tells you anything different is most likely just trying to collect a fee to make you *think* they can do it better.

If you understand and believe this, then I'm hopeful you'll also believe there *has* to be a better way to invest than handing your money over to a monkey named Leonard—a way that takes the guesswork out of investing, makes things more predictable, and greatly increases your chances for *sustained* and *consistent* success. After all, if you were to successfully guess what is going to happen next, you would be either one of the extremely few market geniuses in the world or just plain downright lucky. And when it comes to trying to get rich, how much do you want to base your chances of success on getting lucky? Personally, I want to base *zero* of my chances to get rich on that thing called luck. To me, there has to be a better way, and that is what this chapter is all about.

This brings us to one of the most important points of this book: If, with rare exceptions, very few people, if any, can *consistently* predict the markets and we aren't going to rely on luck to get us rich, then what's the answer to getting us to where we need to go?

The answer is actually pretty simple. And if that's inspiring, there's even better news: The answer is so simple that learning to apply it and make it work for you is even simpler.

Before I reveal what this revolutionary thing is that's actually been around for well over a century, let's see what we can learn from real world events about something called risk and return.

What Billy the Bully Teaches Us about Investing

Many neighborhoods have a "Billy" type of kid. Billy typically sports a short, spiked crew cut, and has bright white skin, scattered red freckles, and a slight belly. He wears a heavily wrinkled T-shirt advertising a local pizza place and torn blue jeans with a big hole exposing his recently scraped knee. Over his shoulder, he carries a Louisville Slugger bat, and he's usually chewing an oversized wad of Bazooka. Billy is also every parent's worst nightmare: He's the kid who somehow always seems to manage to hit the ball through *your* window.

Think of a large picture window facing your front yard. Chances are, the view out the window is enhanced when the only thing between you and the great outdoors is a single sheet of glass. However, the problem with one sheet of glass is that when Billy smacks a foul ball through it, the entire thing is gone goodbye.

So, to counter the risk of Billy smacking another one through your picture window and you having to replace the entire sheet of glass, what could you do?

Instead of one large sheet of glass, you might consider dividing it up into smaller panes, right? This way, when (not if) Billy smacks one through your window, only one of the small sections will shatter, certainly not the entire thing. Although the view might be better if there were no dividers, you reduce the risk of Billy's foul ball smashing your entire window by dividing it up into smaller sections. True, the dividers detract somewhat from the view, but so does a gaping hole lined with sharp, jagged glass.

Bottom line: To reduce the risk of a foul ball shattering the entire window, we divide the window up into many small pieces that *reduce the risk* that the whole thing will be gone.

Let's take a look at one more scenario.

Going Down?

What about riding an elevator? What can riding an elevator teach us about the markets?

Suppose you and I are on the top floor of a skyscraper waiting for an elevator to take us down. Two elevators appear at the exact same time and we notice one elevator is suspended by one pulley, while many pulleys support the other.

Which elevator would you get into—the elevator with one pulley holding its weight or the one suspended by many?

Silly question, right? Who wouldn't pick the one suspended by many?

Now, let me try to entice you a bit. Let's say the elevator suspended by one pulley will get us down twice as fast, but due to the speed there's a much greater chance this pulley could snap and send us crashing to the ground. In contrast, the elevator with many pulleys might take a little longer to get us down, but we can rest assured we won't get killed in the process.

Which one would you choose now?

Except for masochistic thrill seekers willing to risk their lives, most people would get into the elevator with many pulleys. Although it will take more time to get down, many would be comforted by the increased level of security.

When it comes to investing, why would you do anything different? Unfortunately, many people take far too many risks trying to get rich quick. As a result, they've had the unfortunate experience of spiraling down and crashing hard to the ground floor or having Billy's foul ball land on their living room floor after it shatters an entire sheet of glass.

Avoiding the accidents comes down to one basic, extremely important rule that you may have heard a thousand times before. But time and time again, many people ignore it, and that's unfortunate. When it comes to successful and efficient investing, there's really only one way to do it right: *diversification*, otherwise known as not putting all your eggs in one basket.

Diversification is all about many pulleys suspending your elevator. It's also about dividing up your large front window into small sections that greatly reduce the risk that one foul ball will shatter the entire thing to pieces.

When it comes to the markets, diversification is all about *investing*, whereas in most cases, picking individual stocks (and hoping to get rich) is what many call *market timing*. No doubt, with a bit of luck or extraordinary talent, trying to time the market can get you rich quickly. I'm all for taking some educated rolls of the dice, but certainly not with *all* my money. For the market timer or gambler in you looking to get high returns, I won't ignore this understandable desire and I'll be sure to provide a few key pointers later on. But just as you most likely wouldn't place all your money on 24 black, investing should be no different.

When it comes to investing in the markets, the purpose of diversification comes down to this: the recognition that with very rare exceptions, no one can *consistently* predict what's going to happen next. And when you're smart enough to realize this, then you're smart enough to realize that taking the guesswork out of the markets is the only way to *consistently* win the game.

There is certainly no doubt doing it otherwise *might* lead to success, and in some cases, a lot of success. I've had my share of these successes, and presumably so have you. But this book is not about "let me show you how to get rich quick." I'll save that for the late night infomercials out there and advisors who on spotty occasions might be able to do it, only to likely give it back soon after they made it. What I want to do is make sure you get to your destination as safely and rewardingly as possible *with the least amount of risk* and *the most consistency*—and this is what solid, efficient, and prudent diversification is all about.

Successful and efficient diversification eliminates the element of emotion, which often gets the best of us. It makes trying to predict what is going to happen next something of the past. Diversification makes investing to get rich a much more peaceful, pragmatic, and rewarding experience—one that if properly implemented and practiced doesn't require nearly as much time, fear, and panic as it takes when trying to time the markets or dodging Billy's foul balls.

Personally, when I think of trying to time the markets, I envision stress and frustration. When I think of diversifying the main portion of my money in the markets, I think of peace, serenity, consistent success, and watching the Mets win another one at Shea.

Swing Easy

Have you ever played golf? I have. And to be honest, I'm not very good at it. If you ever want to feel like Tiger Woods, just invite me out on the course and I can assure you that you'll feel a heck of a lot better about your game.

However, one thing I do know about golf is that when my playing leaves much to be desired, one of the first things I hear is my Dad's kind voice whispering for me to "swing easier." Without a doubt, golf is indeed one of those rare games where the harder you try to hit the ball, the worse things typically get. If you merely remembered this fundamental rule of golf—that the easier you swing, the further the ball typically goes—chances are your score will fare so much better.

Investing isn't much different: The simpler you make things for yourself and the more you stick to the timeless fundamentals of the game, the better your score will likely be at the end of the match.

Diversification

So, what exactly is diversification? To begin with, let's think of Bloomingdale's.

Diversification and Bloomingdale's: A Match Made in Heaven

Ever been to the Bloomingdale's in New York City? I have. And if you've been there or in a department store like it, you'll certainly agree that it is a very large store, to say the least, with departments ranging from cosmetics, men's clothing, women's clothing, and housewares to kids' clothing, toys, and electronics.

Think of your diversified investment portfolio eventually looking like Bloomingdale's, with each department representing a different class of market sectors to invest in. When it comes to investments, the departments you can shop in are typically categories such as domestic stocks, international stocks, bonds, commodities, and cash.

Now, suppose you walk into the women's department of Bloomingdale's. This may be a department, but there can also be subsections within this department, such as suits, casual wear, accessories, and shoes.

We'll see the same thing within a diversified portfolio. The department you are shopping in might be domestic stocks, but domestic stocks will also have subsections such as large-cap stocks, small-cap stocks, mid-cap stocks, and micro-cap stocks.

So, when talking about diversification within a portfolio, just like Bloomingdale's men's department with its subsections of shoes, socks, and suits, each asset class of the markets have subsections inside it as well. It's a very important point, because someone might come along and say real estate isn't doing well, but that's a very broad, generalized, and unfair statement to make. Certainly, there could come a rare time when *all* of real estate isn't doing well, but typically some of the subsections might not be doing well while others are doing just fine. At the time of this writing, the residential housing market is performing terribly, but at the same time, commercial properties are faring quite well. As I mention many times during this book, when it comes to investing, generalizing anything is often grounds for disaster.

Inventory and Monitoring

The next aspect of diversification involves *managing* the store: taking your store's inventory, periodic monitoring of the departments, and evaluating performance. This is followed by making any necessary adjustments by either selling merchandise that isn't performing well, looking for things on sale, buying potential profit makers, or a critical concept called "rebalancing"—which we'll get into in a little while.

Now, when I say "periodic monitoring" of your investments, don't be intimidated. Few people want to stay up late at night poring over the *Wall Street Journal* and analyzing the latest financial news. Not only is that tedious, but having to put in that amount of time and effort typically means that you are swinging the golf club way too hard. It means you are most likely trying to time the market with your money, not *invest* it through the fundamentals of diversification we're just starting to learn about.

Remember: When it comes to diversification and rebalancing, like a good golf swing, the simpler you make things for yourself, the greater your chances are to consistently make more money in the markets than you likely have before. Once your *diversified portfolio* is established, which, quite frankly, is the most time-consuming part of everything I'll be discussing here, monitoring this portfolio should happen periodically during the year. However, the actual *trading* should take place only one or two times a year, and rarely more than that. Again, do it more than that and you are likely trying to time the market, and just like my golf swing, the harder you try, the worse your game is typically going to get.

As for the actively traded part of the portfolio, this should all take place in one sector I refer to as the "flavors of the day," which I'll soon be discussing.

Off to the Races: An Introduction to Asset Allocation

Very few people get rich by being lucky. You get rich by being smart, and when it comes to being smart, one of the first rules of successful investing is that you understand you aren't always going to get it right. Pity the financial advisor or stock picker out there who tries to make it sound like they always get it right. Sorry, that's just not possible. There's no such thing, not even close. And once and for all, and we hope for the rest of your life, we're going to solve all those problems right here.

Diversification means that you recognize that some of the market sectors in your Bloomingdale's department store of investments will end up in first place and others will come in last. And by spreading the bets throughout a diversified pool of sectors, you get the *combined returns* of all of the winners and losers. The trick here is to spread your bets to minimize risk *and* increase the likelihood that the overall return will be positive.

I've heard some say that diversification could be grounds for lackluster returns, but I often find these people fail to address the critical need to rebalance a portfolio. I'll define this concept in a little while, but if you've heard someone mention "lackluster returns" as a result of a diversified portfolio, stick around. I'll be addressing what this rebalancing is and how to overcome this potential concern.

Most investors have heard of diversification, and some might even be able to explain why it's important. However, I often find that even those who seem to know what they're talking about don't always understand or follow their own advice. Let's get deeper into reviewing one of the most important and most fundamental rules of successful investing.

Different Asset Classes

Domestic stocks, international stocks, bonds, real estate, commodities, and cash equivalents perform differently in unpredictable market cycles. Because few people, if any, can predict which market sector is going to come up roses next, because markets are driven mostly by news, and because we certainly aren't going to give a monkey or a dart our money, we are going to let diversification do all the picking and guesswork for us.

In technical terms, different asset classes are known as *uncorrelated*, meaning they move in opposite directions. While some market sectors, or asset classes, are going up, others will be going down. At various times, some sectors may be in favor and more profitable during certain market cycles, others will be out of favor at the same time. And the beauty of diversification and rebalancing is that we will soon learn how to take advantage of those asset classes that are out of favor.

Yes, "take advantage." As you will soon see, taking advantage of asset classes and market sectors that are going down in value will be one of the most important keys to your consistent investment success.

Allocating your assets involves dividing up your investments among these classes, or, using my Bloomingdale's example, dividing things up not only into different departments, but subdepartments as well. *Diversification is simply the process of efficiently spreading your investments across the fundamental and timeless asset classes so that your returns are not dependent on the performance of any one class.*

While diversification doesn't eliminate the risk of loss, it will absolutely help you manage the effects of market volatility on your portfolio. Rather than trying to guess which part of the market will go up and which part will go down in any given period, a diversified portfolio will ride out those fluctuations, reduce risk, and stabilize your returns over time.

As evidence, if you look at a number of asset classes over the past 10 years—large-cap value stocks, large-cap growth stocks, small-cap value stocks, small-cap growth stocks, international stocks, real estate, commodities, and bonds—the best and worst performers have varied every year. The asset class that came in first place one year often dropped much lower the next year. With rare exceptions, no one can predict which horse is going to win the next race.

In Table 2.1 there is a tangible example of what makes asset allocation and diversification so important. At first the vertical strip is going to look like a Chinese mosaic hanging on a take-out restaurant's wall, but I promise, as I walk you through it, it will start to make sense and it will help clarify and support some of the points I'm making. For now, just take a quick peek. You'll get a bit dizzy, but don't worry. I'll make it much simpler in a few moments.

What you are seeing are the returns of various market sectors for the year 1997. The box just below the year 1997 represents the best-performing market sector for that year, while the box at the bottom represents the worst.

- S&P 500 Index represents the 500 largest companies in the United States (large-caps).
- S&P 400 Index represents 400 medium-sized U.S. companies (mid-caps).
- Russell 2000 represents 2,000 small U.S. company stocks (small-caps).
- LB Agg is the Lehman Brothers Aggregate Bond Index, comprised of roughly 6,000 bonds.
- MSCI EAFE represents international stocks traded in 16 countries within Europe, Australasia, and the Far East.
- Indexes Annual Average is *all* sectors in the table bundled together into one neat package. In this example, this represents a diversified portfolio.

So, as an example of why diversification is so important, let's start by looking again at how things were doing in 1997 in Table 2.1.

Table 2.1   Annual Returns for Key Indexes, 1997

1997
S&P 500 Index 33.36%
S&P 400 Index 32.25%
Russell 2000 22.36%
Indexes Annual Average 19.94%
LB Agg 9.66%
MSCI EAFE 2.06%

Here, the best-performing sector for that particular year was the Standard & Poor's 500 index, gaining a very impressive 33.36 percent rate of return. The worst-performing sector at the bottom of the ladder, the stocks in the MSCI EAFE index (Europe, Australasia, and the Far East), returned a meager 2.06 percent.

Here is why asset allocation and diversification are so important, and why those who try to pick the winner of the next horse race are usually not very successful.

In the year 1997, few market timers were paying attention to stocks found within the international sector as represented by the EAFE "horse." Why bother? During 1997, the market timers out there were making much more money in other areas of the market, such as domestic stocks found within places such as the S&P 500.

But then what happened? The following year, in 1998, suddenly the stocks found within the international sector, as represented by the EAFE horse, fared much better, coming in second place. (See Table 2.2.)

All of a sudden, many of the market timers and horse pickers now started to pay attention to international stocks found in the EAFE

Table 2.2   Annual Returns for Key Indexes, 1998

1998
S&P 500 Index 28.57%
MSCI EAFE 20.33%
S&P 400 Index 19.12%
Indexes Annual Average 14.83%
LB Agg 8.68%
Russell 2000 −2.55%

horse. Many market timers said, "International stocks within the EAFE horse are doing fantastic. I want in on some of that action." So what did they do? They likely started taking money out of the worst-performing sectors of the market for that particular year and starting chasing stocks found within the EAFE horse.

Then what happened? The next year, 1999, the international stocks found within the EAFE sector won the race, coming in at the top of the list. (See Table 2.3.)

Fantastic! International stocks found within the EAFE horse finished in first place. Celebration time, champagne bottles popping, corks flying, drinks and partying, everyone is happy. But, wait! The

Table 2.3   Annual Returns for Key Indexes, 1999

1999
MSCI EAFE
27.30%
Russell 2000
21.26%
S&P 500 Index
21.05%
Indexes Annual Average
16.70%
S&P 400 Index
14.72%
LB Agg
−0.83%

next year, 2000, international stocks found within the EAFE horse came in last place. (See Table 2.4.)

Terrible returns, awful. The sector was down almost 14 percent for the year. Many market timers out there got a bit uneasy. Some of them started betting on other stocks found within other sectors, while others hung in for maybe another race.

Check out what happened in the two years that followed, shown in Table 2.5.

Those were two horrible years. The international stocks found within the EAFE sector weren't even horses; they were dogs. So,

Table 2.4   Annual Returns for Key Indexes, 2000

2000
S&P 500 Index 17.51%
LB Agg 11.63%
Indexes Annual Average 0.61%
Russell 2000 -3.02%
S&P 500 Index -9.11%
MSCI EAFE -13.96%

Table 2.5   Annual Returns for Key Indexes, 2001–2002

2001	2002
LB Agg	LB Agg
8.42%	10.27%
Russell 2000	Indexes Annual Average
2.48%	–12.50%
S&P 400 Index	S&P 400 Index
–0.61%	–14.51%
Indexes Annual Average	MSCI EAFE
–4.56%	–15.66%
S&P 500 Index	Russell 2000
–11.88%	–20.48%
MSCI EAFE	S&P 500 Index
–21.21%	–22.10%

during 2001 and 2002, what did those at the racetrack do? Naturally, many started taking their bets off the EAFE dogs and started betting on other horses higher up on the list.

However, as soon as many took their bets from the worst-performing horse, what happened next? You guessed it—the international stocks found within the EAFE sector suddenly moved into the lead, and as a result, many market timers out there missed out on the next three years of fantastic returns where the international stocks found within the EAFE sector came in first place, leading the pack. (See Table 2.6.)

Table 2.6 Annual Returns for Key Indexes, 2003–2006

2003	2004	2005	2006
Russell 2000	MSCI EAFE	MSCI EAFE	MSCI EAFE
47.25%	20.70%	14.02%	26.8%
MSCI EAFE	Russell 2000	S&P 400 Index	Russell 2000
39.17%	18.32%	12.55%	18.35%
S&P 400 Index	S&P 400 Index	Indexes Annual Average	S&P 500 Index
35.64%	16.50%	7.69%	15.80%
Indexes Annual Average	Indexes Annual Average	S&P 500 Index	Indexes Annual Average
30.97%	14.15%	4.89%	15.13%
S&P 500 Index	S&P 500 Index	Russell 2000	S&P 400 Index
28.69%	10.87%	4.55%	10.32%
LB Agg	LB Agg	LB Agg	LB Agg
4.11%	4.34%	2.43%	4.33%

That's what trying to time the market is all about—trying to pick the next winner of the next horse race, trying to chase the winners. Unfortunately, many market timers do not fare all that well, especially when it comes to generating *consistent* and successful rates of return.

It's possible that you could get rich by trying to time the market, but let's face it: Trying to predict the winner of the next horse race is a very difficult, frustrating thing to do, and with very rare exceptions, most people simply cannot do it, nor do they have the *time* to do it. Without a doubt, market timing can be quite stressful. And as far as I'm concerned, as I've mentioned a few times before, if you are going to do it, do it with a smaller portion of your money—the portion you don't mind losing.

Very few of the rich people I have met got that way by being lucky. They got rich by recognizing that with rare exceptions, trying to time the market simply does not work, especially over the long haul. Sure, you can lay down a few dollars in the casino and get some spectacular rates of return, but the rules of a casino are no different than the rules of investing: When it comes to market timing, the longer you play the game, the less chance you have to win. On the flip side, when *investing*, in contrast to market timing, the longer you play the game, the greater the odds are that you will get rich.

Taking it one step further, I'll spell it out: To get rich, do not try to time the market. *Invest* your money by diversifying and rebalancing it.

Diversification is an understanding that you can't predict which market sector is going to come in first next. For the moment, to greatly simplify the concept, the approach I'm talking about is to bet on *all* the *fundamental* sectors *at once*, and not chase after each one.

Using Table 2.7 as an example, diversification is best represented by the middle square or "Indexes Annual Average" box, which is essentially all the market sectors bundled together. If you are having trouble finding it, just look toward the middle of the chart, because that's where a well-diversified investment portfolio typically shows up. Rarely is it found at the top of the list, but certainly not at the bottom, either.

If you plot the annual average square for each year, you will see that the diversified portfolio never came in first place, but to make you feel better, it never came in last place, either. In the diversified portfolio, you rarely get the biggest returns, but you never get the devastating losses like those experienced by the market timers who got badly hurt in the tech crash of 2001–2002.

For those who are hungry to go after higher returns, don't despair. I want them, too, and I'll deal with how to approach this objective in a little while. For now, let's stay on course and continue with the prudent laws of diversification.

Stocks, Funds, or Indexes?

We've now seen how various market sectors such as U.S. stocks, international stocks, and bonds bounce up and down in any given year. We've also recognized that it's very difficult, if not impossible,

Table 2.7 Annual Returns for Key Indexes, 1997–2006

1997	1998	1999	2000	2001	2002	2003	2004	2005	2006
S&P 500 Index 33.36%	S&P 500 Index 28.57%	MSCI EAFE 27.30%	S&P 500 Index 17.51%	LB Agg 8.42%	LB Agg 10.27%	Russell 2000 47.25%	MSCI EAFE 20.70%	MSCI EAFE 14.02%	MSCI EAFE 26.8%
S&P 400 Index 32.25%	MSCI EAFE 20.33%	Russell 2000 21.26%	LB Agg 11.63%	Russell 2000 2.48%	Indexes Annual Average -12.50%	MSCI EAFE 39.17%	Russell 2000 18.32%	S&P 400 Index 12.55%	Russell 2000 18.35%
Russell 2000 22.36%	S&P 400 Index 19.12%	S&P 500 Index 21.05%	Indexes Annual Average 0.61%	S&P 400 Index -0.61%	S&P 400 Index -14.51%	S&P 400 Index 35.64%	S&P 400 Index 16.50%	Indexes Annual Average 7.69%	S&P 500 Index 15.80%
Indexes Annual Average 19.94%	Indexes Annual Average 14.83%	Indexes Annual Average 16.70%	Russell 2000 -3.02%	Indexes Annual Average -4.56%	MSCI EAFE -15.66%	Indexes Annual Average 30.97%	Indexes Annual Average 14.15%	S&P 500 Index 4.89%	Indexes Annual Average 15.13%
LB Agg 9.66%	LB Agg 8.68%	S&P 400 Index 14.72%	S&P 500 Index -9.11%	S&P 500 Index -11.88%	Russell 2000 -20.48%	S&P 500 Index 28.69%	S&P 500 Index 10.87%	Russell 2000 4.55%	S&P 400 Index 10.32%
MSCI EAFE 2.06%	Russell 2000 -2.55%	LB Agg -0.83%	MSCI EAFE -13.96%	MSCI EAFE -21.21%	S&P 500 Index -22.10%	LB Agg 4.11%	LB Agg 4.34%	LB Agg 2.43%	LB Agg 4.33%

to accurately predict which sector is going to be at the top of the list year after year. Lastly, we've seen that the diversified portfolio of the fundamental market sectors typically remains somewhere in the middle of the returns, rarely giving you the biggest gains of the market, but also rarely delivering the big losses.

Recognizing this, the next important step we need to address is *how to represent* each market sector that will ultimately be present in our diversified portfolio. If a sector in Bloomingdale's is men's clothes, then we need to put things in that department to represent it. To accomplish that, we'd likely go out into the marketplace and get men's clothes from various companies that we think would be attractive to the shoppers and thereby make us a nice profit. Maybe we'd place a few Ralph Lauren shirts on the rack, and perhaps we'd add a few Donna Karan pants and a couple of Liz Claiborne jackets.

Similarly, the sectors that typically belong in a diversified portfolio need to be represented by something. Just like the men's department at Bloomingdale's, we need to fill it up with something that belongs in there. And needless to say, the something we use to represent the sector needs to give us the best chances for *profitability* as well.

For example, if one sector in the diversified portfolio needs to be large domestic U.S. companies (large-cap), what do we use to represent that sector? Do we have Leonard the Monkey select a few individual large-cap stocks to represent that sector for us? Do we rely on randomly thrown darts? Do *we* do it ourselves? Do we maybe hire a local financial advisor at a big brokerage firm to do it for us, or what about hiring a professional at a mutual fund company to take care of the job? Or, is there another way to do it?

When it comes to finding a way to represent each sector of a diversified portfolio, we have three choices:

1. Pick individual stocks ourselves.
2. Have an advisor at a brokerage or at a mutual fund company do it.
3. Have no one do it—use an index fund to do it.

To analyze which option is typically the most efficient, let's get a little creative. Let's suppose that we visit a casino where each choice has its own roulette table, and let's evaluate the particular experience one might have when playing at each of the three distinctly different tables.

So, head on over to the casino cage, cash in a few dollars, grab your chips, and let's go searching for the best way to represent each sector in what will soon become our well-diversified investment portfolio.

Roulette Table 1: Picking Individual Stocks

Large crowds of people are standing around a roulette table placing their bets on individual stocks to represent a sector within a diversified portfolio. You've played this roulette game before; you're familiar with it, so you figure you'll give it a go. You look up at a sign that clearly states this roulette area represents securities found within the bond slice of a diversified portfolio.

But for the moment, you don't want bonds. You're not that familiar with them. To make things a bit easier, you're looking to start building your diversified portfolio with something a bit more familiar, large-cap stocks.

So you walk around the large and busy room, past the roulette tables where investors are busy picking individual stocks for their portfolios. There are roulette tables for mid-cap stocks, small-cap stocks, foreign stocks, real estate stocks, energy, pharmaceuticals, health care, banks, consumer goods, and a large variety of other sectors that you eventually might very well consider to earn a place within your diversified portfolio. But for now, all you want to do is to handpick a couple of stocks to represent the large-cap slice of your diversified portfolio, and you finally find that roulette table near the middle of the room.

The roulette table is massive, the biggest one you've ever seen, and it's crowded with investors just like you who are carefully trying to evaluate all the large cap stocks on the table.

You clear past a few people and get a spot to start playing what is essentially choice number one of how to represent the large cap stock slice of your diversified investment portfolio: picking individual stocks yourself.

No problem. All you have to do is pick the number that's going to come up a winner once the little ball drops after the lucky wheel is spun.

Easy, right?

Well, not exactly. At this roulette table of large cap companies, there are hundreds, if not thousands, of stocks to choose from. Which one do you pick? Some of the companies look quite familiar: Coca-Cola, Altria, Wal-Mart, AT&T, 3M, Microsoft, and many, many others. Some companies you've never heard of before. A bit overwhelmed, you take a deep breath. There's an entire diversified portfolio you need to fill up, and this sector is just the first of many roulette tables you're going to have to visit.

Another deep breath and you're on your way. You place a handful of chips on the numbers you think are coming up next and the lucky wheel takes a spin. . . .

Nothing comes up. You try a few more times. On occasion, large-cap big company stocks such as Google, Microsoft, Coca-Cola, and Home Depot may come up winners, but all of a sudden, just when it appears you're on a winning streak, unexpected news flashes—Dell reports bad earnings, a crisis in the Middle East flares, oil prices spike, there's an accounting scandal or unexpected inflation—random news that adversely affects the one particular company you just chose. Whatever the reason, for better or worse, the unexpected news catches everyone by surprise. Round and round she goes, where she stops . . . few people playing this game can really say they actually know.

You research the numbers, and you may win some and lose some; but *consistently* winning is definitely a bit rough. Maybe you played this game years ago when things were easier—the last time you played this, the news that influenced this game wasn't moving so fast. But now, the news is coming in from everywhere and anywhere in real time, and it affects everything that's going on. CNN, Fox News, the Internet, chat rooms—in this game, everyone wants and needs to know the news that could possibly give them some sort of edge as to which number might come up the next big winner.

Things are happening a bit too fast, and you might be having a tough time keeping up. Most of the time, you've been choosing a number based on some research, but most likely a little hunch is thrown in as well. Sometimes you try to base your choice on some form of statistical analysis. For example, you may have been watching the performance of the roulette wheel for a while and think you have figured out the odds of a particular number coming up next.

As you continue doing the best you can, a woman sitting next to you seems to be doing a bit better. You ask her what her secret is, and she points to a bank of nearby television sets suspended from the ceiling. Scouring the TVs, you see a few talk shows that analyze all those large-cap companies sitting in front of you.

Maybe those guys will help give you an edge. . . .

One man on the TV seems downright nuts. He's so excited about his picks that he's busy honking horns, sweating profusely, pulling alarms, throwing chairs, and heaving giant water balloons and mannequins across the room.

You notice another show that is a lot less chaotic. On this show, there is a professional moderator discussing "which number will come up next" with two trustworthy-looking men. The number they are discussing today is number 12. One guest is very optimistic about it. He has analyzed number 12 for many years and is quite confident that number is coming up a winner next. Sounds good. But just as you're about to reach over and place a stack of chips on number 12, the other guy opens his mouth and says he is certain number 12 *won't* come up for a while. So, you pull your money back and now you're confused. Not only do both of these guys look smart, but they *are* smart, and each makes a fantastic argument as to why number 12 will or will not come up next.

To hedge your bet, you figure it couldn't hurt to put just a few chips on number 12. After all, one of them made a very convincing argument as to why that number should come up a winner. You place your bet, and just as the wheel is spun and the ball dropped, a TV news flash announces that the CEO of number 12 just stepped down, making the chances for success less probable, at least for the moment.

Most people shouldn't be betting their money on just one number unless they really understand what they are doing, have a distinct tolerance for pain, or maintain at least some degree of psychic ability. You have to admit that it's tough trying to consistently pick individual winning stocks. As we've just seen, you cannot possibly know every circumstance affecting each stock; who knew that interest rates would go up? For the most part, that's beyond anyone's ability to predict. It can be nerve-wracking trying to hang in there until you've actually made a profit on your money.

Needless to say, picking individual stocks can indeed have some high payoffs, and if you've ever played the markets or the game of roulette, chances are you have had some degree of success, perhaps a lot of success; but when it comes to *sustained* and *consistent* success, that's an entirely different story. I said this earlier and it's so important that I'll say it again: I have no problem investing some money on individual stocks. They can pay off quite nicely, especially when there's at least a concrete reason you want to invest in them—and

I'll get into some of those reasons in a little while. But remember that I also said many people just don't understand what it is they are investing in. For many people, picking a few individual stocks to represent a market sector within your diversified portfolio has a lot of risk and guesswork involved in it.

There is no doubt that if you put all your chips on a single number and win the bet, you'll get a large payoff. After all, the payoff for picking an individual number on the roulette table is something like 35 to 1. However, that fantastic payoff has to cover _all_ of the losing bets you made if you are to at least break even. In roulette, picking the right number is a downright tricky game. And for most people, picking an individual stock is even trickier.

Recognizing this, when trying to find stocks to represent a specific market sector found within a well-diversified portfolio, many people will turn to another type of roulette table in the casino.

Roulette Table 2: Managed Mutual Funds

A bit dejected, you start to wonder if there's anyone around who can give you a helping hand on how to pick a few stocks to represent the large-cap slice of your diversified portfolio.

You head over to casino customer service and find there's a "roulette advisor" sitting there. You explain to the roulette advisor that you're trying to find a few stocks to represent the large-cap slice of your diversified portfolio. You just lost some money playing the do-it-yourself game, and you're looking for someone that can give you a few pointers.

"Forget about doing it yourself," says the roulette advisor. "I can certainly do it for you. I'm a roulette advisor from a large brokerage firm. Sure, I can handpick stocks for you, but to be honest with you, there are some hard-core, very experienced professionals on the other side of the casino who know how to pick them better than anyone else. These guys have been doing it for many years, they have proven track records, and I know the best of the bunch. Follow me!"

Where is the roulette advisor taking you? He's taking you over to choice number two of how to find stocks to represent the large-cap sector of your diversified portfolio: hiring a professional money manager to do it within the confines of a managed mutual fund.

He walks you across the casino to an area where professional stock pickers are at the roulette tables, and the investors are merely spectators. Whereas in choice one the investors were handpicking numbers for themselves, in this area the professionals do the picking for them. And just like before, there are many roulette tables that represent different market sectors often found in a diversified portfolio—sectors such as technology, commodities, utilities, consumer products, construction, and a large variety of others that could eventually wind up in your diversified portfolio. Each sector has many tables, all competing for your money, with attractive assistants handing out all sorts of glossy brochures and literature that show what appears to be impressive rates of return generated by the professional stock picker at each table.

The roulette advisor finally settles near a brightly lit platinum table where the waitress serves drinks to other investors lounging around on plush burgundy velvet chairs. In the center of all the action, standing at the table picking numbers, is a well-dressed fund manager wearing a black Armani suit. The bright, flashing, and somewhat blinding sign above him reads: "Number Selection Experts: We Make Money Picking Large-Cap Stocks." Underneath in bright neon flashes, "Check out our performance!"

The roulette advisor shows you the fund manager's performance, and there's no doubt about it—those returns look pretty impressive. This fund manager has made a lot of people a lot of money, and you are certainly tempted to get in on the action.

To be sure, you sit for a moment to contemplate the fund manager's performance, and someone tells you this guy is doing well. Many people are crowded around because he's been on such a winning streak. As you get ready to reach into your pocket, you take one last look at his track record for the past several years, and sure enough, even you have to admit it really does look good.

As you're about to hand over some chips to the fund manager, the roulette advisor steps in the way. "I'll take care of that for you," he says. He takes your chips and hands you a thick book. Glancing at it, you see there are many paper-thin pages and endless fine print. "What's this?" you ask. "The rules of this game," he replies. "It's a prospectus. But hurry—you do want to get in, don't you?"

And as the roulette advisor hands your chips to the fund manager, something startling happens: You notice the roulette advisor stick a few of your chips into his own pocket.

When you ask the roulette advisor why he did that, he says it's his fee for getting you into this game. "After all," he says, "take a look around. There are many large-cap roulette tables around here, and

I saved you lots of time and money by showing you the best of the bunch."

Although it sounds a bit odd that he is charging you just to get into the game, you figure it certainly does appear that he introduced you to a table with a good track record; so arguably, it'll be worth a few chips. But you can't help thinking about a friend of yours that just recently put a house on the market. He didn't have to pay the real estate agent just to get the sales process started, did he? Doesn't the agent get paid a commission only if she's successful in selling the house? Of course! So why would this game be any different?

You suppose this is the way the strange game is played, and down on your luck by doing it yourself, you figure why not take a chance? What's the worst thing that could happen? If the fund manager loses money, you can take your money off the table at any time, right?

With his fee collected, the roulette advisor shakes your hand and wishes you luck. "I'll check back with you soon," he says.

As the game begins, you just can't help but think it's a bit strange the roulette advisor would pocket some of your money before the fund manager actually wins something for you—but you figure what can you do? You just have to find some stocks to fill up the large-cap slice of your diversified portfolio, and you certainly didn't fare too well picking stocks on your own. Rules are rules, right? So, you sit back in one of the chairs and start watching the action: The fund manager starts betting your money on various large-cap stocks along with the chips he's been entrusted with from everyone else. Sometimes he wins, sometimes he loses. As time ticks by, you're starting to get a slight butterfly in your belly. True, the sign does say, "Past performance does not guarantee future results," but you just can't help thinking that something doesn't feel right here. He's winning, but it just doesn't seem as if he's winning as many times as the performance states.

The game continues. You're keeping a close eye on your money when all of a sudden, out of nowhere, a guy wearing an oversized red, white, and blue hat appears at the table and starts sweeping a bunch of chips off the table, including some of yours.

Alarmed, you get up to approach him, but a guy sitting nearby tells you to relax. He says that's Uncle Sam, and every now and then he makes his rounds because the action at this roulette table creates something called "taxable events." Simply put, "You have to pay up," he says. You argue that you're not even using that money. "Too bad," says the man. "That's the way this game is played."

Without a doubt, this game is starting to get a bit aggravating. How can you make money when the roulette advisor and Uncle Sam are taking their cuts before you even show a profit?

Then, something awful happens. The fund manager starts losing. He hits a bad streak and every spin of the wheel keeps getting worse. After an hour of this, you can't stomach it any longer. You want out. Getting up from your chair, you reach for your chips. However, a security guard stops you, telling you "rules are rules." He points to the prospectus, where the fine print clearly states, "You can't get out of this game until the end of the day when the casino closes."

This is horrible—the fund manager is losing your money and you have to *wait* to quit the game? Just when it appears things can't possibly get any worse, the fund manager sweeps some of your chips off the table and slips them into his pocket. As if that's not enough, he holds back a couple of chips and tosses them over the rail to the roulette advisor, who's passing by.

Appalled, you demand to know what's going on. As you head toward the fund manager, the security guard holds you back and reminds you of the rules detailed in the prospectus: You need to pay the fund manager a fee for his time. "But he's losing me money," you say. "Too bad," says the security guard. "You still have to pay him for his time." "Then what about the roulette advisor? Why is he getting some of my money?" The security guard simply tells you, "Sorry, pal, that's between him and the fund manager. That's how the game works, and the rules are spelled out right there in your prospectus."

This is definitely a game you don't want to play anymore.

Picking your own stocks to represent the large-cap sector of your diversified portfolio is tricky, especially if you don't understand the game well enough to play it profitably. Then there's the roulette advisor who introduced you to the fund manager, who seems to be faring just a tad bit better, but those commissions, fees, and Uncle Sam sweeping some chips off the table eat into your profits regardless of whether the fund manager wins or loses.

You feel misled and disappointed, and just when things could not seem to get any worse, you notice more fine print in the prospectus. When taking a closer look at the fund manager's past performance, you find out the guy betting your chips is completely new to this table; the enticing track record was from a *different* fund manager who *used to* work for Number Selection Experts.

Does the above scenario seem familiar?

You may not think so, but if you've ever invested in a managed mutual fund, you've played this game, albeit with (I hope) much better luck than the hypothetical person playing my game just did. Maybe you didn't pay that commission up front to get into the game, or maybe you played the game at something called a "no-load" table, but I can assure you that there are still fees being paid while the game is being played.

Does this sound like a game that can get *you* rich, or a way for the *casino* to get rich? Common sense tells you that you most likely know the answer to that question.

Sadly, many people either blindly throw their money at something because it sounds good, leaving the investment of their hard-earned dollars to chance, or entrust their money to guys in Armani suits who could very well be playing the game in a hornet's nest buzzing with unnecessary commissions, high fees, and uncontrollable taxes.

Now, in fairness, I need to take a step back. I've obviously not painted a very good picture of roulette advisors or fund managers wearing Armani suits. Most certainly, there are some very good roulette advisors around, and certainly not every fund manager loses people's money.

There are certainly some good mutual funds out there. No doubt, I'm being a bit over the top to make a point. But, that said, if you aren't paying close attention to this game that many are indeed playing, you are doing yourself a horrible disservice, especially when it comes to the cost to play it.

Often, when it comes to fees and taxes, I see people turning the other way. "After all," I often hear, "my mutual fund made me lots of money last year."

Congratulations. That's fantastic news. But that's also the type of attitude that the casinos of Wall Street spend fortunes every year on advertising, marketing, and branding *hoping* you'll end up thinking that way.

Without a doubt, there is another way to do this—a way that is far more effective and efficient, and less costly in terms of fees and taxes; a way that greatly eliminates the guesswork, high fees, uncontrollable taxes, and frustration from the equation. And after I complete my little tale, I'll be certain to back that up with some interesting facts that very few Wall Street firms spend millions of dollars to advertise.

The game of roulette I would prefer to play costs a lot less, gives you total control of when you get in and out of the game and when

Uncle Sam takes his cut. Furthermore, and best of all, the game I prefer to play offers returns that are often much higher than those at all the tables we just gambled at.

After all, by paying less in fees and taxes, isn't it logical that you are already one big step ahead of the game?

Getting rich often means looking at things with a different perspective—ignoring the flashy magazine ads, burgundy velvet chairs, and well-produced TV commercials. Getting rich means having the confidence to maintain a contrarian's view, a perspective that goes against the grain of millions of dollars spent on advertising that tries so very hard to do one thing: get your money and make you think you need someone to pick individual stocks for you.

To win the game, you must search for concepts that you may have once heard about, but that have very likely been buried in the rubble of advertising, marketing, and advisors potentially clouding your mind. So, grab a shovel and let's start digging to explore the last choice you have to once and for all find a way to fill up the large-cap sector of your diversified portfolio.

Roulette Table 3: Index Funds

Neither trying to pick individual stocks by yourself nor having someone do it for you through a mutual fund was a very good experience. On your way out of the casino, you catch sight of something interesting—there's another roulette table in a distant corner. This area is the index investing part of the casino, representing choice number three of how to pick stocks for the large-cap sector of your diversified investment portfolio.

This area is dimly lit and it's not as flashy as the other area you just left. In fact, it's a no-frills type of place. There are no plush velvet reclining chairs, waitresses, flashing lights, or platinum tables.

As dim and unappealing as it is, something about this area seems a bit interesting. Brave, or perhaps curious, you look past the no-frills nature of this game and take a few steps closer. You notice that here, everyone around this no-frills table seems to be in a peaceful mood. When you take a look at what's going on, you notice that *all* large-cap stocks on the table are covered; they are all picked, taking the emotion and the guesswork out of the game. Oddly, there's not even a fund manager standing at the table picking anything. There are no up-front fees paid to roulette advisors, and because there are no fund managers picking and choosing which number might come up next, the cost to play this game is quite inexpensive, especially when compared to paying the roulette advisor and the fund manager to do it for you.

You carefully check the rules, and things look even better. In this game, you can take your money off the table at any time and, to make matters even better, you find out Uncle Sam doesn't visit this table until *you* decide it's time to invite him over. Just when you thought it couldn't get any better, you see the track record of this mindless game: Most of the time, it's clear that you will make more money playing at this table than at the one where the professional fund manager is picking away. Thinking about it, something seems logical here: No one picking which large-cap stocks he thinks will be best? No fund manager who could have been recruited to another table because he was doing a great job, leaving you with some guy who basically has no track record?

Better performance? Lower fees? *You* control the taxes *and* when you get in and out of the game? You ask a guy nearby, "Why doesn't everyone play this?" He answers, "That's simple. Over here, there are no flashy signs, fancy service, or velvet chairs. Know what I mean?"

Something tells you that *this* is the game to play. It just *feels* a lot smarter. You toss a few chips on the table, no one takes a cut, and as the wheel is spun, you are doing well. Why are you winning more often than the fund manager did? Wasn't he supposed to be the expert? The answer is simple: *All* the large-cap stocks on this table are covered, providing a significantly better chance of winning. This one requires little guesswork, no emotion, less news, no monkeys, no randomly thrown darts, and certainly not having to watch a guy on TV hurling chairs or slinging water balloons across the room.

Over on this side of the casino, we find what is commonly known as index investing.

Index investing is the third, and as far as I'm concerned, most powerful way to select stocks to represent each sector of your diversified portfolio. Index investing takes much of the guesswork out of investing. Unless you, your advisor, or your fund manager is one of the very rare exceptions who can successfully pick winning stocks on a *consistent* basis, there's no doubt: When it comes to making money in the markets, for many reasons, this is by far the most efficient game for most people to be playing.

Let's take a closer look.

The Index Advantage

Is it possible to get higher rates of return on your money over time with reduced risk? While it may sound a bit fishy at first, read on to find out why it *is* possible.

A divorced woman in her mid-50s came into my office wanting a second opinion. Joyce sensed that things could be better when it came to her investments. She had been with the same advisor for over 10 years, and just as she occasionally brings her car in for a tune-up, she wanted a second opinion to see if her engine of investments was running as efficiently as possible.

Joyce's money was held at a fairly large brokerage firm. What was taking place in her investment engine wasn't all that unusual; in fact, from what I have seen over the years, it's unfortunately quite common.

To try to diversify her $500,000 portfolio, Joyce's advisor selected a portfolio of managed mutual funds to represent the various market sectors of her somewhat diversified portfolio. Most of the mutual funds were proprietary funds, which simply means these funds are available only to clients of the brokerage itself. As an example, if the name of the brokerage was Alan Haft Brokerage, then the proprietary funds would be named something such as Alan Haft Mutual Funds, and only clients of Alan Haft Brokerage would have the ability to purchase Alan Haft Mutual Funds.

Propriety mutual funds are generally not a good sign. Often (but certainly not always) these funds have higher overall fees than most others of the same group. As for performance, it's not uncommon for them to rank lower than their peers as well.

As soon as I saw Joyce's portfolio, I knew there could be some concern. After researching her funds through various sources, I calculated she initially paid over $10,000 in sales commissions just to set up the portfolio. Joyce was aware of this, but defended her current advisor by stating that a different one had initially sold her the funds.

Some people may be reading this and thinking, "I never purchase front-end load mutual funds that charge a commission. I purchase only no-load funds." If you are of that mind-set, congratulations. You are a step ahead of the game. Unfortunately, the *internal* fees inside mutual funds *once you are invested in them* can sometimes be fairly steep. (For the mutual fund investors out there curious to find out how much you are paying in your mutual funds, be sure to check out Lipper's www.personalfund.com, a fantastic resource for the fee-conscious investor and what I sometimes refer to as "the mutual fund killer").

In Joyce's case, the cost to run her investment engine every year, regardless of whether she was making or losing money is broken down as shown in Table 2.8.

It cost Joyce over 5 percent per year to invest in the mutual funds and have her newer advisor watch over them. On a portfolio valued at approximately $500,000, for the 10 years she was in the funds the total cost to her in fees and taxes was over $250,000.

Needless to say, that is a lot of money to pay in fees and taxes, and it is certainly not the way people get rich.

Was Joyce's advisor a bad guy? In many cases, not at all. As retired Securities and Exchange Commission Chairman Arthur Levitt writes in his fantastic book, *Take On the Street*, brokers such as this are often "good people in a bad system." It's not their fault that the funds have high fees; it's just that the business of brokerage firms *requires* their brokers to generate them.

The fact of the matter is that if you are not paying attention to fees, you are likely doing yourself a terrible disservice.

Starting out a year of investing at *minus* 5 percent like Joyce obviously did makes earning money much more difficult. With those types of fees, it's as if her money had a ball and chain wrapped around it, and it's no wonder Joyce was sensing her investment engine wasn't running at maximum efficiency.

When I pointed out the fees to Joyce, her instinctive reaction was to first defend the broker she's been with. "But over the years," she said, "my account has gone up in value."

True, there was no denying that, but unfortunately, this is exactly what the broker and the fund companies want you to be thinking. Through the low cost and highly efficient indexes, she could have still been diversified in the markets but at a much lower cost in terms

Table 2.8   Joyce's Investment Expenses

Internal Fees to the Fund	1.40%
Transaction Fees	.84%
Distribution Fees	1.00%
Taxes Distributed	.75%
Annual Management Fee to Advisor	1.50%
Total Annual Cost	**5.49%**

of fees and taxes. With this efficiency, her account could have been worth far more than it was today.

Would you be interested in:

- Easily picking stocks to represent each sector of your diversified portfolio?
- Keeping fees to an absolute minimum?
- Controlling when you want to pay tax?
- Controlling exactly when you want to be in or out of the market?
- Best of all, statistically speaking, having a greater chance of getting higher rates of return than when someone does the stock picking for you?

Who wouldn't say yes to all of these? And the answer is to stay in the no-frills area of the casino of the markets known as index investing.

What Exactly Is Indexing?

Think of an index as a roulette table where all the numbers for the particular sector are covered with your chips. If the roulette table represents the large-cap sector within your portfolio, then instead of you, your advisor or a professional fund manager trying to pick the *best* large-cap companies out there, the index says, "I don't know which large-cap companies will be the best, so I'm simply going to pick *all* of them."

Index investing is a *passive* investment strategy, meaning "hands off." It is sometimes referred to as lazy investing, because no one is really trying to pick the stocks. In an index, *all* the stocks within a very specific sector are included, and from there, the stocks within the index are rarely changed.

An index is a group of stocks selected to represent a certain portion of the stock market. The Standard & Poor's (S&P) 500 index, which consists of 500 large-cap domestic stocks, such as Microsoft and General Electric, is widely considered to be the best representative of the market as a whole. The Russell 2000 index consists of small-company stocks. The Morgan Stanley Capital International Europe, Australasia, Far East (MSCI EAFE) index holds international stocks. You will find that there is an index for just about every sector of the market, including highly specialized sectors such as health care stocks, real estate, oil and exploration, nano technology, water companies, currencies, commodities, clean energy companies and many other departments that can be found within the "Bloomingdale's department store" of investments.

I sometimes find it odd that many advisors challenge the efficiency of index investing. After all, as I'll momentarily point out, not only do some of the most successful investors and fund managers in the country openly advocate index investing, but many have revealed it's the manner in which they invest *their own* money. If some of the greatest, most successful minds of Wall Street follow this advice, why isn't your advisor doing so? These are questions that are sometimes tough to ask, but the challenge is often one well worth making.

Here's a handful of quotes some advisors and many fund companies certainly aren't going to openly advertise:

- "Let me add a few thoughts about your own investments. Most investors, both institutional and individuals, will find that the best way to own common stocks is through an index fund that charges minimal fees. Those following this path are sure to beat the net results (after fees and expenses) delivered by the great majority of investment professionals."—Warren Buffett, Berkshire Hathaway Annual Report, 1996.
- "A low-cost index fund will *always* outperform the collective performance of active investors in the same market sector. Last year, a majority of funds failed to beat their benchmark index in *eight of the nine categories*. The five-year results are equally bad, with funds again striking out in eight of the nine categories."—Jonathan Clements, "Getting Actively Passive," *Wall Street Journal,* January 12, 2005.
- "The truth is, any lazy portfolio index strategy is better than wasting your time chasing hot stocks and the other 8,000-plus actively managed funds, 80 to 85 percent of which underperforms the market every year. So in the long run, any one of the indexing strategies is a better choice than virtually any load fund."—Paul B. Farrell, *MarketWatch,* January 16, 2007.
- "Only 19 percent of all actively managed funds beat the Standard & Poor's 500 stock index this year."—Shefali Anand, "Strong Markets Had Few Losers," *Wall Street Journal,* December 29, 2006.
- "Reams of statistics prove that most of the fund industry's stock pickers fail to beat the market." The solution, says Jonathan

Clements, is to "ditch actively managed funds and buy market-tracking index funds instead." As for fees and taxes, he states, "Loads, like taxes, are ignored by most surveys of mutual-fund performance. But if loads were included, the results for actively managed funds would look even worse."—Jonathan Clements, "Only Fools Believe in Managed Funds," *Wall Street Journal*, September 15, 2002.

- "Even the hotshots working full-time in the financial world follow the same strategy with the bulk of their assets. It's their biggest secret. Mutual fund managers making an average $400,000-plus playing the market with your money often lock away the bulk of their retirement assets in safe, untouchable portfolios using a variation of a lazy portfolio strategy."—Paul B. Farrell, "'Lazy Portfolios' Win Again, Beat S&P 500!" *MarketWatch*, January 16, 2007.

- "When indexing is discussed by brokers, fund-company executives, and others on Wall Street, it is often in scathing terms. Make no mistake: These derogatory comments are entirely self-serving."—Jonathan Clements, "Investors Cling to Managed Funds Despite Performance of Indexing," *Wall Street Journal*, July 29, 2001.

- "Wall Street doesn't want you to use this Nobel Prize-winning strategy because it can't rake off enough in transactions fees from index funds."—Paul B. Farrell, *MarketWatch*, January 16, 2007.

So, if many mutual funds are not so spectacular, why do so many people still invest in them? I believe the answer as to why mutual funds remain so popular comes down to two things: (1) advisors make more money touting them, and (2) through massive advertising, the fund companies have done a fantastic job of convincing many Main Street investors that the fund managers can do it better than anyone else.

Have you ever done something as utterly boring as I have and counted the number of ads mutual fund companies place in some of the most popular investment magazines in the country, such as *Money* magazine? It probably won't surprise you that the number of ads placed by the mutual fund companies is often far greater than the number of ads for any other type of investment. It's no wonder that in mainstream media, we often don't hear a lot about the pitfalls of mutual funds when those companies are providing much of the advertising revenue that supports the media themselves.

Speaking of ads, have you ever read the small print? You may be surprised when taking a closer look at it. Take, for example, excerpts of one particular fund's tiny print, which I found just recently in a leading financial magazine:

- "During the period shown, some of the Fund's fees were waived or expenses reimbursed; otherwise, total return would have been lower."
- "If the Fund's performance had been readjusted to reflect estimated expenses of the Fund for its first fiscal year, the performance would have been lower."

Many fund ads eliminate sales charges, fees, and tax ramifications from their stated returns. If critical elements such as these were included, the returns would not only be lower, but most likely *much* lower.

As Jonathan Clements well points out in his 2002 *Wall Street Journal* article mentioned earlier, "Paying a load makes it awfully tough to earn superior returns. If you invest $1,000 in a fund that charges a 5.75 percent load, your account balance starts out at $942.50. That means you have to earn 6.1 percent, just to get back to even."

Another reason I believe mutual funds remain so popular is because the investor does not have to actually write a check for the fees. I often use the experience I had with Joyce's $500,000 mutual fund portfolio to make a point. I sometimes ask investors the following questions:

1. Would they be interested in paying over $10,000 just to start the investment process?
2. Would they be interested in paying fees and taxes of over $20,000 per year regardless of whether the account ever makes money?
3. And the final offer: Over a 10-year period, would they be interested in paying fees and taxes of over $200,000 on their investments?

Certainly, in the perspective of *dollars* and not *percentages*, most people would never take up any of these offers. But the ironic thing is many people *are* doing such a thing; they just haven't taken the time to realize it.

I equate this to the way casinos operate. Many years ago, while the movie *Casino* was being filmed in Las Vegas, I had the chance to spend some considerable time with people in upper echelons of the Caesar's Palace organization. One of the top executives told me that when it came to the business of gambling, if chips were ever replaced with cash, he felt the casinos would easily lose well over half of their business.

The same thing would probably happen if investors had to write checks for their fund fees. If every year a woman such as Joyce had to physically write a check for over $20,000 to stay invested in her funds, I'd bet anything she would have been much more motivated to find a less expensive way to invest.

So, the next time you look at your mutual fund statement, or the next time someone out there recommends that you represent a market sector within your diversified portfolio with managed mutual funds, just take a step back and imagine yourself physically writing a check for the fees. You might possibly feel *better* writing that check, but in my experience, this mental exercise often inspires the investor to seek a less costly direction.

The answer to lowering your costs and taxes and typically increasing your returns is found in index investing.

Investing in the Indexes

Index funds invest in whichever stocks are in a particular index. They don't hire analysts with Ivy League MBAs, and they usually don't develop a lot of slick marketing materials trying to convince you that their fund is the best. This significantly reduces the fees the fund charges shareholders, which quite simply leaves more of your money to grow.

Moreover, actively traded mutual funds do just that—they actively trade. When a mutual fund sells stocks, the capital gains are passed on to you, meaning you have to pay taxes even if you haven't sold anything. Typically, trading is done within an index fund only when the composition of the index it represents changes. The result is a much smaller tax bill for you, given the fact that these changes are usually highly infrequent.

There are two types of products available to invest in indexes: index *mutual funds* and one of my favorite products to hit Wall Street in recent years, index *exchange-traded funds* (ETFs). Both types of funds replicate an index. Index mutual funds, as the name implies, are mutual funds. You obtain them through a brokerage, your financial advisor, or any mutual fund company that sells directly to the public.

Exchange-traded funds, in contrast, are bought and sold like regular stocks and even have stock symbols. Index ETFs that track the S&P 500 include Spiders (SPY) and iShares (IVV is one example). One of the leading providers of ETFs is Barclays; you can check out its selection of ETFs at www.ishares.com. Vanguard also has many ETFs, as do many other companies, making these highly efficient investment tools widely available throughout the market.

One thing you will want to watch out for, whichever you choose, are the fees you're paying. Before you invest, check the fund's expense ratio, which is calculated as a percentage of the amount you invest. Generally, I would advise investing in an index fund or ETF that has an operating expense of less than 0.4 percent, which is typically the case. The internal fees of many ETFs are even as low as 0.2 percent per year, which is certainly light-years less than the fees Joyce was paying per year on her account.

For Joyce, saving 5 percent in fees and taxes per year instantly earns her 5 percent more per year on her investments. On an account worth $500,000, that's over $20,000 more per year remaining in her account, and over a 10-year period that's an astonishing difference of over $200,000.

Does that sound like a way to help you get rich? I think it does.

At the beginning of this section, do you recall I said I'd show a way to generate higher returns on your investment at no risk? This is the answer: In Joyce's case, it was for her to lower her fees and taxes. After all, the less you pay, the more you keep, correct? Maybe after a careful analysis of your portfolio you'll wind up feeling the same way.

As for performance, the returns on index mutual funds and ETFs representing the same index are typically the same, given that the stocks within the index are usually identical. However, there are a few reasons you may want to consider one over the other. Since ETFs are bought and sold just like stocks, with rare exception, you will pay a transaction fee each time you buy and sell. If you were adding money into your portfolio on a regular basis, you would likely be better off investing in the index as a mutual fund instead of through an ETF. The reason for this is that most index mutual funds do not charge trading fees when adding or withdrawing money.

One distinct advantage that ETFs have over index mutual funds, however, is that they can be traded on a moment's notice—intraday, as it is technically referred to—whereas shares of a mutual fund aren't sold until the end of the day.

In addition, because an ETF trades like a stock, it offers protective measures that one cannot take advantage of when investing in a mutual fund: first, the ability to establish a safety net such as a stop-loss order that could potentially protect you by selling your position at a predetermined level if the share price drops in value; and second, the ability to purchase something called "put options" on the position. If your ETF drops in value, your owning a put obligates someone to purchase the ETF from you at a future price greater than the price it is then trading at. Buying put options, which is generally considered to be a conservative strategy given that the maximum one can lose is the cost of the option itself, is a fantastic way to insure a portfolio of ETFs against significant loss (or, for that matter, individual stocks as well). There are other option strategies that could be considered, but because options are an entire subject of their own, I'll quickly move past these otherwise advanced concepts.

(That said, I can't resist: If you are reading this book and have large holdings in individual stocks and/or ETFs, I would strongly recommend you learn a little about various option strategies that could protect your holdings, especially if you are of the mind-set that you won't sell your stocks in exchange for a more diversified portfolio.)

Getting back on track . . . Should you invest in an index mutual fund or an index exchange-traded fund? My preference has always been in favor of index exchange-traded funds, simply because they essentially do the same thing as an index mutual fund but provide you with maximum control that could protect the investment.

When I see an investment portfolio filled with brand-name and propriety mutual funds such as Joyce's, I typically determine if it makes practical sense to replicate portions of the portfolio with the lower-cost indexes.

In Joyce's case, the fee structure would have been dramatically different. Instead of paying fees and taxes of over $200,000 for the 10-year period she was invested in the funds, her account would have cost her only a few thousand dollars in total fees and hardly anything in tax. She would have had more control over her investments, and, according to the statistics, would likely had a higher return on her investments.

- Lower fees?
- Less tax?
- Much greater control of your money?
- According to the statistics, higher returns on your investments?

That's the way people get rich.

Building the House

Let's take a step back and quickly summarize what we've covered so far:

- Diversification is the key to taking the guesswork out of investing.
- If you want to speculate for the high returns, do it with a small portion of your money outside your diversified portfolio that you are willing to lose.
- The most efficient way to pick stocks to represent an asset class within a diversified portfolio is *not* to pick individual stocks or have a broker or mutual fund manager do it for you. The most efficient way to do it is to invest in the indexes, preferably through an exchange-traded fund (if you are making frequent contributions to the portfolio, use an index mutual fund instead).

Remember: Although diversification certainly won't guarantee against loss, it is a key strategy in helping you minimize risk. As mentioned earlier, some believe diversification is also a recipe for lackluster returns, and as promised, I will be sure to address how to best overcome this belief. That subject is coming up soon.

To diversify, one must first develop what's known as an asset allocation model, and that's what this section is all about.

As a reminder, asset allocation is the process of spreading your investments among different asset classes. At the highest level, major asset classes are typically defined as stocks, bonds, and shorter-term safer investments such as cash equivalents. Although international stocks are technically a subcategory of the stock asset class, many people consider it to be one of the top-level asset classes as well.

Remember Bloomingdale's? The highest-level asset classes are represented by departments such as menswear, while the subclasses, as we'll soon start exploring, are represented by things *within* menswear such as shoes, hats, suits, and ties.

When it comes to actually diversifying a portfolio, let's say you are investing for what many people do it for: investing for retirement. If you won't be retiring for many years, you would obviously want to accumulate as much as possible and will therefore allocate more of your investments to the areas of the markets that have historically produced the highest rates of return (stocks), since you'll probably be seeking growth and have some time to ride out the ups and downs of the market.

As you get closer to retirement, though, prudent planning says you should start shifting the diversified portfolio of stocks toward more conservative, reliable, and predictable investments, such as bonds, that will help minimize exposure to market volatility, preserve your money as much as possible, and allow you to *reliably* live off the nest egg you've presumably spent many years working to accumulate.

I, and many others typically refer to the working years as the accumulation stage, during which you are obviously trying to build up as much wealth as possible. Once in retirement, for most people it's time to generate as much reliable income from the portfolio as possible. Many people call this stage different things, such as the distribution stage, but I often refer to it as the time in our lives when we'll want to generate *reliable returns* to get us the *income* we want.

- The accumulation stage is typically the most speculative, given that it's during this period of time that most people are often heavily invested in the stock market, seeking maximum growth. And because the growth of stocks is speculative (no one can ever be sure what the returns will be), this is obviously the riskiest stage of investing.
- The reliable returns stage is typically the time when we move closer to or are already in retirement. Transitioning and shifting growth investments from the accumulation stage to investments that will generate reliable returns, especially for income, should take place here.
- There's also the preservation stage, or, as some people call it, the transfer stage. This is usually defined as the period of time late into retirement when safety of principal is of paramount importance, with an outlook on how to best transfer the assets to heirs.

In the rest of this chapter, I'll be addressing how to construct a portfolio for the accumulation stage. In the next chapter, I'll discuss concepts on generating reliable returns, especially for the income-hungry investor who is often found in the reliable returns stage; and late into the book, I'll mention a few important concepts to consider when in the preservation or transfer stage.

However, just as a good movie script weaves together all aspects of the plot, although the stages obviously take place at different points in our lives, there is no doubt they are interwoven together right here and right now. So please, don't for a moment think that learning a few things about the preservation stage is not applicable to you. Quite frankly, the more you understand about each stage, the better your own personal movie will play out now and, of course, further on down the road.

Time to Roll Up the Sleeves

We're about to start building our diversified portfolio house. Grab a couple of tools and let's get started.

Diversification is all about developing an asset allocation strategy in each of the major asset classes. Within each of the major asset classes—stocks, bonds, and cash—as mentioned, there are also subcategories, such as domestic and international stocks, growth and value stocks, and investment-grade and high-yield bonds.

For example, you may want to divide your stock allocation between domestic and international stocks. Or, you might choose to allocate a higher percentage of your portfolio to stocks that focus on a certain industry or sector, such as technology or health care stocks. Again, the closer you are in needing to live off your assets, the more conservatively you will need to invest.

If you are 35 years old and investing for retirement, you will likely want to allocate more of your investments to midsize domestic, international, and sector-specific indexes such as technology, which can be riskier (and offer greater opportunity for growth) than a sector such as large-cap domestic stocks. As you near retirement, however, you will absolutely want to shift assets away from those riskier sectors toward more conservative sectors that I'll soon be discussing.

Unfortunately, given personal tastes, risk tolerances, and a wide variety of other factors, there is no exact and precise science as to what *your* portfolio should look like. However, I will provide you with some concrete examples that could very well wind up being the portfolio you select. But just as if you were creating your own Bloomingdale's department store, a certain level of customization depending on your personal needs, goals, and desires will need to be factored in.

As if you were building a house that you are going to live in for a long time, taking the time to determine the sectors you want to be included in your portfolio is very important. As we'll soon learn later in the chapter, for your investments to be *consistent, sustainable,* and *rewarding,* the intent is to select sectors that are going to be like giving birth to a bunch of new children; it's as if you were giving birth to sectors that should remain in your house for quite some period of time.

While at first that might seem a bit scary, intimidating, or overwhelming, I'll soon show you why and how it's not. But make no bones about it; if you want to be an investor and make things easy and rewarding for yourself, selecting sectors that belong in your portfolio for the long haul is going to require a bit of work up front.

But here's the honest and truly best part of all: As soon as this up-front work is done, living in this house with your new children will require less maintenance than you very likely imagine. In fact, the less maintenance you typically put into it, the more effective it usually is.

The Rule of 120

Sometimes the simplest rules are the most effective. Let's begin with a very general rule that will help you at least form a framework for your house.

Many years ago, a very Wall Street trader who amassed extraordinary wealth in the markets introduced me to one of the simplest asset allocation rules I have ever come across. You might have heard of this rule, commonly referred to as the Rule of 100. But because people are living longer and longer, the timeless, prudent rule has been updated to the Rule of 120.

The Rule of 120 very simply states that in order to determine the percentages of your portfolio that should be in stocks (for growth) and in a sector such as bonds (for increased safety and preservation), all you need to do is subtract your age from 120. The result is the percentage of stocks you should have exposure to.

For simplicity, suppose I am 45 years old and I have $100,000 in savings. To provide me with a general guideline for the percentage of my portfolio that should be in stocks and the percentage to be in more conservative investments such as bonds, the following steps would give me a basis for understanding:

- $120 - 45 = 75$.
- Therefore, 75 percent (or \$75,000) of my portfolio should be in stocks for growth.
- The remaining 25 percent (or \$25,000) should be in bonds.

Having a hard time believing that something so simple could be so effective, many years ago I ventured out to find something that would be more accurate. I figured there was no way something so ridiculously simple could ever be so efficient. After researching virtually every asset allocation modeling software available on the market, I finally settled on one and spent quite a few dollars to purchase it. I installed it and spent weeks to understand every aspect of it, only to come to the realization that, looking past all the complicated, colorful, and fancy charts (and the highly detailed reports the software generated that virtually no one ever seemed to read), the end results were really no different from the Rule of 120.

Thankfully, the Rule of 120 is a very simple formula to remember, especially since I'll be referring back to it several times during the course of this chapter and throughout the book.

Now, let's move forward. . . .

As mentioned, in a book such as this, generalizing a one-size-fits-all portfolio for everyone is virtually impossible. Everyone is different, and as such, your portfolio will be best determined by who you are, your tolerance for taking risks, your age and time horizon to retirement, how much income you anticipate needing at retirement, and a variety of other factors.

I have met plenty of people very late into retirement who are absolutely comfortable keeping 100 percent of their money in speculative stocks regardless of what the fundamental guidelines of prudent planning tell us. To each his or her own, and if that's what makes someone happy, then so be it.

As an advisor, I believe my job is to merely to help people make sure they fully understand the choices available in the marketplace, what could go wrong with their current plan, why their current course of action might not be the most effective, and what the alternatives are. As long as someone understands and is comfortable in their current plan as well as understanding all the risks associated with it, then their plan could very well be the perfect one for them.

To give you an idea of what a diversified portfolio could look like during the accumulation stage, you may want to use the guide in Table 2.9 as a starting point to help you construct the foundation for your diversified portfolio.

Table 2.9 Model Portfolios

Sector	% of Portfolio Allocated to Sector
More Than 10 Years until Retirement	
Low Risk	
Bonds	30%
Foreign	20%
Large Caps	30%
Small Caps	20%
Medium Risk	
Bonds	25%
Foreign	20%
Large Caps	35%
Small Caps	20%
More Risk	
Bonds	20%
Foreign	20%
Large Caps	40%
Small Caps	20%
Five to 10 Years Until Retirement	
Low Risk	
Bonds	50%
Foreign	15%
Large Caps	25%
Small Caps	10%
Medium Risk	
Bonds	45%
Foreign	15%
Large Caps	30%
Small Caps	10%
More Risk	
Bonds	40%
Foreign	15%
Large Caps	30%
Small Caps	15%

Table 2.9   (*Continued*)

Sector	% of Portfolio Allocated to Sector
Three to Five Years until Retirement	
Low Risk	
Bonds	70%
Foreign	10%
Large Caps	15%
Small Caps	5%
Medium Risk	
Bonds	65%
Foreign	10%
Large Caps	20%
Small Caps	5%
More Risk	
Bonds	60%
Foreign	10%
Large Caps	20%
Small Caps	10%

A few things to keep in mind:

- Table 2.9 should serve as a general guideline only and should not be construed as a recommendation for your exact portfolio. That can only be determined by gaining a much better understanding of your personal situation.
- To represent each sector mentioned, I would use index exchange-traded funds (ETFs). Some of the largest providers of ETFs are Barclays iShares (www.ishares.com), Vanguard (www.vanguard.com), PowerShares (www.powershares.com), Wisdom-Tree (www.wisdomtree.com), ProFunds (www.profunds.com), and StreetTracks (www.ssgafunds.com). For simplicity, I would suggest first exploring Barclays. A search for all sectors to be included in your diversified portfolio could very well end there.
- As mentioned and explained earlier, you might be better off investing in index mutual funds instead (especially if you are adding additional monies into your positions on a frequent

basis). For index mutual funds, I would recommend you consider Vanguard (www.vanguard.com).

- *For the bonds sector:* I might consider investing in the ETF ticker symbol "AGG," which represents the Lehman Brothers Aggregate Bond index.
- *For the international sector:* I might consider investing in the ETF ticker symbol "EFA," which represents the MSCI EAFE index of international stocks found in Europe, Australasia, and the Far East.
- *For the large caps sector:* I might consider investing in the ETF ticker symbol "SPY," which represents the S&P 500 index of large U.S.-based company stocks.
- *For the small caps sector:* I might consider investing in the ETF ticker symbol "IWO," which represents the Russell 2000 growth index of small U.S.-based company stocks.

Table 2.9 is a quick guide that could possibly serve as the foundation for the portfolio. I'll give an example of how to apply this shortly.

The Process of Building a Portfolio

The following is an example of how one could go about building a diversified portfolio. As a first step, the stock and bond portions of the portfolio should be determined by the Rule of 120. If, for example, I'm 45 years old, then as outlined, 75 percent of my portfolio would be allocated to stocks (120 − 45 = 75 percent stocks). The remaining 25 percent of my portfolio would be allocated to bonds.

Furthermore, suppose I consider myself an investor who is more than 10 years from retirement and willing to tolerate medium risk. Using Table 2.9 as my guide, my buy-and-hold portfolio might be as shown in Table 2.10.

The portfolio might simply end there, and for most people it really should. Typically, for many investors, there's no reason to make things any more complicated than this. However, some people might want to further diversify and fine-tune the portfolio to better meet their own personal desires. This is important to recognize now, because later in this chapter when I discuss rebalancing, I'll be detailing why this portfolio will be most effective as a buy-and-hold, core group of holdings that should change as little as possible. Remember: The simpler you make your golf swing, the better your score typically gets.

Table 2.10   Sample Diversified Portfolio

Assuming $100,000 Portfolio		
Sector	Percent	Dollar Amount
Bond Index	25%	$25,000
Foreign Index	20%	$20,000
Large Cap Index	35%	$35,000
Small Cap Index	20%	$20,000

Leaving Room for Other Sectors

Suppose, as an example, I want to add some additional market sectors to my buy-and-hold portfolio that I believe are worthy of holding for the long run—common sectors such as technology and real estate. In order to free up some of the buy-and-hold portfolio, I would need to make some room, wouldn't I?

To do that, I'd simply reduce the percentages of each stock index by a few points—as an example, by 3 percent. Doing so would add room in the portfolio for these technology and real estate indexes.

Keeping in mind that I am adding stock indexes, therefore, the only allocations I want to modify are the stock sectors. The bond allocation is not modified, because, as always, I am strictly enforcing my Rule of 120 and I'm holding the balance of the portfolio steady at 75 percent stocks and 25 percent bonds.

After the adjustments are made, my diversified portfolio might look something like Table 2.11.

Table 2.11   Sample Diversified Portfolio with Additional Indexes

Assuming $100,000 Portfolio		
Sector	Percent	Dollar Amount
Bond Index	25%	$25,000
Foreign Index	17%	$17,000
Large Cap Index	32%	$32,000
Small Cap Index	17%	$17,000
Added:		
Real Estate Index	4.5%	$4,500
Technology Index	4.5%	$4,500

Leaving Room for Flavors of the Day

Taking this one final step further, suppose I want to leave room for trading individual stocks or adding sectors of the market that are trending well but do not necessarily belong in the buy-and-hold portfolio for the long haul.

To avoid having to remove fundamental sectors from the core buy-and-hold foundation established in the previous examples, it would be most prudent to create what I commonly refer to as the "flavors of the day" sector in the portfolio itself.

In order to do this, I would once again have to make room in the portfolio to add yet another sector, in this case, the flavors of the day sector. To make room, I would once again further reduce the percentages of the stock indexes to free up some money. Remember: I never deviate from the Rule of 120; I am keeping the bond percentage the same—I'm merely modifying the stock portion and nothing else.

In such a case, the portfolio might be modified to look something like Table 2.12.

Some of the more speculative investors may want to increase the percentage of the "flavors of the day" sector from 9 percent (in my example) to 15 percent, or as high as 20 percent, but I wouldn't recommend much more than that, given that doing so would mean only one thing: You are speculating with too much of your money, not *investing* it.

Table 2.12   Sample Diversified Portfolio with Additional Indexes and Flavors of the Day

Assuming $100,000 Portfolio		
Sector	Percent	Dollar Amount
Bond Index	25.0%	$25,000
Foreign Index	14.0%	$14,000
Large Cap Index	29.0%	$29,000
Small Cap Index	14.0%	$14,000
Real Estate Index	4.5%	$4,500
Technology Index	4.5%	$4,500
Added:		
*Flavors of the Day	9%	$9,000

*Includes anything I desire; this is the only actively traded part of the portfolio.

Applying a strategy such as this means that you recognize that the core holdings of your portfolio represent the foundation and majority of your investment house, and the roof is reserved for speculative opportunities as they arise. After all, if a violent wind blows the roof off (the "flavors of the day" section of the portfolio), there will still always be a house to live in (the fundamental sectors found within a diversified portfolio). Within the "flavors of the day," you might invest in individual stocks or indexes that represent anything your speculative heart desires, such as narrow market sectors that are trending favorably at any given period in time (some examples: currency indexes, specific country indexes such as China, oil exploration companies, health service companies, biotechnology, gold, silver, other commodities, water service companies—far too many possibilities to list here). For some of the more creative sector indexes available, check out ETF providers such as PowerShares (www.powershares.com) and ProFunds (www.profunds.com).

The key point, however, is that when it comes to picking individual stocks or highly specialized market sectors that you want to take advantage of for a more brief period of time, the portion of your portfolio reserved for the flavors of the day should be *the only area of your investment portfolio that you are actively trading.*

The "flavors of the day" sector is the only place in the house where the market timer or speculator within us should be allowed to live. If you lost money within this sector, it would certainly be upsetting; but, because it should represent a smaller slice of the portfolio, it wouldn't affect the *investor* who is living in all other parts of the well-constructed, diversified house for the long haul.

One practice I've found very helpful to many investors is to create a "flavors of the day" account that is completely separate from the one where the core diversified portfolio resides. For example, suppose my total portfolio is worth $100,000, and I want to create a "flavors of the day" sector with $20,000. Instead of having the entire $100,000 lumped into one account, I would recommend creating a second account with this $20,000 that remains separate from the diversified portfolio, which is then worth $80,000. Doing so typically helps an investor maintain discipline in using this $20,000 account as the only place where the market timer and speculator is allowed to reside.

Individual Stocks Living in Your "Flavors of the Day" Sector

With rare exceptions, and for reasons I believe I've made clear, whether we're discussing the core portfolio or the "flavors of the day" sector, I prefer using indexes as the investment vehicle of choice. However, there will undoubtedly come a time when you get an itch to invest in an individual stock. Many people do; therefore, this is a good moment to make a few comments on how to pick an individual stock. Once we move past this section, I'll return to the diversified portfolio and give you a few examples of some real-world portfolios used by some of the brightest minds out there, and a few other interesting ideas.

But for the moment, let's digress with a few words on how to pick an individual stock that might very well be used to satisfy the "flavors of the day" portion of your diversified portfolio. And when picking individual stocks to satisfy the "flavors of the day" itch, what better way to do it than the Warren Buffett way?

How to Pick a Stock Like Warren Buffett

Although I have clearly preached the concept of representing each section of your diversified portfolio with indexes as opposed to managed mutual funds or picking individual stocks, every once in a while I, along with countless others, simply cannot resist the urge to invest in an individual company. That said, when picking an individual company to bet on, I would strongly suggest not just tossing your chips on black 23 on the roulette table. There's a better way to do it, and learning a few things from Warren Buffett is certainly a decent place to start.

So, if you are interested in learning how to pick individual stocks that can turn $1,000 into over $40 billion, this section is for you.

Pretty easy, right? All it takes is a little time and some homework.

Well, not exactly, but if you want to take a shot at it, I would recommend you start by learning some of Warren Buffett's basics. Study the method he used to turn $1,000 into $40 billion; at least maybe then there's a fighting chance.

To begin with, Buffett has often stated that everything he learned about investing he learned from Benjamin Graham, the author of *The Intelligent Investor*, widely considered by many, including myself, to be the greatest, most timeless and relevant book on prudent investing.

Written in 1949, the classic work covers Graham's safe and sound principles for investing—principles that have been tested and alive for well over 50 years. The foundation of Graham's philosophy of value investing is a matter of setting and following structured rules of investing, which, he once said, involves "picking good stocks at good times and staying with them as long as they remain good companies."

While the definition of "good stocks" is subject to interpretation, in Buffett's case it involves a very specific and defined set of criteria, much of which is based on Graham's ideology. Consider that Buffett built Berkshire Hathaway and his financial empire by investing in solid, no-nonsense companies (like Coca-Cola, H&R Block, American Express, and Comcast) that offered him four key foundational components:

1. Steady growth.
2. Good management.
3. No surprises.
4. An easily understood business model.

Buffett is known for being, like Graham, a value investor, meaning he looks for stocks that are priced unjustifiably low compared to their intrinsic worth.

But what does that mean?

He isn't giving away all of his secrets to the public, but here are some of his basic tips. Keep in mind that these aren't the only things Buffett looks at when analyzing a stock, but they should give you an idea of how he thinks. Don't be afraid of the technical nature of the tips; I'll wrap them up with a simplified version of my own.

- *Understand the business in which you are investing.* Buffett will invest only in a business that he fully understands. He admits that he doesn't understand what a lot of today's technology companies actually do, which is one reason why he rarely invests in them and missed the dot-com revolution of the late 1990s.
- *Look for companies with distinguishable products.* Buffett tends to avoid companies whose products are indistinguishable from those of their competitors (those that rely on a commodity such as oil or gas, for example). His reasoning: Any characteristic that is hard to replicate creates a competitive advantage, which Buffett calls an

"economic moat." The wider the moat, the tougher it is for a competitor to gain market share. Is the product truly unique? If it is, then that's a great start.

• *Analyze the company's fundamentals.* According to Buffett, investors should seek out companies that have solid fundamentals. For example, he likes companies that generate earnings growth from shareholder equity as opposed to borrowed money. As a result, he looks at something called a company's debt-to-equity ratio, which, for any techies out there reading this, is determined by dividing the company's total liabilities (or long-term debt) by its shareholder equity. The higher the number, the more debt incurred by the company. To a value investor, a high debt-to-equity ratio is generally not a good thing.

Buffett also looks for companies that have consistently performed well relative to other companies in the same industry. As a result, he calculates return on equity (ROE), which reveals the rate at which shareholders are earning income on their shares. ROE is calculated by dividing the company's net income by its shareholder equity.

Another example: Buffett looks for companies with high—and increasing—profit margins. A company with a high profit margin has likely been executing its business well, and an increasing profit margin indicates that a company has been efficient at controlling expenses. To determine profit margin, you divide net income by net sales.

For those of you who may possibly want to research some of these criteria, this information is usually simple to find on the internet in sites such as Yahoo! Finance and others.

• *Look for stocks selling at a 25 percent discount to their real value.* If you thought some of the formulas mentioned so far are tricky, here is where Buffett's investing strategy can get *really* tricky. Finding companies that meet the criteria listed earlier is easy if you do some legwork; much of the data is available in each company's annual report. However, finding companies that are also significantly undervalued can be tough, especially since every human being who is devoted to stock trading is typically looking for the same thing.

To find a company that is undervalued, one must determine a variety of things, especially what is known as the intrinsic value of a company by analyzing a number of business fundamentals including earnings, revenues, and assets. Once Buffett determines the intrinsic value of a company, he compares the value to the company's current market capitalization. If his measurement of intrinsic value is at least 25 percent higher than the company's market capitalization, Buffett sees the company as one that is undervalued.

Sound difficult? It is, and this is where Buffett excels—and where he generally keeps a bit quiet. After all, if we all knew what Buffett knows, we'd all be worth around $40 billion today.

A Simpler Way to Pick Individual Stocks

For those who insist on picking individual stocks and understandably have a difficult time analyzing things the way Buffett would, the simplest recommendation I can make on how to pick an individual stock is to keep your eyes wide open for products that you feel you absolutely cannot live without. Amazingly, finding a product that your life cannot be without is often an indicator that the company manufacturing it might fit Buffett's value investing criteria.

Personally, I'm always keeping an eye out for a product my life cannot be without, and once in a great while I find one. When their products first came out, companies such as America Online (graphics interface for the Internet), Research in Motion (BlackBerry), and Apple Computer (iPod) were some examples of stocks I bought within the "flavors of the day" portion of my diversified portfolio that I certainly don't regret.

There have also been a few others I've had great success with (and some I have not). As simple as it may sound, I can honestly say that despite analyzing balance sheets, charts, and graphs, when it comes to the most successful stocks I have ever picked, finding an excellent product has ironically been the best first step for me to start the evaluation process on whether or not to invest in the company.

In the absence of the ability to analyze stocks the way Warren Buffett does, you may not be able to turn your $1,000 into $40 billion. However, for those of you who want a few "flavors of the day" individual stocks layered on your diversified core holdings portfolio, falling madly in love with the product and investing in the company is the simplest strategy to begin the process of selecting individual stocks and one that I have had great success with.

Real-World Sample Portfolios

Let's get back to the accumulation stage of your life and get an idea on what your diversified portfolio may look like.

Remember: When it comes to a diversified portfolio, you cannot expect all of your choices to perform well all of the time. The idea behind a diversified portfolio and asset allocation is that you develop a portfolio that is designed to meet your needs (i.e., your desire for growth, your risk tolerance, and your time horizon). In time, some of your investments will falter while, presumably, others will perform well, resulting in an overall return with which you are comfortable.

Here are a few real-world examples used by some well-known people who share the same belief.

Aronson Family Portfolio

Ted Aronson's name may not be familiar to you, but on Wall Street he is a very well known and highly respected individual. He runs the $28 billion AJO Partners Fund, an institutional retirement fund closed to Main Street investors. In a January 16, 2007, *MarketWatch* article, he revealed the secret ingredients of his personal diversified investment portfolio. An interesting note: *None* of his money is with money managers (including himself) trying to pick individual stocks at the roulette table; it is all invested in low-cost index mutual funds:

- Vanguard 500 Index
- Vanguard Emerging Markets Stock Index
- Vanguard European Stock Index
- Vanguard Extended Market Index
- Vanguard High-Yield Corporate
- Vanguard Inflation-Protected Securities
- Vanguard Long-Term U.S. Treasury
- Vanguard Pacific Stock Index
- Vanguard Small Cap Growth Index
- Vanguard Small Cap Value Index
- Vanguard Total Stock Market Index

David Swensen of Yale University

Next up is David Swensen, a legendary money manager who oversees the endowment fund for Yale University and has maintained an extremely impressive average rate of return of 16 percent per year for the last 20 years.

Where does he invest his money? His portfolio was revealed in the January 16, 2007, CBS *MarketWatch* article as well. Again, not surprisingly, he doesn't pick individual stocks, nor does he invest any money with fund managers trying to do the same. Like many recognizing the difficulty of winning the investment game by picking individual stocks, he invests in low-cost, passive index funds. Note how few funds he invests in, supporting my overall claim that it doesn't have to be complicated for a portfolio to be effective. In fact, his portfolio is as simple as it gets and the results have been quite impressive.

- Vanguard Inflation-Protected Securities
- Vanguard REIT Index
- Vanguard Short-Term Treasury Index
- Vanguard Total International Stock Index
- Vanguard Total Stock Market Index

Alan Greenspan, Suze Orman, and Groucho Marx: Matches Made in Heaven

Who would have thought that Alan Greenspan, Suze Orman, and Groucho Marx were so alike?

Surprisingly, their styles of investing are very much the same. In an interview with the *New York Times*, Alan Greenspan mentioned that nearly all of his money is invested in short-term government treasuries.

In another *New York Times* interview, Suze Orman revealed that most of her money was invested in AAA-rated and insured municipal bonds. She said that only 4 percent of her money is in stocks. Such safe investments at her young age (55)—why would someone want to do that? Number one, because that's what makes her happy. The second reason is best described using something that Groucho Marx allegedly once said.

When touring the New York Stock Exchange, according to Wall Street legend, someone asked Groucho where he invested his money. He replied, "All in Treasury bonds." "But they don't make any money," an inquisitor said. Groucho responded, "They do if you have enough of them."

My Personal Portfolio

Approximately 80 percent of my portfolio is invested in a core holdings portfolio of various plain-vanilla index ETFs and index mutual funds. I don't have much invested in bonds—maybe around 10 percent, which is slightly less than the Rule of 120 tells me to (as mentioned, the Rule of 120 is merely a guideline, certainly not an absolute).

I consider this my buy-and-hold portfolio, and I seldom trade it. I'm very satisfied with the returns I've been receiving over the years; especially with the annual rebalancing I do to ensure my long-term success. It's a boring portfolio, but I recognize that just like my golf game, the easier I swing, the better my score usually is.

The only portion of my portfolio that I actively trade is what I refer to as the flavors of the day—the 20 percent that is outside my core buy-and-hold portfolio. I've been using that 20 percent to invest in various international indexes, currencies, a few individual stocks, options, and some creative, alternative investments beyond the scope of this book.

Over the past few years, I was (and in many cases, continue to be) heavily invested in the international markets—specifically, emerging markets such as those in Latin America, China, and India, and sometimes in often-overlooked foreign countries such as Mexico and developing European nations showing strong signs for continued growth.

Ask me which companies in these foreign markets to invest in, and it would be a challenge to tell you. I generally don't have a deep enough understanding of the *local* companies within those countries, but I do have an understanding of their economies and how they fit within the framework of what is rapidly becoming, as Thomas Friedman put it so well in his brilliant best-selling book, a "flat world." Some of these countries, such as China, maintain state control over the companies listed on their exchanges; capitalism in its truest sense may very well be on the rise, but it's not there yet and likely won't be for many years to come. As always, diversification is the key to reducing the risk, and doing it within an index ETF gives me the greatest peace of mind.

I've also been investing quite a bit in various metals, such as gold. With geopolitical instability in the world, metals such as this have historically provided a good hedge in the overall portfolio. And lastly, recognizing that "the world is flat," I've also invested quite a few dollars in foreign currencies such as the euro to hedge the risk that the dollar will continue to drop in value, as it has generally been during the time I've been writing this book.

Over these past few years, the rewards for these investments have been tremendous, posting what I consider impressive returns. As I watched some of these areas grow and grow and grow, though, not once did I think that I should shift any money from my core holdings into the flavors of the day.

On average, I religiously rebalance my diversified portfolio once a year, and I have no problems selling gains in order to invest in other areas of the market that, presumably, few people are paying attention to because those areas are not currently trending well. For a long time I let emotion get the best of me, but now I consider myself quite mechanical in my habits. While I monitor my portfolio many times during the year, the majority of my portfolio just sits there. Barring an economic disaster of some kind, for the most part, when it comes to the diversified portion of my portfolio, my life as an investor has become a bit boring.

Quite simply, when it comes to investing, the majority of my portfolio is as boring as it can possibly get. When it comes to my diversified portfolio, in my now peaceful state of mind, the returns I'm getting are far better than they were a long time ago when I actively traded *all* my accounts, and I am also certain my returns are considerably better than those who still haven't seen the light and continue to believe they can beat the market. If nothing else inspires me to invest differently, right around New Year's Day, like clockwork, I rebalance my portfolio; and as a result, I'm very pleased with the returns I'm getting year after year, especially within the flavors of the day residing outside my core holdings.

For those reading this and perhaps feel a bit overwhelmed, there are a few more ideas I want to share that could simplify all these concepts even further. To find out, let's explore a little more.

How to Beat Wall Street in Nine Seconds Flat

I read as many books on investing as I possibly can. Sitting on my bookshelf are stacks of the timeless classics such as *The Intelligent Investor* by Benjamin Graham, *Where Are All the Customers' Yachts?* by Fred Schwed, *A Random Walk Down Wall Street* by Burton G. Malkiel, *The Great Mutual Fund Trap* by Gregory Baer and Gary Gensler, and many, many others.

There are also books such as David Bach's *The Automatic Millionaire,* which suggests that you can get rich automatically, and Phil Town's *Rule #1,* which tells you all it takes is 15 minutes a month to get it done. (For the record, I think both of these books have great value and I often recommend them to people I meet.)

On the far end of the spectrum are books that make "automatic" seem like a lot of work and "15 minutes" seem like an eternity. A while back, one of my friends gave me a book that literally suggests you can get rich by doing absolutely nothing else but going to bed at night and spending a few minutes merely *thinking* about it. I tried that one, but after a few months of not seeing any results, I found that such a strategy didn't exactly wind up paying for my New York strip steak over at Morton's.

Similar to diets that claim you can lose 60 pounds next month while eating as many Carvel cakes as you want, it seems some of the more successful books on investing are the ones that make the bold claim you can get rich with no effort. Who knows? Maybe the book that says you can get rich merely by thinking about it will completely outsell this one. I certainly hope not, but for the fun of it, on occasion I have asked myself, "What's the fastest portfolio one could put together that, statistically speaking, will outperform most professional money managers?"

After figuring out what the portfolio would be, I clocked how long it would take to set it up, and it came down to a mere nine seconds. As crazy as it sounds, yes, it's true. All the time would take for you to set up an investment portfolio that beats most professional money managers is a grand total of nine seconds flat.

So, what is it?, you ask. Come on, not so fast. I have to keep a little suspense here, don't I? I can't give it all away in just one sentence— that wouldn't be fair. So, I'm going to try to build a little suspense by first asking if you'd be interest in . . .

- A highly diversified portfolio that will take you nine seconds to set up.
- A highly diversified portfolio that, statistically speaking, has outperformed most professional money managers on Wall Street.
- A highly diversified portfolio that should cost you somewhere around $7 to set up.
- Once set up, annual fees on the portfolio that will cost you a mere 0.2 percent per year to maintain it.
- Finally, a portfolio that has a track record several decades long and that has averaged a return of over 10 percent per year.

Would you be interested in knowing what that portfolio is? Okay, there's one last thing before I tell you: To invest in this, all you first have to do is send some money to a discount brokerage. Once the account is set up and your money is ready to be invested, you simply go to the area of the web site where you buy a *stock*.

Once at that screen . . . get ready . . . get set . . . the countdown begins . . .

Enter ticker symbol "SPY" and buy it. By the time the confirmation screens are complete, it should have taken you roughly nine seconds to make the purchase. Do you know what you just purchased? You just purchased (you've probably guessed it by now) the S&P 500 index—specifically, the exchange-traded fund (ETF) of the 500 largest U.S. companies all wrapped up into one neat little package.

Think I'm joking around? Hardly. Here are two great quotes that summarize it well:

- "The S&P 500 is a wonderful thing to put your money in. If some-body said, 'I've got a fund here with a really low cost, that's tax efficient, with a 15-to-20-year record of beating almost everybody,' why wouldn't you want it?"—Bill Miller, portfolio manager, Legg Mason, in *Wizards of Wall Street* by Kirk Kazanjian (Bill Miller is the only fund manager out of thousands to successfully beat the S&P 500 index more than 10 years in a row).
- "Eighty-eight percent of managed mutual funds underper-form the S&P 500 over time."—*CFO*, 2004.

Needless to say, I would certainly not advocate you invest 100 percent of your money in the S&P 500. Based on everything I just wrote about in the prior sections, that wouldn't make sense. But as ridiculous as it may sound, there is indeed a kernel of truth embed-ded in doing so based on the fact that many people trying to time the market are going to underperform the S&P 500. As for those who deny it, here's something important to keep in mind:

- "Whenever index funds come under assault, you ought to be suspicious, because the critics aren't exactly disinterested observers. . . . Wall Street sees them as a threat to its profit margins because The Street can make a whole lot more money flogging actively managed funds."—"Indexes Still Win," *Wall Street Journal,* January 12, 2005.

If you believe in the statistics that don't lie, sometimes one must occasionally ask, why bother doing anything else?

Lifestyle Funds

You may be reading this and, although hopefully learning a few things, may find yourself thinking something such as, "There's not a chance I'm going to take a minute to do this stuff. No matter what, it's still confusing to me and I have much better things to do."

The mutual fund industry recognizes that some of you might feel this way, and as a result has decided to try to capitalize on this mindset by inventing something called lifestyle funds. A lifestyle fund manager not only manages a diversified portfolio of stocks and bonds for you, but also adjusts the asset allocation percentages as well.

Remember the Rule of 120? To remind you: Generally, to find out how much of your portfolio should be divided between stocks and bonds, you subtract your age from 120, and the result is the percentage of your portfolio that should be allocated to stocks (the rest to bonds).

In a lifestyle fund, adjustments in allocations are not made by you, but by the fund manager in accordance with a few variables, including but not limited to:

- Your current age.
- Estimated years until retirement
- Your tolerance for risk.

Once this information is determined, your investment then goes into a managed pool of money for investors just like yourself. The fund manager then invests everyone's money "as if it were one" according to the same underlying parameters, presumably in a diversified portfolio of stocks and bonds.

So, if I am 40 years old with a moderate risk tolerance and plan on retiring in 20 years, the fund manager might very well manage a portfolio that consists of, for example, 80 percent stocks and 20 percent bonds (following the general Rule of 120). Then, as the years move along, the fund manager will periodically rebalance the portfolio so that the closer one gets to retirement, the greater the shift toward safer, more reliable investments.

Companies such as Fidelity, Vanguard, and T. Rowe Price now offer lifestyle funds. They are typically called something like "Target Retirement 2045" funds; in this case, the year 2045 represents the year I think I'm going to retire. I've taken a peek at quite a few lifestyle funds, and for investors who are rarely going to pay any attention to their investments, a lifestyle fund is certainly something to consider. After all, if you admit to yourself that you are never going to look at any of your investments, then there's little argument against having someone else do it for you.

If you were going to consider an autopilot investment such as a lifestyle fund, I would strongly urge you to stick with, as always, lifestyle funds that offer index investing rather than managed funds. For reasons I've already discussed, the index investments typically (but not always) outperform the managed mutual funds, and the fees are considerably lower. However, many of the lifestyle funds I've investigated have considerable fees and, needless to say, those fees can really weigh down your returns. In addition, also beware of the tax ramifications some of these funds have. Some of them might be trading much more often than others, causing more taxable events than you or I would prefer.

You may be asking yourself, "If someone can do all this for me, why bother with anything else?"

An autopilot lifestyle fund basically assumes that the thousands and thousands of investors in the fund are all basically the same person, when I believe there's little reality in that. I have dealt with scores of investors, and I can honestly say that there are very few who are alike. Everyone's needs, tolerances, and desires are different, sometimes vastly different even though at first glance they *appear* to be the same. And generalizing everyone into one big vat of age, risk tolerance, and years until retirement is just that: a generalization. A lifestyle fund manager cannot possibly know some of the nuances that make you who you are, and adjust the portfolio accordingly. Only you could know that.

And when it comes to investing, anytime someone generalizes, I believe that's not the most efficient philosophy by any means. After all, which would you prefer—flying from Los Angeles to New York on autopilot or flying in a plane with a very experienced pilot who can customize adjustments according to who you are along the way? Personally, I would much rather personalize a portfolio according to my exact needs, not the needs of a general population.

All that said, if indeed you are someone who will not take any time to monitor your portfolio and to make minor adjustments once or twice a year, considering a lifestyle fund for a portion(s) of your investments would be better than not doing or watching anything at all. After all, one fund manager sticking to the basic, general laws of diversification and rebalancing is certainly better than having no one do it at all.

The Fine Art of Buying Low and Selling High

Up until now we've covered the following key points:

- *Why diversification is the key to investing success.* No one can accurately predict the markets, and diversification takes much of the guesswork and stress out of investing.
- *The ingredients to fill up each sector within the diversified portfolio.* Instead of individual stocks or managed mutual funds, by now I hope you will prefer passive and lazy stock market indexes using exchange-traded funds or index mutual funds.
- *How to diversify the portfolio.* The Rule of 120 provides us with a general balance between stocks and bonds in accordance with our age.
- *Sample diversified portfolios.* We've reviewed sample portfolios that could help get you started, and we've also taken a look at a few real-world portfolios being used by some of the most successful money managers in the country.

While we've covered quite a bit of ground, there is one very significant piece missing. This critical piece has nothing to do with what's *in* the portfolio; rather, it has to do with the *management* of the portfolio itself.

What I'm referring to here is something called rebalancing, and it's truly one of the most important concepts that you need to take home with you after reading this book. In previous sections I referred to the occasional belief that diversified portfolios offer lackluster returns. If you're looking for ways to greatly minimize such a possibility, this section provides the answers.

Failure to rebalance a portfolio would be like ending a good golf swing right at the moment of impact. End the swing at impact and the ball won't go very far. But *follow through* with the swing, and you could wind up giving Tiger Woods a run for his money. In the world of Bloomingdale's, forgetting to rebalance your diversified portfolio would be like filling up the store with fantastic merchandise, but rarely returning to update products and make sure everything is in order. Fail to do that, and the success of the store is destined to fade away.

Before I discuss what rebalancing is and why it's so critical to your sustained and consistent success, there are a few things I need to cover. First, when it comes to managing your diversified portfolio, I need to begin by addressing what I deem to be the "Most Difficult Investment Formula in the World."

While at first glance it may appear like the simplest formula you have ever seen, I have to warn you: Out of anything you'll ever come across in any book on investing, it will hands down be the most difficult formula to abide by. Only the bravest and most dedicated investors have overcome the Most Difficult Investment Formula in the World. Some of the smartest and sharpest-minded investors have been completely destroyed by failing to heed it. In fact, and I kid you not, entire fortunes have been lost by not abiding by it.

Personally, it took me years to finally abide by the Most Difficult Investment Formula in the World. But once I truly obeyed it and engraved it into my mind forever, I have become a better investor beyond my wildest dreams.

Is the Most Difficult Investment Formula in the World some sort of ancient spell cast on investors that dooms them to oblivion? Is it some sort of biblical plague that's been unleashed on investors all across the planet? As strange as it may seem, yes, it absolutely is. Various forms of the Most Difficult Investment Formula in the World have been around since the dawn of time. It may not have exactly addressed investing, but various versions of it have existed since Adam walked in the Garden with Eve.

So, what is the Most Difficult Investment Formula in the World? What is this thing that has ruined kings and caused fortunes to be lost? Remember: At first glance, it will seem like the easiest formula you will ever come across, but don't take it for granted, because failure to respect it *for the rest of your life* will no doubt cause you irreparable harm.

Fasten your seatbelt and take a deep breath. Here it is, the Most Difficult Investment Formula in the World:

$$\text{Investing} - \text{Emotion} = \text{Success}$$

Simple, right?

Not exactly. Failure to remember that formula has caused losses of untold fortunes in the unforgiving abyss of the stock markets.

We're Our Own Worst Enemy

Emotions get the best of us. When it comes to investing, one of the hardest things for anyone to do is sell something (whether it's going up in value or down). The immortal Benjamin Graham (author of *The Intelligent Investor* that I've mentioned before) summed it up perfectly when he stated, "The investor's chief problem—and even his worst enemy—is likely to be himself."

Especially when it comes to investing, we've all had the experience of being our own worst enemy. Many of us have bought a stock and watched it go way up in value, never knowing when to sell it. Many of us have also had the experience of buying a stock and watching it go way down in value, and also never knowing when to sell it. Oftentimes, we've seen it go way up in value, then down, and we just can't get rid of it, remembering what it was once worth. And as we watch things go up, and down, and up again, it can drive us absolutely nuts.

Getting into the markets is often the easiest part of investing. For better and worse, it's knowing when to get *out* of the markets that is hands down the most difficult thing to do.

Diversification of your investments through stock market indexes takes the guesswork out of *where* to invest. Certainly, that solves the problem of trying to figure out where to place your bets on the market's many roulette tables. But diversification of your investments through stock market indexes only *establishes* the portfolio; it merely opens up your Bloomingdale's department store for business, and that's it.

The next step is to *manage* and *oversee* it. And because emotions typically get the best of us, because it is often so very difficult to know when to sell or leave alone, to complete the efficient process of diversification, we need to find a way to take the guesswork out of managing the portfolio as well. After all, as soon as we inject our emotions into the management of the diversified portfolio, quite frankly, with rare exceptions, most of us are doomed to fail—not because we aren't smart or intelligent, but because no one can predict the unpredictable. We cannot possibly know what's coming around the corner. The inability to predict, especially when it comes to random global news that drives so much of today's stock markets, makes it quite difficult to achieve sustained and consistent success investing in the markets.

Therefore, there has to be a system of how to predict the unpredictable. And the good news is that the system of how to overcome the guesswork of buying and selling should be the simplest and easiest part of this entire book. What makes it often impossible to do is when our emotions get in the way.

The something I'm talking about that makes investing simple, easy, and highly rewarding is this thing I've mentioned a few times already, rebalancing. You may have heard about it before, but perhaps never quite understood it. Or you may have understood it but not implemented it.

Either way, rebalancing a portfolio is by far the easiest, most rewarding, and most efficient way to manage your portfolio. And once that diversified portfolio is established, the great news is that rebalancing should take no more than a few hours *a year*.

Crazy? Not at all. Because all rebalancing really comes down to is the simplest form of arithmetic, as we'll soon come to see.

Is it worth a few hours a year to give you the best possible chance to "buy low and sell high"? Is it worth a few hours or so a year to greatly reduce the stress that plagues most investors? Is it worth an hour or so a year to give you the absolute best possibility for sustained success in the markets?

I think it is, especially since I have seen stellar returns as a result of a few hours of truly effortless and unemotional work. I also think it's worth it given that the mechanical and unemotional management of my portfolio eliminates guesswork and stress from investing. When I rebalance, I see everything as math, not as a stock index that I can't figure out whether to buy or hold, and not as something I love or hate because its made or lost me money.

Your New Babies and Why You Need to Love Them

As I alluded to before, establishing your diversified portfolio filled with the essential fundamental market sectors is like giving birth to a handful of new children. Seeing it this way will help crystallize the important concept of rebalancing and diversification.

Congratulations to you, new parent. You have a handful of new market sector kids, and if established correctly, these children should be with you presumably for a very long time, maybe even your entire life. On any given moment, just like having real kids, you may like one more than the other, but you should always *love them the same.* Maybe the "large-cap growth stocks" child is acting up and causing all sorts of trouble in the kitchen while at that same moment the "international stocks" child is busy cleaning up the entire house, making you feel really happy. But just like having real kids, we all know that as good as the "international stocks" child is at the moment, in a flash, this kid might wind up spray painting the walls, while the "large-cap growth stocks" kid who was once hurling bone china against the mirror suddenly stops tossing dishes and starts mowing the lawn.

While this is all going on, what should *never* happen? Again, just like having real kids, although there are times you will definitely feel like getting rid of any child at any given time, in practice, I would hope you never actually would. We hold on to our children for life because we love them dearly; sure, at times one might be acting up while the other is doing just fine, but at the end of the day, they are all here to stay—you just need to figure out how to manage them. And when it comes to investing, managing them most efficiently simply means taking your emotion out of the equation and rebalancing them.

Do that and you will no doubt realize that over time, all the children will be highly rewarding to you. For some, it may not happen this year or next. But there's no doubt that over time, you will wind up loving them all just the same. Truly, just as with your kids, when it comes to the diversified portfolio consisting of the fundamental and essential market sectors, there are never any favorites. Over time, because all market sectors cycle in and out of favor, I promise you will wind up *loving them all the same.*

This is exactly why when someone asks me, "What do you recommend right now in stocks?," I often half-jokingly respond, "Nothing." If I were to answer that question, I am allowing myself to assume the role of a market timer or speculator. And when it comes to making money in the markets, for the majority of my money, I do not want to be a speculator or market timer. With rare exceptions, market timers rely on luck. Maybe they'll get lucky and win a few bucks, but over time, they are destined to do one thing: lose. On the other side of the fence is me, the investor, where over time, I am destined to do only one thing: win. And not only win, but also win without having to rely on luck.

So, when someone asks me, "What do you recommend right now in stocks?," it's like asking me, "Which one of your children in your diversified investment portfolio do you love more than the others?" I'll never love one more than the others. Sure, I'll *like* one a bit more than another depending on the moment, but when it comes down to which I love or would "recommend" over the others, that's an impossible question to answer given that I will always love them all the same.

As for better answering the question, "What do you recommend in stocks?," the answer can only relate to one place and one place only: the "flavors of the day" portion of my portfolio where I am the speculator, where I *do* actively trade my accounts, often on a weekly basis. The flavors of the day is the *only* place, albeit small, where I allow myself to play the role of the day trader or market timer and make educated recommendations on individual stocks or other investments.

Rebalancing Defined

Now that we recognize that the market index sectors comprising our diversified portfolio are just like our children, let's dig a little deeper into this concept of rebalancing.

To begin with, to buy low and sell high you must first find the discipline and guts to take emotion completely out of the equation. By eliminating emotion and following very simple guidelines, you will find yourself closer to becoming the investment genius you never thought you could be. Best of all, you won't need Wall Street to do it, you'll save yourself a lot of money in fees and taxes, and you'll get higher sustained and consistent returns than you most likely ever have received before. You may think I'm kidding, but really, this is far from any joke.

Rebalancing also recognizes that as the years progress, not only does your body, career, and virtually everything else about you change, but so too should the way you invest.

In terms of investing, in the broadest sense, the allocation between stocks (for growth) and bonds (for preservation) needs to change. A person investing for retirement at age 20 should have most of the money in stocks. On the opposite end of the spectrum, someone in their 80s should generally have very little invested in the market. As the years progress, there needs to be a gradual shift in the balance between "trying to accumulate money for my retirement" and "preserving my money."

This, and a number of other factors I'm about to address, is accomplished through monitoring your portfolio during the year and rebalancing it typically on an annual basis. Doing so provides the greatest chance to do what I mentioned before, "buy low and sell high."

The next logical question is likely, "Okay, how do I do that?"

To begin with, let's first start with a very tangible historical example of how rebalancing really would have helped many people. Let's turn back the clock and say it's the roaring 1990s all over again. The technology sector is surging beyond our wildest dreams. You wake up and find that the technology sector of your diversified stock portfolio is skyrocketing (or, if in your diversified portfolio you didn't select a narrow index sector such as technology, but rather, a plain-vanilla growth sector such as large-cap stocks like the S&P 500, the same principles would most certainly have applied).

During the same period of time that tech was surging, market sectors such as precious metals, international stocks, and real estate were ice-cold in comparison. Who was showing the love to these nasty children? The *market timers* out there certainly weren't, whereas *investors* like us might have been because remember: We love all our children all the same.

So, you awaken to find that tech is on a great run, but other sectors are doing poorly in comparison. This is the exact moment that really "separates the men from the boys." This is the moment when the market timers would have likely neglected the critical need to respect the Most Difficult Investment Formula in the World. For many, this is the moment that forgetting about the Most Difficult Investment Formula in the World starts to cause all sorts of havoc, turmoil, frustration, and regret. Why? Because those who don't respect the Most Difficult Investment Formula in the World simply let their emotions get in the way of prudent investing. This is the moment in time that the investor unfortunately turns into the market timer. As soon as investors start to think they can predict what will happen next or that they know more than the market does, the train wrecks often begin.

Tech is way up, whereas sectors such as international are down and in comparison doing just awful. But what do the gods of diversification and rebalancing say you should never do? They say you should *never try to predict* what's going to happen next. The gods of investing say you need to *get rid of your emotion* and remember that each sector within a diversified portfolio is just like your children—you always need to feed them, love them, and pay attention to them even though they might be acting naughty, because at any moment in time they will turn around for the better.

In this case, even though a sector such as international is ice-cold during this time, not only should you still own it because it represents an essential slice of your well-diversified portfolio, but you should invest *more into it.*

Again, this is exactly the point in time when you would have absolutely needed to respect the Most Difficult Investment Formula in the World and stood firmly by it. Because at this point, your emotions would be staring at your naughty international child and saying, "I want to get rid of that child. It's losing me money." And to think that you should invest *more* money into these international children? Here, the emotions in your head start to whisper, "Have you gone insane? . . . You read a book that told you to do *what?!?*" But it's at this exact moment in time that you need to say, "The only insane thing is thinking that I can predict what's going to happen next. Thousands of professionals can't do it. Cramer can't do it. There's a monkey and a bunch of darts that can *almost* do it. I am not insane. I am an investor, and I need to take care of all my children, even the ones who are acting up."

At this point in time, if you were truly able to eliminate emotion from your portfolio, what would have happened? You would have been adding money in ice-cold sectors such as international *while they were on sale.* And where would you have been raising the money to invest in the ice-cold sector when it was on sale? From a sector such as technology that was *not* on sale, but *surging* in value.

Crazy, right? Insane? It may sound like it, but stay with me on this.

When tech was red-hot and surging in value, according to the laws of rebalancing, this is the exact point in time when you would have been *selling* the profits to scale that sector back down to the *original percentage you allocated in the first place.* Seeing that tech is way too heavy, you trim the gains (rebalance) to bring that slice of the diversified portfolio back down to its original percentage. And what have you just done? You just *sold* tech *high* and pocketed the profits.

Now, once you sell off the profits of tech, where do you invest them?

You use those profits to refill the sectors that have gone down in value and are below the percentage you originally allocated. You've taken those profits from tech and used them to refill sectors such as real estate, international stocks, and precious metals that during those years were going down in value; you were feeding the children in your portfolio who were losing weight. And by following this mechanical and unemotional process of rebalancing, what have you just done?

You guessed it.

Congratulations. You just did what every single investor during the late 1990s *wished* they would have done: sold technology at the high and bought into sectors such as real estate, international stocks, and precious metals when they were at their lows.

Who was not able to do that? The market timers, those who let their emotions get in the way of investing and did not respect the Most Difficult Investment Formula in the World.

I know, it sounds so simple. But guess what? It's certainly not easy to do, and that's why I call it the Most Difficult Investment Formula in the World. During those years when tech was hot and a sector such as international was ice-cold, selling tech to invest in something not doing well would have easily caused your emotions to say, "Invest in international? Now? Are you crazy? Get out of tech while it's red-hot?"

These are emotions speaking to you. This is the market timer or speculator in the casino, not the investor we need to be. Remember: You are an investor; you need to take emotion out of the equation; you are not trying to guess or predict what's going to happen next; and as hard as it is, as impossible as it may seem, you will be immensely rewarded for it.

I have personally seen it. I have seen it for my money and for the many people I've helped. I've seen the stressed-out market timer finally get out of the casino and into the peaceful world of investing. I have seen the housewife beat the performance of the professional mutual fund managers she used to pay a lot of fees to. And I have seen the very bright day trader who used to spend every last waking moment trying to guess what was going to happen next but now, since becoming an investor and taking his emotion out of the market, he, like many others, is consistently earning more than he ever did, while spending only a fraction of the time to do it.

The Big Payoff

That's the hard part—seeing something like tech on a great run, selling it off, and adding the gains in ice-cold sectors such as international in that period of time. But here's where the big payoff comes: Seemingly out of nowhere, what happened next, and what typically happens when you feed the children who are losing way too much weight? Let's let history tell us.

Tech finally crashed. As all sectors do, it merely went through its cycle. Just about everything in that sector took a total and complete nosedive.

A few months later, the markets finally hit rock bottom and leveled off, and then what was it time for?

It was then time for the naughty child who was busy tossing crystal at the mirrors to start cleaning the bathrooms. And the once favorite child of technology who was once pristinely cleaning the house then started hurling fish across the room. When one child turns nasty and evil, by the laws of natural childhood, another kid in the house is due to turn for the better. But which child is it going to be? We have no idea, because we know, and admit, that very few people can predict the child we're going to like next.

Do the gods of investing call and tell everyone which child is going to be the next good kid? Certainly not. Back then, and as always, no one knows which sector is going to be the next profitable one.

But because you took emotion out of the investing equation, because you got rid of the perpetual insanity of trying to time the market, of trying to guess the next winner of the next horse race, the sectors that take off next are often those sectors that you acquired more of while they were *on sale*. During the years that followed the tech crash, not surprisingly, sectors such as real estate, precious metals, international stocks, and emerging markets then started performing really well.

Those sectors rocketed up in value and went on a five-year tear, posting fantastic gains. And while they are going way up, what were investors doing? You guessed it—they were once again taking emotion out of the equation. As difficult as it was, they remembered the Most Difficult Investment Formula in the World. They spent a few hours or so rebalancing their portfolios, presumably adding more money into ice-cold sectors such as technology where, now years after the bad crash, it is starting to heat up again. And because the investors realized that they need to love all their market sector children the same, by rebalancing, they never miss a good run-up in one particular area because they never got rid of any children.

This is what rebalancing and diversification are all about. Markets are greatly affected by news and no one can predict tomorrow's headlines. Crisis in the Middle East? The price of oil could very well go up along with that of gold, and when this happens, certain areas of the portfolio will spring up in value while others plummet. Inflation rearing its head? Fed lowering interest rates? The only thing certain during uncertain times should be the *un*emotional fine-tuning of a diversified portfolio through the magical, timeless art of rebalancing.

This is why, when first establishing your diversified portfolio and carving it up into sectors using the indexes, it is so important to get it right the first time. Remember what I've been saying, that the sector indexes you pick for your diversified portfolio should be construed as *your children*. You want to presumably keep them all for the rest of your life because you are an *investor*. You recognize that at any given time, you may like one better than the other, but you *love them all the same.*

This is also what makes a buy-and-hold portfolio of fundamental and timeless asset classes truly buy-and-hold. Have you ever asked an advisor *why* a portfolio should be diversified and largely a buy-and-hold? Many cannot answer this question, or if they can, they may simply say something like "To spread the risk." But what does that really mean? *Why* spread the risk? What's underneath the critical need to do that, and how can you really maximize profits?

Many market timers and advisors don't truly understand the underlying mechanics of what makes a buy-and-hold portfolio so successful. Furthermore, many advisors do not religiously practice rebalancing the portfolio. Frankly, I seldom see rebalancing being done. Far too often, the diversified sectors, if there are diversified sectors at all, are completely out of balance or they grossly overlap. As an example, for the past few years, the international and emerging markets sectors have been surging, and if someone has exposure to these areas of the market, it is not uncommon to see they have gone way, way up in value. One portfolio I saw recently had gains of 90-plus percent in places such as Latin America, China, and India. Who's not rebalancing those sectors? Either lazy advisors who aren't updating a portfolio or market timers who are trying to guess when to sell them. Insanity, that's what it is. It's time to take the emotion out of the equation.

Hold that position, watch it go up some more, and what is destined to happen? Just like technology once did, it *will* retreat. Rebalancing it, however, means that you sell and use the gain to invest into something else that is now on sale.

It is hoped that by reading this you will understand what many advisors do not: why buying and holding the fundamental asset classes combined with rebalancing within a well-diversified portfolio most often provides the best chances for sustained and consistent success in the stock markets.

By rebalancing the buy-and-hold portfolio, I know that I will always have some hot sectors as well as some cold sectors, but over time, just like my real kids, I love them all the same. I am certain that during various cycles over my lifetime, all of them will wind up paying off. The only problem is that no one knows when that will happen. And to solve that problem, I simply buy and hold my stock index children and rebalance them accordingly—and all along the way, *I take emotion out of the equation.*

If I want to have emotion and try to time the market or take momentary advantage of speculative investments that don't belong in my buy-and-hold portfolio, it's no problem. I'll let those desires live in the "flavors of the day" portion of my portfolio, but I never allow guessing and emotions to enter the buy-and-hold area. For me, emotions and trying to time the market are banned for life from ever entering my precious children's lives in the precious core holdings area.

Wrapping It Up

When you're standing around a craps table that is red-hot, the toughest thing in the world to do is to walk away—especially when you are walking away from a winning table filled with screaming happy people making boatloads of money—and to place chips at a table that no one is playing at, a table that is ice-cold and deserted.

But remember: No table goes on a run forever. Likewise, no one can really predict when the turn for the better or worse is coming. It is for this reason that those who follow the laws of diversification and rebalancing, those who take *emotion* out of the equation, are the ones who will have the greatest chances for *sustained* and *consistent* success.

A diversified investment portfolio using indexes injected with the *un*emotional art of rebalancing offers the greatest chance of consistent and sustained investment success. Period. The results are often excellent, and the only thing that typically prevents you from success is when you allow emotions and the market timers to enter your primary residence.

Stick with the fundamentals and I promise you will never, ever look back.

That's how people get rich.

How Much Should I Be Saving?

Building a diversified engine to empower your investment vehicle and rebalancing it is quite an important step, but establishing the vehicle is just the beginning.

The next step is obviously to drive that car to the local gas station and fill it up. Without fuel, your car isn't going to get very far, and, needless to say, the more you put in, the farther it's going to go.

The fuel I'm talking about isn't premium, diesel, or regular; it's that thing called *money*. How much money you pour into your diversified engine of investments is certainly going to help determine how long it's going to take to get to your destination.

It's the million-dollar question that many people are asking: How much do I need to save for retirement? The answer to this question isn't as simple as throwing out a figure or a percentage of salary you should save, because it will differ from person to person. However, there is a simple process you could use to determine just how much you will need to save.

The first thing you must consider is how much annual income it will take to sustain your lifestyle through retirement. Many people will simply reply with one of two likely responses: (1) "As much as humanly possible" or (2) "I have absolutely no idea."

I can certainly understand and respect either one of those. However, most people won't ever take a moment to grasp how much they are saving and investing and what that plan will mean once they get into retirement. Without any goal for retirement, how can you possibly know if you're on track?

I had dinner recently with a successful friend who informed me that he has absolutely no plan for his investing or retirement. For many, this might sound familiar. His plan is to toss a "few bucks" into a "couple" of investments he thinks are going to do well whenever he "gets the chance or feels like it," and beyond that, "whatever happens happens."

While his laid back attitude is certainly at the extreme end of the spectrum, I'm quite sure there are many people out there who have never really taken a moment to consider where they are headed. In fact, many investment companies have done extensive studies that all pretty much conclude that most people don't really take any time to plan anything at all and aren't saving nearly enough for retirement.

If you're reading this book, however, congratulations. I can only hope that once we're through, you will be inspired to start doing a little something for yourself, at the very least. The fact that you bought this book and have already made it this far means that you are doing great—most likely better than many of your peers. Not only have you pushed through my attempts to make the various facets of an otherwise challenging subject interesting to read, but you can consider yourself one of the fortunate few who are attempting to bring your current and future plans to fruition.

Let's shed some light, then, on the age-old question, "How much do I need to save for retirement?" We can at least gain an understanding of how much income you need as the starting point toward meeting your target at retirement.

Imagine being the coach in the locker room before a football game. If you promised alumni that the team would score 70 points or more, you'd need to tell the quarterback to heave Hail Marys into the end zone each and every play. However, if you are expecting a lower-scoring game and will also be relying on your defense to keep the other team away from the end zone, then obviously you can take a much more pragmatic and realistic approach to win the game.

A popular technique within various financial planning circles suggests you should start by assuming you'll need 70 percent to 100 percent of your current income, depending on how well you want to live. From my experience seeing many people transitioning into retirement, I would lean toward the higher end of the scale where one should expect to live off 90 to 100 percent of current income. For illustrative purposes, let's assume you'll need $70,000 a year in retirement.

Once you have an income target, you can begin to look at where that money will come from. How much, if any, will come from pensions you expect to receive? The first pension you could expect to receive, provided it is still around once you get into retirement, could likely be Social Security.

Use the statements you should be receiving from the Social Security Administration to get an idea of how much you can expect in Social

Security benefits. We will assume for this brief exercise that the amount you'll receive is expected to be $20,000 a year. Suffice it to say that relying on Social Security alone is a pretty tough thing to do, especially since many people could not imagine living off that amount.

The next step is to determine how much money you'll want or need to receive each year from your investments—investments that might include a company pension, a 401(k) plan, and/or some individual retirement accounts (IRAs). (Speaking of 401(k)s, one of the most basic, elementary rules of prudent planning that I'll later address in more detail is often to do everything possible to contribute up to the maximum amounts allowable per year, especially if your company matches contributions.) To determine how much money you'll want or need to receive each year from your investments, you simply subtract the amount you expect to receive from Social Security from your target income. For illustration, if we were expecting $20,000 from Social Security, we would then need an additional $50,000 to maintain our lifestyle.

Here is the part of the projections some people choke over. I'll refrain from throwing complicated formulas at you, but allow me to share the simplest one I know of that gives a reasonable indication of how much you'd need to save in order to live on (in this case $50,000). Taking inflation into account, multiply the target income amount of $50,000 by a factor of 25, which equals $1,250,000. Multiplying your target income by 25 will give you a very general idea of how much money you'll need in order to make it through approximately 30 years in retirement. This assumes you will keep your annual withdrawals limited to approximately 3 to 4 percent of your nest egg's value per year, and only adjust it for inflation to keep your purchasing power constant.

You might be looking at that $1.25 million and saying to yourself that you are so far from being there that it seems pointless to even try. While there are most certainly no shortcuts, if you are in the later stages of your working life and rapidly approaching retirement, there are several powerful income strategies I'll be discussing that could really help you out. There are also some very interesting strategies on how one can safely convert a small portion of equity in one's house into some of the most reliable forms of retirement income available. More on this in a little while.

Back to that $1.25 million. The next question is, "how can you possibly generate such a nest egg?" Besides the obvious—picking good investments, reducing fees, and maximizing returns while reducing risks—how much you *save* is a huge factor as well.

Needless to say, you'll obviously need to save as much as possible each year so that your current savings grow into your target nest egg. You certainly didn't need to buy this book to hear that, but it is indeed the obvious truth. Formulas to figure this out can be quite cumbersome and complicated, but there are some great tools out there that can give us a more concrete idea as to how much we need to save. The tools I'm referring to are the many Internet retirement calculators. You plug in your target income at retirement along with the amount you've already saved and several other factors, and the calculator will reveal your target rate of savings.

As with everything else in this guide, the calculation is by no means definitive; there is no one-size-fits-all solution. You probably have several types of accounts, each with different tax treatments and different rates of return. You also need to predict your future rate of return, which is obviously not concrete. However, these calculations will at least give you a basic idea as to how much you need to save, and you can always consult an advisor if you want a more sophisticated calculation. He or she can run through various scenarios, including what's known as a Monte Carlo simulation. A Monte Carlo simulation will analyze all of the variables in your investment scenario and predict a return and/or an expected income at retirement—and thus a savings target—based on the results.

Most Internet brokerage and fund companies have retirement calculators that do a good job of running you through various scenarios. Over the years, these calculators have become quite common on many financial web sites. My personal favorites are the retirement calculators offered by Yahoo! Finance (http://finance.yahoo .com) and T. Rowe Price (www.troweprice.com). These calculators do a fantastic job of giving you an understanding of how much you should be saving in order to achieve your retirement income goals.

For those seeking a more detailed blueprint as to how much gasoline you need to put into your engine, I would strongly recommend spending time exploring these retirement calculators. After all, you don't want to run out of gas halfway to where you wanted to go. And if you feel all hope is lost, don't despair. When it comes to maximizing your income at retirement, there are some very interesting and powerful strategies one can take advantage of to really help out.

Speaking of maximizing income at retirement, the next section is all about how to maximize it *during* retirement. After all, we just spent the last few sections discussing how to *accumulate* wealth; now it's time to most efficiently discuss how to *distribute* it in the form of income.

CHAPTER 3

Reliable Returns

Earlier in the book, I highlighted three primary investment stages that take place during your life. Let's review the stage we just left and look ahead to the one we are about to enter.

The accumulation stage is typically the most speculative, given that it is during this period of time that most people are usually heavily invested in stocks for *growth*. The accumulation stage most often takes place during the working years. Quite simply, you are trying to save and earn as much as possible so that when it is time to retire, you can live off your nest egg. Up until now, we have spent all of our time discussing efficient ways to accumulate money.

The reliable returns stage represents the time we shift closer to, or are already in, retirement. It's at this stage that, in strict accordance with our own personal Rule of 120, we should be shifting our money slowly but surely away from accumulation to generating reliable returns, presumably to meet our *income* needs.

As you'll soon find out, I have a lot to say about this stage, which some refer to as the distribution or withdrawal stage. I often find that many people never really enter this stage. As they get a bit older, although their lifestyle starts to greatly change, their investment style unfortunately does not. Their money often merely lingers in the accumulation stage, and when they start drawing income from their accumulation stage portfolios, this is exactly when panic, fear, and frustration sometimes set in. It's at this stage that, all too often, what I commonly refer to as the Most Dangerous Game starts to play out.

Moving closer to retirement? Already in it? Or maybe when designing your diversified portfolio you want to include a sector or two filled with various investments that will ensure that you generate at least some measure of reliable returns.

Refill that bag of popcorn. Grab another box of Junior Mints, and save a couple of those for me. Mother nature calling? Maybe take a quick dash to the restroom. Then, be sure to get back to your seat, because this movie is far from over.

Some of my favorite parts are just about to begin.

Generating Reliable Returns

First things first, and it's important I make this clear before I risk losing you: If you are still in the accumulation stage, don't skip this very important chapter. While this reliable returns stage is certainly of great importance to those of you close to or already in retirement, for reasons you'll soon find out, many concepts I'll be discussing in this chapter can and will likely deserve a place within your diversified portfolio during the accumulation stage of investing.

In the prior chapter we explored the accumulation stage of life. When investing for growth, the only thing that remains certain is the *uncertainty* of the returns. As much as a diversified portfolio rebalanced periodically can be designed to generate promising and consistent results, and as much as historical market data demonstrates this, there are certainly no guaranteed returns within a well-diversified portfolio.

Recognizing this, it is certainly possible that during the accumulation stage of investing you'll want to at least consider a sector within the diversified portfolio that offers a "bird in the hand," and not always "two in the bush."

Reliable rates of return are a prudent part of any diversified portfolio. In fact, we've already touched on them in the last chapter. For the younger investor seeking growth, reliable rates of return offer birds in the hand during potential turbulent market periods. For the investor approaching retirement, or those already retired, reliable rates of return are absolutely essential, especially for those looking to generate income from their investments.

If you stick to the guidelines set forth in the preceding chapter on diversification, rebalancing, and following the Rule of 120, by the time you get closer to retirement you should have an increasingly larger portion of your money in safer, more reliable investments—those designed to generate reliable rates of return.

As far as I'm concerned, generating income from your investments during retirement is synonymous to generating reliable returns during your accumulation years. After all, if you are seeking an answer to "How do I *make sure* my money is growing?" and the overall stock markets are not performing well, then certainly there has to be other investments incorporated within a diversified portfolio to ensure that at least some measure of growth continues. Again, we've touched on some of these investments in the last chapter but we didn't go into very much detail about them or, for that matter, anything else out there that could provide our overall diversified portfolio with reliable rates of return.

So, whether you are in retirement trying to ensure reliable returns for income or you are light years from retirement but are looking to ensure that at least one sector within your diversified portfolio is generating at least some growth, incorporating investments that offer these "bird in the hand" returns is something you will likely want to consider.

First, let's start with how generating reliable returns is an essential part of someone's life as they approach or are in retirement. Later in the chapter I adapt the same principles for someone who might very well be years away from retirement, but who can certainly benefit from incorporating reliable returns into the portfolio as well.

The Shift Toward Retirement

Even if you aren't there yet, you can be certain that at some point in your future you will "retire." Maybe, like quite a few people "in retirement," you might decide to maintain a part time job, not only to earn a few extra dollars but also to keep the mind and body busy as well.

Suffice it to say, one day you will retire and when that time comes, many things in your life will change. The way you eat, the way you play, the things you do . . . life won't look the same as it did while you were working.

When it comes to investing, many investors' *mind-sets* unfortunately don't change as much as they should. In retirement, you are presumably no longer trying to accumulate as much as you used to;

rather, you are typically focusing on preserving your money while generating as much *reliable* and *sustainable* income as possible from it. The failure to shift an investment portfolio from the accumulation stage to one designed to generate *reliable returns* leads many people into playing what I call the Most Dangerous Game.

The Most Dangerous Game

The Most Dangerous Game many people play in retirement is to rely on the *speculative* possibility that their stocks will grow enough to give them the income they need.

And who can blame them? After all, by the time you retire, you've likely just spent many years investing like you did in the previous chapter: purely for *growth*. Such a habit is undoubtedly a bit difficult to break.

All of a sudden, you retire and now need to live off of what you have. When that happens, no one calls you and says, "Good job and congratulations. You've just retired and now it's time to invest differently." Typically, an investment portfolio gradually and steadily should evolve over time. Following the Rule of 120 should be doing this for us—as time goes on, we should be reducing our exposure to stocks and increasing our exposure to investments that generate reliable returns such as bonds and other interesting choices I'll soon be discussing. But all too often, especially in the early stages of retirement, the evolution is far too slow, and this is exactly when the Most Dangerous Game's most lethal and devastating train wrecks can take place.

The Story of Dave and Donna

As an example of how an investment portfolio failing to evolve properly can cause train wrecks, let's visit the story of Dave and Donna. Their situation is quite universal, especially for the baby boomers out there.

In the late 1990s, Dave and Donna made a lot of money in the markets, accumulating nearly $2 million in individual stocks. A financial advisor they consulted with assured them they could meet their retirement income goals with "no problem." To keep things simple, their investments needed to generate a 7 percent return to give them the before-tax income they needed, something their advisor assured them he could deliver.

After all, the markets always trend up, don't they? Furthermore, the track record of the managed mutual funds the advisor was suggesting showed impressive rates of return that would certainly provide the income they needed from the potential *growth* of stocks.

Comforted by what they were hearing, and after reviewing the track records of the fund managers, Dave decided to retire.

Over the next year or so, things went fine. Between their individual stocks and stock mutual funds, Dave and Donna were making a substantial enough return to provide them with the income they needed; whatever they pulled out for income was easily being replenished by the continued growth of their stocks.

Making things better, not only was their income being replenished by growth from the stocks, but there was even some excess growth they were reinvesting for future needs.

Everything looked great. The markets were strong, Dave's golf handicap was getting lower by the day, and Donna's tennis game was fantastic. Then, seemingly out of nowhere, the market started taking a turn for the worse.

Thankfully, their investments were somewhat diversified. The advisor had them invested in a scattered few areas of the market, but it was certainly not the type of portfolio that I would truly deem well diversified. However, even with a somewhat diversified portfolio, their investments took a considerable hit, losing roughly 15 percent of their value—which wasn't bad, especially when compared to some other portfolios that fared much worse during those years.

But wait—did they lose only 15 percent? Not exactly. The value of the stocks went down 15 percent, but what else was taking place at the time the market was getting destroyed? From their bathtub of life, at the same time water was going down the drain, they were also removing some of it to live on.

In percentages, they took 7 percent out of their bathtub to live on, but they also lost 15 percent due to water going down the drain, bringing their total loss to 22 percent.

Worried, they consulted with their advisor who, on several occasions, assured them that the professional stock pickers in the mutual funds would "make it back."

With his confidence, they sat tight for another year . . . and that didn't turn out so well, either. In another bad year, they lost 10 percent of value, plus another 7 percent that they withdrew to cover their income needs.

By the time the bad markets stabilized, Dave and Donna's portfolio had lost significant value. It took only two short years to turn what should have been a peaceful retirement into one of great worry and despair. Making matters worse, no thanks to inflation and a few other unforeseen events in their life, by the time the markets finally stabilized, they now needed to generate even *more* income.

When applying this to their portfolio, Dave and Donna had a rude awakening, and, presumably, so did their advisor. Doing the math, it was discovered that with the losses they had suffered, they no longer needed a 7 percent rate of return, but well over a *10 percent rate of return* to give them the income they required.

With well over a 10 percent rate of return needed to provide them with their income, they finally realized they were playing the worst game of all—the gambler's game. Their advisor was relying on the appreciation of their stocks to give them the income they needed, which, as they very quickly learned the hard way, is the Most Dangerous Game to play, during or especially right at retirement.

A client of ours recommended Dave and Donna come see us. Having heard a little about generating reliable returns when in retirement and how to avoid the Most Dangerous Game, they wanted to hear more about investments that were predictable and did not count on the possibility that stocks would always go up in value.

However, as much as we wanted to help them, the damage was already done. Unfortunately, they no longer had the option of repositioning their portfolio into investments that offered reliable returns. Sure, a portion of their portfolio was repositioned to generate more reliable returns. But their need to generate such a high rate of return meant that the majority of their money had to remain heavily invested in the stock markets, keeping their money at risk, albeit in a more diversified portfolio.

As a result of playing the Most Dangerous Game, Dave and Donna no longer have the option their previous advisor once did. Back when Dave retired, if the advisor had simply repositioned portions of the portfolio to produce reliable returns, chances are we wouldn't have met them in the first place.

When evaluating how much income could reliably be generated from their investments, their advisor did not ask himself the single most important question everyone should always ask: What's the worst thing that can happen to this portfolio if things go wrong?

Coming out of the bad market years of 2001 and 2002, we saw many "Dave and Donnas." The results were not pretty; in fact, some were downright tragic and set many people back years from retirement. Worse, some plans were completely derailed, calling for drastic measures, a change in lifestyle, or even worse.

To sum it up, as far as I'm concerned, this was all caused by their advisor playing the Most Dangerous Game of all: *relying on the speculative appreciation of stocks to provide the income someone needs.*

The Numbers Don't Lie

The following is a conceptual guide you can use to get a very basic idea as to how a portfolio could shift from accumulation to one that offers reliable returns. As previously mentioned, be sure to consult with a qualified advisor before any actions are taken on your investments, given that everyone's situation will be unique.

With that in mind, here are six steps to conceptually determine whether repositioning a portfolio into investments that offer reliable returns would make any sense at all. Please note, I am using a before-tax scenario. Because everyone's tax situation is unique, it would be difficult to address all possible variables. For an exact analysis, I urge you to discuss your personal situation with a qualified tax and/or investment advisor.

1. Determine the approximate amount of income you need (expenses, etc.).
2. Reduce this amount by any pension, earnings, or Social Security you receive or expect to receive.
3. The result represents the dollar amount of income your investments need to generate.
4. Divide this amount into the total liquid assets you have available. (Liquid assets would be stocks, bonds, IRAs, 401(k)s, CDs, savings, mutual funds, and the like. Liquid assets do not include real estate, ownership interests in a company, and limited partnerships, which generally are not liquid.)
5. To get the decimal point in the right place, multiply this amount by 100.
6. The result represents the before-tax *rate of return* the portfolio needs to generate in order to receive the desired income.

To help clarify these steps, let's walk through a conceptual example. The numbers and amounts I'm using are greatly simplified just to help you understand the general premise.

Suppose I just retired. I no longer have any earned wages and I am not yet collecting Social Security, but I do have a small pension. Using the six steps as my guide, here's how I'd determine an approximate rate of return my investments need to generate in order to provide the income I require:

1. Determine the amount of income needed per year: *As an example, suppose I need a total income of $35,000 per year.*
2. Reduce that amount by any pension, earnings, or Social Security you receive. *As an example, suppose I receive a pension that pays me $12,000, so the $35,000 I need in step 1 is reduced by the pension.*
3. The result represents the amount of income your investments need to generate. *Therefore, the amount of income my investments need to generate is $23,000 per year ($35,000 − $12,000 = $23,000 income needed from investments).*
4. Divide this amount into the total liquid assets you have available. *Here, I add up all my savings and investments. Suppose the amount is $350,000. I now divide the $23,000 from step 3 into the $350,000, which equals 0.067.*
5. To get the decimal point in the right place, multiply this amount by 100. *$0.067 \times 100 = 6.7\%$.*
6. This result represents the before-tax *rate of return* the portfolio needs to generate in order to get the desired income.

If the result is a single-digit percentage, then you most likely have a good chance of being able to generate reliable income from investments other than stocks. If the result were higher, you might need to remain heavily invested in the stock markets. How much you need to keep invested depends on a number of factors.

As an example, one person we recently met wanted to generate as much income as possible from investments that offered reliable rates of return. After a quick analysis, we determined that to get the income he desired, his portfolio would need to generate over a 15 percent return, which is far greater than nearly all return reliable investments offer. In general, the only place to get such a high rate of return for income would be to try getting it from the *speculative* appreciation of stocks. But what does this do? It causes someone to play the Most Dangerous Game.

At such a high return, our advice to this particular individual was: (1) continue striving for higher rates of return in stocks, which would unfortunately keep him playing the Most Dangerous Game; (2) get a part-time job to supplement the income reliable returns can comfortably generate; (3) reduce expenses; (4) delay retirement a few years; and/or (5) downsize to a smaller residence (to free up more money) or refinance his house, which comes with its own set of issues too complex to address here.

At such a high required rate of return, this person did not have the option of peacefully repositioning investments from his accumulation stage portfolio into investments that generate reliable returns for income, an option that Dave and Donna once had.

So, if you are like Dave and Donna and you *have* the opportunity they once had to reposition portions of their investments into ones that efficiently produce reliable returns, this could easily be the most important section in this book.

Let's continue.

How to Avoid the Most Dangerous Game

As simplistic as it sounds, Dave and Donna's problem could have been completely avoided.

The problem was that when the time came for them to generate income from their accounts, their advisor did not reposition any of their portfolio into investments to produce reliable income, defined as: *a rate of return one can generally rely on regardless if the value of stocks in a portfolio goes up or down.*

Especially when it comes to producing income, the first consideration should be to use the safest and the most reliable investments— investments that, as much as possible, do not rely on the speculative possibility that stocks might go up in value. Plain and simple, relying on the growth of stocks to generate the income one needs is just downright *un*reliable, no matter how well the markets are currently performing or how appealing a stock picker's track record appears.

Two mind-sets that often prevent a shift from the accumulation stage to the reliable returns stage are those of an investor who believes the stock markets go nowhere but up and a tax-conscious investor. Many people gravitating toward retirement hesitate to sell stocks that have appreciated quite well because they don't want to pay the capital gains tax. Even though they can reposition their assets to go into investments that will create more reliable bird-in-the-hand returns, they simply won't do it because they'll have to pay tax.

My gosh. Do you know how many people we met coming off the highs of the late 1990s who would give their right arm and left leg to be able to turn back the clock, sell some growth, pay the tax, and invest in reliable income-producing investments?

Sometimes paying the tax on growth stocks, especially at retirement, would be the *best* deal you could ever find.

So, what are the investments out there that provide reliable returns? There are quite a few, some of which I'll be discussing in this important chapter. But before going any further, let's make sure we're clear on what a reliable return is:

The reliable return investments I'm talking about can be as simplistic as bank certificates of deposit (CDs). Certainly there are many other investments that produce considerably higher rates of reliable return that I'll soon be discussing, but a CD does provide a rate of return that is reliable. The return will be there regardless of whether or not the stock portion of the diversified portfolio goes up or down in value.

If I have $100,000 in CDs paying me 5 percent, then the $5,000 of interest is a return that I can safely rely on, regardless of how my stocks perform. This return is totally and completely independent of the value of my stocks. Of course, for a variety of reasons I'll be discussing, it certainly wouldn't be prudent for most people to invest a large portion of their money in CDs. Coming up, we will soon see there are many other investments that can generate significantly higher reliable rates of return and the opportunity for growth as well, but for now, I'm using the lowly CD just to illustrate the point.

I cannot stress it enough: When it comes to avoiding the Most Dangerous Game, the return an investment portfolio generates must *not* rely on stocks going up in value. As much as possible, to avoid the Most Dangerous Game, reliable returns needs to exist in the portfolio, especially in the worst-case scenarios.

Are You Playing the Most Dangerous Game?

Are you getting close to retirement? Are you already there? Do you know whether or not you are playing the Most Dangerous Game?

Most people have no idea, and as of this very moment, that's okay. You're reading this book and I'm working to help you figure it out.

If you are nearing retirement or are in it, one of the quickest ways to get a preliminary idea as to how much you are currently relying on the speculative growth of stocks to generate the income you need is to take a look at your brokerage statements. These statements generally provide much of the information you need.

Each brokerage statement, especially if issued by one of the larger firms, typically has a line item, often on the first page or in the back summary, that reports the total annual income a portfolio generates from something called dividends and interest. This line item typically is separate from the *value* of your stocks.

Often, this will be stated as a dollar figure.

In Dave and Donna's case, a quick look at their statements revealed that the total income their investments were generating was $20,000 (through dividends and interest). This $20,000 represented the reliable return their portfolio was generating that did not depend on the speculative growth of their stocks. This $20,000 return was *separate* from their stocks going up or down in value. It's a very important distinction to make and it cannot be emphasized enough.

Regardless of whether the value of their stocks went up or down, this $20,000 should generally remain constant. In their case, it was the only reliable return within their portfolio—everything else was based on the pure speculation of stocks growing in value. This reliable return represented dividends and interest from their portfolio, and this amount was completely independent from the value of their stocks.

If it sounds a bit confusing, stay with me. It's about to get clearer.

The $20,000 of dividends and interest (the reliable return) in Dave and Donna's investments represented a 1 percent return on the entire portfolio of investments. The return their portfolio was producing, separate from the possibility of growth, was simply 1 percent, when in fact they initially needed 7 percent. Therefore, the 6 percent they needed *above* this 1 percent *might* come from one place and one place only: the *possibility* that their stocks would increase in value, a possibility that Dave and Donna learned the hard way is not guaranteed by any means, regardless of how impressive the mutual fund manager's track record first appeared. As the old saying goes, "Past performance does not guarantee future results," and in Dave and Donna's unfortunate case, that couldn't have been closer to the truth.

Investors withdrawing money from a stock portfolio could mistakenly believe their investments are doing just fine. In Dave and Donna's case, if they received over 7 percent *growth* on their investments it could *appear* the portfolio is reliably producing the income they need. However, without carefully evaluating the *reliable* return portion of their portfolio, they eventually got a nasty surprise the moment their stocks did not perform well.

Therefore, to avoid playing the Most Dangerous Game, one should strongly consider repositioning enough of your accumulation assets into investments that generate reliable returns. With enough accumulation assets repositioned into investments that offer reliable returns, ideally, the "total income" line item found on a brokerage statement would be *at least equal* to the amount of income one needs. In the prior example of the man needing over a 15 percent return on his investments in order to provide him with the income he needs, we saw that this is not always possible by any means.

A Simple Demonstration of Repositioning Assets for Reliable Income

I'm going to be simplistic about this, but it does help clarify the point. I'm going to walk you through a conceptual restructuring of a portfolio that is in the accumulation stage and now needs to generate reliable returns for income. Doing so I'm sure will help you better understand the concept of the Most Dangerous Game.

Suppose I'm retired and I have a nest egg of $1.2 million that needs to generate $58,000 of before-tax income (to supplement possible Social Security, pension, etc.). Remember: This nest egg may seem large or small to you, but relatively speaking, the concept could remain the same regardless of the amount of money one may have.

If I kept the majority of my $1.2 million nest egg invested in the following portfolio, I'm playing the Most Dangerous Game. Why? Because I'm relying on the *possibility* that my stocks will increase enough in value to provide me with the income I need.

Hypothetically, let's assume the $1.2 million portfolio is currently structured as in Table 3.1.

If my before-tax income goal is $58,000, then I need $41,800 in addition to the $16,200 reliable income. The $41,800 can come from one place only: the *possible* growth of my stocks.

Table 3.1   The Most Dangerous Game: Before

Investment Type	Allocation	Dividend or Interest %	Reliable Income in $
Individual stocks and stock mutual funds	$840,000	0%	$0
Bond mutual funds	$360,000	4.5%	$16,200
		Reliable Income:	$16,200

In this hypothetical scenario, there is no income (dividends) paid from the stocks, revealing that the equities portfolio is invested in pure growth stocks (which, by the way, is true of many indexes one might use in a portfolio described in the previous chapter). Sure, if the stocks increase in value greater than or equal to the amount I withdraw, I might *perceive* I am doing fine. I would not be accelerating losses, nor am I digging into my own principal. But relying on the *possible* growth of stocks to generate the income I need is what someone playing the Most Dangerous Game does. And remember: Whether in the accumulation stage or in the reliable return stage, most of us should speculate as little as possible.

In Dave and Donna's case, their advisor was working with the belief that the *growth* of stocks would provide them with the income they need. Over time, I might endorse this belief. But as one enters or approaches retirement, one rarely has time to make up a possible loss. As mentioned, the advisor was not asking, "What's the worst thing that can happen to this portfolio?" He was not reminding himself, "If a bad market causes Dave and Donna's stocks to lose value and they are withdrawing money from this place at the same time, overall losses would be accelerated." I like to compare this to a bathtub of water: If you are withdrawing water to live on from a single tub, God forbid the drain pops open at the same time.

So, instead of relying on the speculative growth of stocks to provide me with the income I need, for most people, a far better approach would be to reallocate enough of the $1.2 million into investments that offer reliable returns *so that the income goal is achieved without needing the stocks to increase in value.*

How much do I need to reallocate? The answer comes down to a few factors, including, but not limited to age, risk tolerance, tax bracket, and how much income is required. In addition, tax consequences for reallocating the portfolio and the reliable returns currently available in the marketplace need to be factored in as well.

To keep it simple, if I need $58,000 of before-tax income and various investments discussed later in this chapter currently offer reliable returns of 7 percent, then I'd need to fund the portfolio of reliable investments with $840,000 ($840,000 generating 7 percent would provide just over $58,000 of income).

The amount left over that I don't need to produce income from should generally remain in a diversified portfolio of growth stocks. If the stocks do not grow in value, my income should not be affected, nor will I *accelerate* possible loss by drawing money from this area, as Dave and Donna unfortunately did. Remember them? Their account lost 22 percent in one year because they withdrew 7 percent from the same pot of stocks that lost 15 percent of their value.

There are many ways I can restructure my portfolio above to avoid playing the Most Dangerous Game. *One* way of restructuring it would be as shown in Table 3.2, but keep in mind that this is only one of many possibilities that we'll be exploring during this chapter.

By *separating* reliable income-producing investments from investments that are intended to provide nothing but growth, one now avoids playing the Most Dangerous Game.

As time goes by and the stock portion of my investments presumably increases in value, when I need additional income to compensate for things such as inflation, I merely *shift* money from the diversified

Table 3.2   The Most Dangerous Game: After

Investment Type	Allocation	Dividend or Interest %	Reliable Income in $
Individual stocks and stock mutual funds *(portions left over from the "Before" portfolio)*	$360,000	0%	$0
Bond ladder combined with other reliable income-producing investments, including dividend-producing stocks for income *and* possible growth	$840,000	7%	$58,800
		Reliable Income:	$58,800

stock portfolio into the investments providing me with reliable returns. Doing so will naturally increase my income.

So, what have I essentially done here?

After repositioning dollars from growth stocks to investments that offer reliable returns, when looking at my brokerage statement I now see my total income (dividends and interest) *equals* my target of $58,000 per year.

In this case, not only has repositioning my investments nearly *tripled* my income, but it has also made it *reliable*. Furthermore, my portfolio is now considerably safer due to the reduced exposure to stocks along with an inclusion of well-diversified *laddered* bonds that offer *maturity* dates—the date investors generally know their money is going to be returned to them—rather than bond *mutual funds* in the "before" portfolio that do *not* offer maturity dates (which we'll explore in more detail shortly).

As mentioned, this is a hypothetical example. Depending on an investor's personal situation, the portfolio would very likely need to be allocated differently.

If it appears simplistic, you might be surprised to know that there are many investors still playing the Most Dangerous Game. Now that you've learned a few things about the game, don't be afraid to speak up and ask questions. It is *your* money; you have every right to evaluate the methods being used to produce the income you require. A year or two following a dip in the stock market is *not* the right time to stop playing the Most Dangerous Game. At that point in time, it could be too late to give yourself the opportunity to make changes for the better.

The best time to shift investments away from playing the Most Dangerous Game is *before* the time you need them to generate reliable returns. So, even if a growth portfolio is doing fantastically well, be sure to remember the Most Difficult Investment Formula in the World: Investing − Emotion = Success.

Fund manager on a legendary tear? Stocks surging in value? Taxes to be paid if you move money around? It rarely matters to me. Someone can tell me his or her stocks are "doing great." I've heard this many times, but it often makes little difference to me. I've seen the destruction one bad market moment at the wrong time can cause, and I can only hope it doesn't happen to you. After all, this is money I'm sure you've worked hard for and it would certainly be a tragic shame if some of it were lost due to playing the Most Dangerous Game when that game didn't need to be played at all.

When it comes to my money, with the exception of the portion invested into the flavors of the day, I am not a speculator. I am an *investor*, and I hope you are, too. Few people get rich by *hoping* to make money in the market. Rich people get wealthy by being smart. They get rich by taking action and anticipating future events. As Wayne Gretzky said, "Skate to where the puck is going, not to where it currently is."

Need income? Speculating on the possibility that your stocks *might* increase enough in value to generate the income you need? Don't experience what Dave and Donna did. Always ask the question, "What's the worst thing that can happen here?" If your portfolio can afford it, take the profits, pay the tax, do whatever it takes to get into more reliable investments, and let the speculators out there live through the uncertainty of the markets.

This is your life we're talking about, remember?

Stock Market Stan Teaches Us a Lesson

Until this point, I've discussed people such as Dave and Donna who once had the opportunity to reposition portions of their portfolio into safer, more reliable income-producing investments. But at the beginning of this chapter, I mentioned that reliable return strategies are not just for the retired person looking to generate income, but for the investor merely seeking growth as well.

As mentioned, investments that offer reliable returns not only generate income, but they also can help buffer bad markets. If stocks go down in value, then the money allocated to reliable return investments can at least offer some return for the overall portfolio.

In some cases, investing the majority of a portfolio into investments that offer *only* reliable returns even when income is not the priority can make sense as well. To illustrate the point, a person I will call "Stock Market Stan" provides a great example.

Stock Market Stan is one of those individuals who really doesn't have much of a reason to be in the stock market at all. Relative to the value of his nest egg, the returns he can safely generate from reliable investments will provide him with more returns than he'll ever need.

Now, your first inclination might be that I'm referring to people who have amassed a lot of money. But that isn't always the case. I've met many people who could be construed as having just a little bit of money. But given that they need so little income from their investments, in some cases, there are many people who can afford to keep the majority of their nest egg in investments that offer reliable returns.

We often find many people who need very little income remain very heavily invested in the stock markets. Chances are they are still heavily invested in stocks for any one of the following reasons: They know of no other way to invest, they believe the markets will always go up, old habits are hard to break, greed, or the plain old-fashioned love of the action.

Any one of these reasons can certainly be valid. After all, it's not my life, nor is it my money, and as a result, who am I to judge? But that said, many people out there *do* want to know if there's a better or safer way; they are open to hearing or want other ideas, and perhaps learning a few things about Stock Market Stan could help.

Stock Market Stan

When I first met him, Stock Market Stan had just turned 60. Over the years, he had managed to do a fantastic job for himself and his wife. Thanks to the sale of a business, he amassed an investment portfolio of well over $5 million. Now, before I proceed, keep in mind: While over $5 million is certainly a lot of money, this same scenario can easily apply to someone with less money, especially if they are well into retirement. Relatively speaking, it's the percentages that count most, not the dollar amounts.

Thanks to various real estate holdings outside Stock Market Stan's $5 million-plus portfolio, he and his wife withdraw very little from their investments. In percentages, Stan's portfolio needs to generate less than 1 percent return each year to produce the occasional income they require.

Stock Market Stan came in one day wanting to hear some thoughts on how to leave more money to his kids. After learning a few things about Stan and his wife, I asked how much of their money was invested in stocks. He replied, "Most of it." I asked why someone with over $5 million, needing less than a 1 percent rate of return to cover occasional cash flow needs, would be so heavily invested in stocks. He couldn't really answer the question; an advisor up north was managing his investments.

My response to Stan: After considering taxes, sell most of the stocks and make the majority of the money safe. Want to leave more money to the kids? For reasons I'll later discuss, consider investing a small amount in a life insurance policy. As for the rest of the money, invest it in high-quality municipal bonds and other safe investments that offer reliable returns.

With the reliable returns these investments produce, the tax-free interest they provide would far exceed Stan's occasional income requirement. From these reliable returns, withdraw the occasional income he needs, and as for the remaining amount, use *that* money to invest in stocks. Worst-case scenario, some of the stocks go down in value. But the following year, the cycle repeats. The nest egg will always be there, and so will his reliable returns that provide not only his occasional income needs, but new money to invest in stocks as well.

While repositioning the majority of his portfolio into safer, reliable investments might sound like a radical idea, in their interviews with the *New York Times*, this is exactly what Alan Greenspan and Suze Orman mentioned they do. And please, don't always assume this is only for the "rich people." As stated before, the same rules can apply to anyone—it's not always about the dollar amount of the portfolio; it's much more about the portfolio relative to who the person is and what he or she needs it to accomplish.

In her *New York Times* interview, Suze Orman stated her net worth is somewhere around $30 million. If she generates 5 percent returns from safe investments such as municipal bonds (which is where she said she invests most of her money), that's $1.5 million per year in reliable returns.

Can she live off that $1.5 million? Probably. Can she gamble that $1.5 million and lose it all in the markets? Sure, because she knows her $30 million is completely safe and it will always be there next year, and the year after that, and the year after that.

And what about Carole Smith? Carole is a friend of ours in her 80s. Not including her house, she has a total net worth of $250,000. Her pension and Social Security provide her with more income than she needs, and her health care expenses are well taken care of thanks to a rock-solid government plan. Requiring no income from her portfolio, wouldn't it be prudent to reposition much of her individual stock portfolio into investments that provide safe and reliable returns? Carole agreed, and as a result, she decided to reposition much of her portfolio into investments that provide reliable returns. The most important result, however, is that Carole now leads a far less stressful investment life that doesn't require her to panic every time the stock market has a problem.

After learning about Carole, Suze, and Stock Market Stan, if you can afford it, perhaps you will consider doing the same for large, medium, or small portions of your investments. Bottom line: If you don't need the *potential* return, why take the risk?

Where Do You Fit In?

So, where do you fall in the investment spectrum? Are you a Stock Market Stan who can afford to place most of your money in investments that offer reliable returns?

Or are you a Dave and Donna, newly retired, who could have benefited from balancing between stocks and investments that offer reliable rates of return to generate the income they need?

Many people nearing or entering retirement—especially the baby boomers—are finding themselves a bit short of where they need to be. They simply cannot afford to put their investments into the safest things possible, given that they don't have the luxury of the Stans, Suzes, and Caroles of the world who could generate more return than they'll ever need from reliable investments.

For some people, realizing their goals might not be as easily attainable as they once thought (and there are no doubt a lot of people out there like this). Therefore, generating reliable returns poses its own set of unique challenges.

Getting Away from the Most Dangerous Game

Let's go back to baby boomers Dave and Donna.

If you recall, Dave and Donna calculated their annual income needs and with the help of an advisor, determined they would need a 7 percent rate of return on their investments to maintain their lifestyle. However, they were playing the Most Dangerous Game, because their advisor believed getting a 7 percent return in the markets was easy. As they learned the hard way, only 1 percent of that return was being generated from reliable investments. The additional 6 percent needed for their income was coming from the *speculative possibility* that their stocks would increase in value, which unfortunately just did not happen.

This Most Dangerous Game is one played by far too many investors and advisors who seem to have too much trust in the market's appreciation. In the long term, I would absolutely agree that the markets *should* provide a return of 7 percent or better to get Dave and Donna the income they needed. But when in retirement, or approaching it, "the long term" certainly won't help if things go bad, as we witnessed in Dave and Donna's case. If things go bad, there quite simply won't be enough time to recover the loss.

No one wants to lose money. But if you are going to take a loss, it's certainly better to do so when you are working and accumulating money during those years. In these cases, you, a fund manager, or I can afford to recover or make up a few losses along the way. However, in retirement (especially during the early stages) it's a totally different story. All it took to start Dave and Donna's perpetual downward spiral was two short years.

As I've stated, for people like Dave and Donna, or others who need to generate income from their investments, counting on the speculative growth of stocks to deliver the return is the Most Dangerous Game.

This statement, I'm sure, can leave you wondering, "Okay, so can I generate *reliable* income from my investment portfolio, while at the same time, especially during the early years of retirement, *also* grow my money?"

Challenging? Not exactly. There are a few key places to invest that are much more reliable than the possibility of stocks growing in value to generate the income one needs. And there are also investments that can give you the potential for both: reliable returns for income and the possibility for growth. It may at first sound like magic, but I can assure you, it's really not.

The following possibilities are some of my favorite investments that offer reliable returns, but by no means are they the only choices out there.

Bear in mind that to generate reliable returns, this group of investment types is not intended as a "pick one and run with it" kind of deal. Typically, a reliable return portfolio should consist of a diversified *combination* of investments. So, when it comes to generating reliable returns that do not rely on the speculative growth of stocks to provide the income one needs, here are a few possibilities that can get the job done.

Bonds

Bonds have a stated rate of return—a "bird in the hand." For example, a bond may pay you 7 percent on your investment. That's a bird in the hand. When you invest in a bond, you know the return you'll get.

Furthermore, investment grade (good quality) bonds typically ensure that your money is safe. The downside to bonds is that they generally offer little growth, if any. If you are deep into retirement, it may make sense to have most of your money in bonds, but most of us moving toward retirement or are in the early stages of it should certainly not rely on this one instrument alone.

Preferred Stocks

This hybrid of a stock and a bond often appears in investment engines designed to generate income. Because they are so often used, I'll give a quick description of what they are. However, I won't spend as much time on them as I will with the other choices, given something I refer to as the "heads I win, tails you lose" nature of some preferred stocks.

Dividend Stocks

Dividends are cash payments from stocks; they are often used to generate income and can be an excellent way to get both income and the possibility of growth. Dividends can change and are not guaranteed. At any time, without warning, a company may even eliminate them, but we are going to learn some ways to minimize this risk. Receiving dividends while at the same time having the possibility of growth is a particularly strong strategy for many baby boomers who generally need both things at the same time: income and growth from their investments.

Annuities

These contracts offered by insurance companies are specifically designed for those moving closer to, or are already in retirement, especially during the initial years of it. Annuities offer some interesting benefits that cannot be found anywhere else, and I'll highlight a few of these features shortly.

Growth CDs

Have you heard about CDs that could pay greater than 10 percent? We'll soon be exploring these interesting investments many have not heard of.

Private Pension

One of my truly favorite retirement income strategies is to create what we commonly refer to as the "Private Pension." With company pensions slowly fading away, the Private Pension is hands down one of the most fascinating concepts for people in retirement looking to generate a simple, effortless, and highly attractive reliable income stream they cannot outlive. Whether you are in or far from retirement, planning for a Private Pension can easily be one of the most valuable strategies you glean from this book.

Because the Private Pension is insurance-based, it makes better sense to address it in the next chapter; but please be sure not to skip what could be a very powerful income strategy for one to consider.

Let's take a look at each possibility in greater detail.

Bonds

As the old saying goes, "You make your money in stocks and you keep it in bonds."

When it comes to generating reliable returns, especially for income, bonds are an essential part of most diversified portfolios. As a result, I start out by addressing bonds not because they are my favorite, but because they are so often used—and for good reason.

Bonds Defined

Let's start at the very beginning by first asking, "What is a bond?" After all, if you don't really know what it is, then everything else to follow is not going to make much sense.

Simply put, a bond is a loan an investor makes to a corporation or government. In exchange for lending them money, they pay you interest on your investment, and at the end of the term, they will return the money that you gave them.

Suppose you own a business and need money. I give you $50,000 for a term of five years. And for each of those five years, you're going to pay me $3,000 (which represents a 6 percent return per year). So, at the end of the five years, I'll have accumulated $15,000 ($3,000 of interest per year for five years). In addition to keeping my $15,000 of interest, I also get my $50,000 back at the end of the five-year term—that is, at maturity. In its absolute simplest form, this is what a bond does. It provides me with a stated rate of return (in this case, 6 percent per year) for a period of time (in this case, five years).

Let's look at another example of how this could work, incorporating some additional aspects of a bond.

Suppose I am General Electric (GE) and am looking to borrow money. I offer you a bond that says: "Give me your money for five years, and for each year that I have your money, I'm going to give you 7 percent interest. At the end of five years, I'll give you your money back."

Sounds simple, right?

Okay, but what if a guy named Skip who owns a lemonade stand offers the same thing? He says, "Give me your money for five years, and for each year I have your money, I'm going to give you the same interest—7 percent. And, at the end of five years, I'll give you your money back as well."

What would your first concern be?

Most likely, something such as, "How do I know some guy named Skip won't skip out on me with my money? How do I know he will still be in business in five years?" In this case, wouldn't it make much more sense to lend a company such as GE your money, given it has been around for a very long time and as a result you know it'll still be around in five years?

Knowing this, Skip, who is a sharp guy, comes back to you and ups the ante: For each year he has your money, he's going to give you *15 percent* interest, and at the end of five years, he'll give you your money back. At that rate of return, you might be tempted to give Skip some of your money. True, there is more risk, but now you're being paid more for the higher risk and it's somewhat enticing.

What we're talking about here is another component of a bond, its credit quality. In general, the *lower* the credit quality, the *higher* the interest. In addition, the *longer* the period of time someone is borrowing your money, the *higher* the interest rate typically is. After all, if they are keeping your money for a longer period of time, then there is an increased chance more things can go wrong, and you should be rewarded for that risk, which is typically the case.

Among other factors to consider when investing in a bond, another important thing you should know about bonds is how marketable or *liquid* your investment would be. Would anyone else be willing to take over that bond if you needed to sell it? Perhaps you lent GE money for those five years, but let's say two years in, for whatever reason, you wanted to get your money out of the investment by selling it to someone else.

To get your money out, you would need to offer that GE bond into something called the secondary market, the area of the investment universe where others presumably seek what you have and make offers on it. In the secondary market, however, you might not get back the same amount you first invested. If you held it for the five years (to the bond's maturity date), unless GE had significant problems, you would get your money back; but here you are looking to sell it early, which means that you could get back more *or* less than you invested.

Here's why:

The Seesaw Effect of Bonds

Suppose you buy that GE bond for $10,000 and it has an interest rate of 7 percent. A little while later, you want to sell that bond to someone else. However, people can now buy new bonds of the same credit quality and maturity date that pay 10 percent interest, not 7 percent.

Who would want to buy your bond paying 7 percent? No one unless the math was adjusted.

The only way someone would want to buy that bond is if they can get a *comparable* return of 10 percent. So, how would they make it comparable to 10 percent? Simple: They will give you less money for that bond so that their return is essentially the same as if they were buying a new bond offering 10 percent.

The same thing works in reverse. Suppose you wanted to sell that bond paying 7 percent, but at that time the same type of bonds are paying only 4 percent. The only way it would make sense for you to sell that bond is if someone paid you *more* than what you had invested.

If it sounds a bit confusing, think of this little visual I learned while in elementary school. While it doesn't solve the math, it'll help you understand what's known as the "inverse" relationship between the values and interest rates of bonds. It has stayed in my mind since somewhere around the fifth grade and maybe it'll help you as well.

If you've ever been to a playground, you most likely know what a seesaw is. Two kids sit facing each other on opposite ends of a long board. Between them is a block supporting the board off the ground. As one kid goes up, the other goes down.

One kid is named "Interest Rate" and the other is "Value." As one goes up, the other goes down, and vice versa. If the Interest Rate kid goes up, Value goes down. The same thing happens in reverse: If Interest Rate goes down, Value goes up.

"One thing going up while the other thing goes down" is known as the inverse relationship between bond value and interest rates: They move in opposite directions from each other.

Taking it one step further, the *length* of that seesaw is also important. The length—or in terms of bonds, the maturity date (how many years you have to hold that bond before you get your money back)—is also deserving of a visual: The longer the seesaw, the more the value will typically be affected.

You will frequently hear bonds classified as short-term, intermediate-term, and long-term. A quick explanation of each should help you gain a better understanding of the pros and cons, as well as the way that the length of the term affects the value.

- *Short-term bonds (less than five years to maturity).* Building on the seesaw example, assume that the two kids are sitting very, very close to each other on opposite ends of the short board. When the Interest Rate kid goes up, the Value kid goes down. However, because they are sitting so close to each other, there isn't much of a change in their movement. This visual demonstrates the trends seen in short-term bonds, which typically do not fluctuate much in value. Because short-term bonds have less fluctuation in value, they are generally assumed to be *safer* than longer-term bonds.

- *Long-term bonds (over 10 years to maturity).* Now imagine a very, very long seesaw. This one is called a long-term bond. As the Interest Rate kid rises, Value on the other end drops. In long-term bonds, the fluctuation in value can be quite dramatic, and they are therefore assumed to be riskier. If you want to get your money out before the maturity date, then there is a more significant chance the value could be far more or less than the amount you initially invested.

- *Intermediate-term bonds (5 to 10 years to maturity).* Intermediate bonds, as their name suggests, fall between the short- and long-term bonds.

Bottom line: The longer the seesaw (maturity date), the more the value of the bond can fluctuate. Logically, then, in case someone had to sell a bond prior to the maturity date, wouldn't most people prefer to stay in short-term bonds? Not always. In general, the longer the maturity date, the higher the interest rate is on the bond. While that is not always the case, it is typical and therefore the reason people often invest some of their money in longer-term bonds to get the higher reliable return they desire. (More on this coming soon.)

Now that you understand a bit more about bonds and the way they operate, let's take a closer look at how to invest in them so that you can generate some reliable rates of return for your diversified portfolio.

Individual Bonds versus Bond Mutual Funds

When investing in bonds to produce a reliable return, one can invest in an individual bond or, commonly, a diversified pool of bonds. For many people, investing in a diversified pool of bonds is often done by investing into a bond *mutual fund.*

In general, I advise people, especially those in retirement, to stay away from investing in bond mutual funds as much as possible. Only if someone has a small amount of money to invest ($50,000 or less) should they consider using a bond mutual fund.

However, bond funds are a mainstay for many investors seeking reliable income and the stability of a diversified investment portfolio, and with understandable reason. Because a bond fund is a group of bonds chosen and managed by a money manager, it provides professional management and quick diversification among a large number of different bonds. This could help cushion a portfolio from one of the bonds defaulting (not paying interest or going bankrupt), which brings us to another important point about bonds.

Whereas investing in bonds is generally safer than investing in stocks, they are certainly not without risk. Aside from the possibility that a company may go out of business, when interest rates rise the value of the bonds will likely fall, as will the value of the bond mutual fund as a whole.

Unlike an individual bond, a bond mutual fund does not have a maturity date—the wonderful date every investor looks forward to, when you know the money you invested is going to be returned to you. This is obviously a very attractive feature of an individual bond that a bond mutual fund doesn't offer.

If the value of an individual bond goes down, you know the date (maturity) when you are getting your money back.

Conversely, if the value of a bond mutual fund goes down, you do *not* know when you will get your money back, because there is no maturity date. You don't know when the value of the bond fund might return to its initial value, if at all. It is for this reason I generally recommend individual bonds when investing to achieve reliable rates of return with as little risk as possible.

But as with all investment strategies, there are advantages and disadvantages. I wish it were simpler; it would save us all a bit of time and paper, but unfortunately, when it comes to investing, things are never quite as black-and-white as we'd like. No doubt, this is where having to choose between a bond and a bond mutual fund can get somewhat confusing. Thankfully, however, when it comes to bonds, I do believe there is an answer that satisfies the advantages and disadvantages of both. More on this coming up.

On the one hand, investing in an individual bond means there is a date (the maturity date) when you are due to get your money back. That's great, but when investing in an individual bond, there is certainly risk that the company you lent your money to could go out of business.

On the other hand, if you invest in a bond mutual fund, you have many bonds working for you. If one company defaults (goes out of business), it won't have a dramatic effect on your overall investment because there are many other bonds in the mix to buffer one evil bond's demise.

So, the *diversification* of having many bonds in a fund certainly decreases the risk; if one hair on the head is lost, there are many others on the head to still keep things looking pretty. But here's where the paradox comes in: The disadvantage to the bond fund, as mentioned before, is that if interest rates rise and the value of the fund goes down, you have no idea when your investment will "come back." Certainly, many advisors will tell you to diversify and to hold on until it does come back, but remember: We are not market timers or gamblers. We are investors, and every single step of the way, as much as possible, we are always looking to give ourselves the best chances for success while asking ourselves the constant question, "What's the worst thing that can go wrong with this portfolio?"

With that, when it comes to wanting the diversification of a bond fund *and* the maturity date that an individual bond offers, in this case there is a way to have your cake and eat it, too.

Before I reveal the timeless answer, it is important that you understand where the risks and rewards are when choosing between

Table 3.3   Bond Fund versus Bond Ladder

	Bond Fund	Bond Ladder
Maturity Date (is there a *date* when investors know they will likely get their investment back?)	No	Yes
Risk	Less than an individual bond due to increased diversification	More than a bond fund due to less diversification
Income	Can be the same	

an individual bond and a bond mutual fund. To help summarize the advantages and disadvantages, Table 3.3 is a quick summary of a few important differences between an individual bond and a bond mutual fund.

As you can see, the attractive features one has that the other does not make choosing between the two a bit difficult. So, is there a way to get the best of *both* worlds? To take the good of both and as much as possible eliminate the bad?

There sure is, and the answer is one of my favorite reliable return investment strategies, designed to preserve your money *and* create a reliable return that is independent from stocks. The answer is: Create your own bond mutual fund, otherwise known as a bond ladder.

Bond Ladders

Bond ladders provide the advantages of both individual bonds and bond mutual funds. We'll soon find out why. The main disadvantage of bond ladders is that they are not as simple to invest in as, in comparison, a bond fund generally is.

But, I firmly believe the rewards of investing in a bond ladder far outweigh the additional time it takes to create one. No doubt, if you have never created a bond ladder for yourself, this is definitely one area of your investment portfolio that you'll want to get some assistance on. And by reading this section, you'll have a great head start in working with your advisor in creating one. And who knows? Maybe you'll even teach the advisor a thing or two, given that many advisors rarely use it, perhaps because of the additional time it takes to create one or, perhaps, the higher fees earned on many mutual funds.

Suppose I have $100,000 to invest, and let's also suppose that I need to generate some reliable returns from this money. In case the stock indexes in my diversified portfolio go down in value, I want a hedge to ensure that at least one part of my portfolio is delivering reliable returns for my income needs.

There could be many reasons why I would invest in a bond ladder, but the bottom line is this: At this moment in time, for whatever reason, suppose I need to get myself a 6 percent rate of return, or in dollars, $6,000 off my $100,000 investment.

After reading and understanding the differences between various investment vehicles we have discussed to this point, I don't want to play the Most Dangerous Game by counting on stock appreciation to try to give me that return. I want to invest that $100,000 in something secure and reliable that will deliver the $6,000 I need without the speculation that it *might* happen in the stock markets.

So, after investigating various possible choices, I like the idea of bonds. I venture out into the marketplace and feel really lucky when I find that GE, a very solid company with great credit quality, has a bond that will pay me 6 percent. With this reliable return meeting my investment requirements, I figure, "I'll take it. Why invest anywhere else?"

Comfortable in my decision, through the bond, I lend GE my $100,000 and all is fine. I'm happy with my 6 percent return per year and it seems that I've made the right choice. But then the bond matures (I get my money back at the end of the term), or it gets called. ("Called" simply means GE has the right to return my money at any time before the maturity date. This is a common feature of many bonds, and typically when a bond is called it's not a good thing, for reasons I'm about to explain.)

I get my money back, and have to start searching the bond market for another bond. I like the idea that the GE bond offers safety of principal (at maturity when you get your money back) and that I am provided with the "bird in the hand" reliable return of 6 percent.

While it's nice that I got my money back (at maturity or when GE called it), in this hypothetical example, I am disappointed to learn GE bonds and others like it are not paying 6 percent any longer; they are only paying, as an example, 4 percent.

That's not good. I need 6 percent to satisfy my reliable return requirements and there are no good credit quality bonds available in the marketplace that can provide me with this return. The risk of this happening is what's known as interest rate risk or reinvestment risk, and it's a risk that investors who rely on bonds may run into from time to time; when a bond matures or gets called and you get your money back, you may not find another bond with an equal rate of return, years to maturity, and quality.

To give you the best possible chance to avoid these risks, a bond ladder does the following:

- Minimizes interest rate and reinvestment risk.
- Diversifies your bond portfolio.
- Includes many maturity dates, the dates where you typically get back your original investment.
- Maintains a reliable and predictable rate of return to help hedge the possibility that the stock portion of the portfolio may go down in value.

A bond ladder is simply a portfolio of individual bonds with staggered (different) maturity dates. Think of a bond ladder as your very own bond mutual fund, without the management fees and *with* maturity dates (the date at which you know your money is being returned to you). This is a highly efficient strategy that many advisors and investors often overlook. I find the reason it is often overlooked is because setting up a bond ladder requires more work than investing in a mutual fund does. But is it worth the extra time? In most cases, I absolutely think so.

Suppose you have $100,000 to invest in your own bond ladder. You don't have one bond paying you 6 percent, but you might have 10 bonds with a value of $10,000 each. In a well-structured bond ladder, the bonds would have varying maturities, with one bond maturing in a year, another in two years, another in three years, and so forth. The resulting portfolio would look like a ladder, as you will see shortly in my example. Most important, the *entire ladder,* not just one bond, pays you an aggregate total of 6 percent (needless to say, this 6 percent is just an example—rates can be higher or lower depending on many different factors and economic conditions).

The main benefit of this investment strategy is that by laddering, or staggering, the maturity dates of the bonds, you won't be locked into any particular bond for any significant length of time, which gives you much greater flexibility on a number of levels.

Let's say that you invest your $100,000 in that single GE bond with a 6 percent yield and a 10-year maturity. During the 10 years that you're going to hold that bond, interest rates are likely to rise and fall and the bond value will follow suit.

As mentioned, if interest rates are low at the time your bond matures—and you're ready to invest in another bond—you'll be stuck buying a bond with a low interest rate. Not good.

However, if you have constructed a bond ladder, only *one* of the many bonds in your portfolio will mature at any given time. So although interest rates may be low when one bond matures, chances are the interest rate environment will be different when the other bonds mature, thereby giving you a much better chance of sustaining the rate of return that made you comfortable to invest in the bond ladder in the first place.

Bond laddering is particularly beneficial in a rising interest rate environment because it allows you to readily move your money out of lower-yielding bonds and into those with higher yields as interest rates rise. One could argue that if you buy shares of a bond fund, the portfolio manager would do this for you, but again, just remember that bond mutual funds have no maturity dates. If the value of the fund drops, you have no idea when your investment is going to be returned to you, if ever.

Remember that important consideration I mentioned before: Investors looking at their portfolios should always be asking themselves the question, "What is the worst thing that can happen here?"

In a portfolio of bond mutual funds, the worst thing that can happen is that interest rates can rise, causing the values of the funds to go down, and if investors need to remove money from this area, they will be getting back less than the amount invested. Or, if the value of the funds goes down and investors need more income, then they have to sell at a loss and possibly reinvest the smaller amount somewhere else to try to give themselves a higher return.

Those are certainly not the best options. These are scenarios that should be considered when asking, "What's the worst thing that can happen here?" And it's the reason that, as much as possible, I tend to shy away from bond mutual funds that cannot assure an investor that if the fund loses value, they will get their money back. I'd much prefer the reduced risk that comes with a well-diversified portfolio of quality, laddered individual bonds.

Bond Ladders Offer Flexibility of Interest Rates

A secondary benefit of bond laddering is that it lets you or your advisor adjust the interest you receive from the bonds. With a single bond, what you see is what you get. With bond laddering, you have plenty of room to tweak your portfolio to generate results that work best for you.

Suppose your bond ladder provides you with a combined return of 6 percent, but for whatever reason, you need an extra percentage point, 7 percent. To get that extra percentage point, you can usually swap one bond on the ladder for another. Typically, to get that extra yield you would either increase the maturity length of a bond or invest in a bond of a lesser credit quality.

Incorporating one of these elements, or a combination of the two, will usually get you that extra yield. Needless to say, adjusting maturity dates and credit quality can bring additional risk into the ladder. Therefore, you never want to overload an investment into one bond, but rather spread the risk out among many bonds.

Let's take a look at an example:

Suppose you are investing in bonds and want or need to generate that reliable return of $6,000 per year. You have $100,000 to invest. You can certainly put the full $100,000 into that one GE bond paying 6 percent. But that puts all your eggs in one basket, and furthermore it won't provide you with the flexibility you'd have from laddering the $100,000 into several bonds, as shown in Table 3.4.

Table 3.4   Sample Bond Ladder

Bond	Amount	Yield	Income
1	10,000	4.0%	$400
2	10,000	4.5%	$450
3	10,000	5.0%	$500
4	10,000	5.5%	$550
5	10,000	6.0%	$600
6	10,000	6.0%	$600
7	10,000	7.0%	$700
8	10,000	7.0%	$700
9	10,000	7.0%	$700
10	10,000	8.0%	$800
	Return:	6.0%	$6,000

You're still getting your 6 percent for income, but you are not painting yourself into a corner with just one bond. As the years roll on and bonds in the ladder mature one after the other, you would be continually rolling into a new bond to maintain the reliable return requirements. Even as I write this in a relatively low interest rate environment, maturing bonds are being reallocated into other bonds that are maintaining the reliable return requirements.

Am I Locked into a Bond Ladder?

The entire bond ladder is liquid and can be sold off at any time. Just know that while you own the bonds, the yield won't change but the *value* of the bonds could. Depending on what happens with interest rates during the bond ladder period, the *value* of each bond can rise or fall. As bond values rise and fall, there are many opportunities for adjusting the ladder.

For instance, yield and length of maturity can be updated by selling the bond and replacing it with another one. However, selling a bond prior to its maturity date would make sense only if you can invest in a different bond that will provide you with higher yield, while decreasing the length of time until maturity and/or purchasing a bond of equal or higher credit quality.

The locked-in maturity date typically comes into effect only if the bond decreases in value and you want to know when your original investment will be returned to you. The answer, of course, is at maturity when the bond reaches its full face value. Remember, however, that if you sell the bond prior to maturity, you will get whatever value the secondary market places on the bond at the time you sell it.

In summary, bond ladders provide comfort in knowing:

- With good credit quality bonds (investment grade), your investment is generally quite safe, especially when compared to stocks.
- Bond ladders provide a predetermined, reliable, and predictable rate of return, which is helpful toward generating income or hedges against the stock portion of your diversified portfolio if it goes down in value.
- Finally, bond ladders provide flexibility in being able to adjust the ladder when interest rates change.

Before moving to the next area of creating reliable returns, there are a few other things you should know about bonds.

Final Points on Bonds

No discussion about bonds would be complete without mentioning at least a few other key points. Keep in mind; this certainly does not cover *all* other relevant points about bonds. As with any investment, be sure you completely understand as much as possible before anything is invested. With that, here are a few other quick points about bonds not addressed in the previous discussions.

Duration

For instant diversification, ease of investing, or any other reason, you might very well wind up investing in a bond fund. As mentioned, I usually stay away from them, but many people do use them and find that they suit their needs.

For those of you who invest in bond mutual funds, you should at least be aware of two key figures provided by the fund: average maturity and average duration.

Average maturity is the average time period until the bonds in a fund mature, and this period is usually quoted in years. Why look at this number? Generally speaking, bond funds with lower average maturities experience less fluctuation to their value than bond funds with higher average maturities (assuming that both types of funds have comparable credit quality). As a result, bond funds with lower average maturities typically have less interest rate risk.

Average duration is an even better reflection of a bond fund's sensitivity to interest rate changes. Duration indicates the change in the value of a bond fund for each 1 percent change in interest rates. For example, let's say the bonds in Fund A have an average duration of three years. That means that for each 1 percent change in interest rates, the bond fund's value (or price) should move 3 percent (1 percent × 3 years) in the opposite direction of the interest rate change. So in this example, if interest rates rise 1 percent, Fund A's value should fall 3 percent.

Another example: Let's say the bonds in Fund B have an average duration of 10 years. For each 1 percent change in interest rates, the bond fund's price should move 10 percent—again, in the opposite direction of the interest rate change. When interest rates rise 1 percent, the bond fund's price should fall 10 percent.

As the examples illustrate, the lower the average duration of the bonds held in a fund, the less the bond fund's value should fall when interest rates rise. These calculations can get complicated, but most portfolio managers do the work for you by classifying their bond funds according to average duration. Short-term funds, for instance, generally hold bonds that mature within one to four years. Intermediate-term funds generally hold bonds maturing in five to 10 years. And long-term funds generally hold bonds that mature in 10 years or more.

The lesson: If you want to stay in bond funds and minimize the risk as much as possible, find a fund that is classified as short-term, or funds that have short duration. Morningstar's web site (www. morningstar.com) is a good resource to help evaluate the duration of your funds, or funds your advisor might be considering for your money.

Do you understand the concept of duration? I hope so, because if you are going to invest in a bond fund, it's certainly useful to have a grasp of duration, especially since I find some advisors don't always take into consideration the duration of the fund.

Credit Qualities

We've learned that it's important to pay attention to the credit quality of the bonds in your ladder or your mutual fund. The two agencies that are most frequently referred to in assigning ratings to corporate bond issuers are Moody's Investors Service (Moody's) and Standard & Poor's Corporation (S&P). Both firms focus on a company's financial condition and the state of the industry in which it operates at that particular point in time. The agencies often revise their ratings of companies, so it's important to make sure you are looking at current ratings and not the ratings from years ago.

Conceptually, corporate bonds are broken down into two categories: investment grade and below investment grade (aka junk bonds, which, for marketing purposes, the companies have conveniently renamed high-yield bonds).

Investment grade bonds carry less risk than junk bonds. As a rule of thumb, if you see a bond in your ladder paying an abnormally high rate of interest, chances are great that it is a junk bond issued by a company that has a poor credit rating.

Table 3.5 summarizes the different ratings that Moody's and S&P place on bonds.

Table 3.5   Bond Ratings

Investment Grade		
Highest Grades		
Moody's	**Aaa**	Best quality, smallest degree of risk.
S&P	**AAA**	Ability to meet financial obligation on the bond is extremely strong.
High Grades		
Moody's	**Aa1, Aa2, Aa3**	High quality by all standards. Not as strong as highest grade.
S&P	**AA+, AA, AA−**	Ability to meet financial obligation on the bond is very strong.
Upper Medium Grades		
Moody's	**A1, A2, A3**	Many favorable investment attributes, secure.
S&P	**A+, A, A−**	The issuer's capacity to meet its financial obligations is strong.
Medium Grades		
Moody's	**Baa1, Baa2, Baa3**	Speculative characteristics.
S&P	**BBB+, BBB, BBB−**	Adverse conditions are likely to lead to speculative possibilities about whether the issuer will meet its obligations.
Below Investment Grade		
Speculative Grades		
Moody's	**Ba1, Ba2, Ba3; B1, B2, B3**	The future of these bonds cannot be considered as stable.
S&P	**BB+, BB, BB−; B+, B, B−**	These bonds face exposure to adverse business or economic conditions that could lead to an issuer's inadequate capacity to meet its financial commitment.
Highly Speculative Grades		
Moody's	**Caa1, Caa2, Caa3; Ca**	These bonds are of poor standing. Such issuers may be in default, or in significant danger of not meeting obligations.
S&P	**CCC+, CCC, CCC−; CC, C**	These bonds are vulnerable to nonpayment, and are dependent upon favorable economic conditions for the issuer to meet its financial commitment.

Table 3.5   (*Continued*)

Below Investment Grade		
Default		
Moody's	**C**	These bonds are typically in default, with little prospect for recovery of principal or interest.
S&P	**D**	These bonds are in payment default.

Taxes

My previous examples have not included a discussion on taxes. As with any discussion on taxes, given there are so many considerations to take into account based on someone's personal situation, please make sure you discuss your intentions with a qualified tax or investment advisor before taking action.

In general:

- Interest from corporate bonds is fully taxable as ordinary income, which, as we'll find out later on, is the least favorable type of tax.
- Interest from government bonds is generally taxed as ordinary income at the federal level only.
- Interest from municipal bonds is generally tax-free both at the federal level and at the state level (as long as you reside in the state where the bond was issued or you live in an income-tax-free state such as Florida).

When constructing a bond ladder portfolio (or any investment portfolio, for that matter), it is important to consider the actual after-tax return when evaluating the income the ladder produces. On occasion, it will make sense to use municipal bonds within the ladder, given that the interest from these bonds is often tax-free. That said, some people rush a bit too fast into municipal bonds simply because they hear that kind phrase "tax-free." But tax-free isn't always the best way to go.

Let's take a brief look.

Municipal Bonds

"Munis," as municipal bonds are frequently called, are one of the safest investments around, especially if they are AAA-rated and/or insured. Just a tiny fraction of municipal government bonds issued have ever defaulted. The best thing about munis, though, is that the interest they generate is typically tax-free.

Depending on your tax bracket, short-term munis or laddering longer-term munis with different maturity dates could give you attractive reliable returns while still providing a high level of safety. Up until the maturity date, just like corporate bonds, values on munis will fluctuate as well. But thanks to maturity dates, you can be assured that you'll get your money back.

To determine whether a muni bond's tax-free interest provides a higher rate of return than a taxable corporate or government bond, use the following formula (I've tried to refrain from complicated formulas in this book, but to do it right, there's no easy way around this one):

$$\frac{\text{Tax-free yield}}{1 - \text{Your federal tax bracket}}$$

As an example, suppose the yield on a taxable corporate bond is 5 percent, while the yield on a tax-free bond is 3 percent and your federal tax bracket is 28 percent. With this information, you would then take the tax-free yield of 3 percent and divide it by 0.72 (1 − 0.28 = 0.72), giving you an after-tax equivalent yield of 4.1 percent. In this case, the taxable corporate bond yielding 5 percent is higher than the tax-free equivalent muni yield of 4.1 percent, making the corporate bond a better choice. Although the interest from the corporate bond is taxable, the *after-tax* amount is still higher than the *tax-free* muni, making the corporate bond a better choice.

Your tax bracket and the comparison between the taxable and tax-free yields will help determine which bond would provide better results.

That's a wrap on bonds. Let's move to the next type of investment that can generate some reliable returns for your diversified portfolio—the one, the only. . . preferred stock.

Preferred Stocks

Many investors searching for reliable returns often look toward bonds to satisfy the desire. But bonds aren't the only way investors can obtain reliable returns. Certain stocks provide viable features as well.

"Stocks?" you might ask.

Yes, some stocks. Preferred stocks, for example. There are also dividend-paying stocks that we'll discuss in the next section. But preferred stocks are closer in concept to bonds, which we just discussed, so we'll start with them here.

Preferred Stocks Defined

Investing in preferred stock, like common stock, means you have ownership in a publicly held corporation. Yet preferred stockholders are in a different class, which generally gives them priority over common stockholders when it comes to earnings and assets in the event of a bankruptcy. If the company goes bankrupt, preferred stock dividends are paid *after* interest to those holding bonds but before dividends on the company's common stock.

That level of security isn't the only reason to invest in preferred stocks, however. They can also be a worthy element within a diversified portfolio designed to generate reliable returns. That's because just like a bond, preferred stocks have a stated dividend (yield), which must be paid before dividends are distributed to those who hold common stock. Dividends typically range from 5 percent to 9 percent per year and are paid quarterly or monthly. And many preferred stocks are eligible for the attractive 15 percent tax rate on dividends, preferred stocks issued by real estate investment trusts (REITs) being the notable exception. So if you're looking for less volatility than dividend stocks and a higher cash return with generally more liquidity than bonds, preferred stocks are certainly worth considering.

How do you know the stock listed is a preferred stock? If you're interested in seeing an example, check out the local newspaper's business section. Many papers list preferred stocks in a separate category. You can also look at Yahoo! Finance or CNBC. On Yahoo! Finance, preferred stocks are listed by the ticker symbol of the issuing company, followed by an underscore, followed by the letter P, followed by the series letter (if there is one, and there probably is, because companies that issue preferred stocks often have more than one series and use letters of the alphabet to distinguish them). In some places, such as tickers on CNBC, preferred stocks are listed by the company ticker symbol, followed by a vertical PR, followed by a letter indicating the specific issue.

As with any investment, some preferred stocks are better quality than others. One way to determine the quality is by looking at the stock's rating. Similar to bonds, preferred stocks are rated by

Standard & Poor's and Moody's. Although the agencies use different scales, the general rule of thumb is much like a school report card: You want to get an A, and the more As the better. Anything below a B grade is not very good in terms of credit quality.

It's a good idea, however, to know a little more about what you're buying before you dive in. So once you find a preferred stock you think you like or your advisor is recommending, take a look at the details and get down to business. It's important to understand what the company issuing the stock does, just as you would want to before buying any stock. But you also need to do a risk analysis just like you would do with bonds. In other words, how likely is it that the company will not be able to pay its preferred dividends?

Analyzing this can be pretty tricky stuff, and it's for this reason that when investing in preferred stocks, many investors will often turn to mutual funds or closed-end funds to have a manager make the selection.

For the curious minded or techie out there looking to understand how risky it is that the company might not be able to pay its preferred dividends, one way to figure that out is to determine something called the coverage ratio. If you're in the mood to get technical or are having a difficult time falling asleep, figuring out a preferred stock's coverage ratio should help to satisfy either desire.

To calculate the coverage ratio, you divide the company's earnings before interest, taxes, depreciation, and amortization (EBITDA) by interest expense plus preferred dividends. The higher the coverage ratio, the better the chance for success. These numbers can typically be found on web sites such as Yahoo! Finance and many other places.

Of course, that may be more work than most investors want to do, and I certainly can't blame them. This is where a financial advisor usually comes in handy. He or she can help you analyze a company's risk of default and answer a number of other key questions about investing in preferred stock. For example, are the dividends cumulative? Are the shares redeemable, and if so, when? What is the likelihood of redemption? These are all key technical terms that many Main Street investors most likely aren't familiar with, which is perfectly understandable.

Another key detail to understand: the maturity date, which on preferred stocks can often be quite lengthy. Similar to a bond, preferred stocks do have a maturity date, and those dates are sometimes very far off in the distant future. As much as you can, stay away from the long maturities—just like a bond, the higher interest rates go up, the more the value on the preferred will drop.

What does this all mean?

Putting all the technical stuff aside that few people will take time to analyze (which I can completely understand, given the complexity) let me try to shed some light on this stuff for you.

Preferred stocks are often used for the portion of a portfolio that is seeking reliable returns, especially for the income-hungry investor. Without a doubt, they can make a worthy addition to a well-diversified investment portfolio.

However, a long time ago someone told me to watch out for the "heads I win, tails you lose" type of game that is sometimes found in the preferred stock world. Here's why.

Heads I Win, Tails You Lose

Many preferred stocks have what's known as a long maturity date. If you recall the previous section on bonds, the maturity date simply means that as long as the company doesn't default, maturity is the date you get your money back. By "long" maturity dates, I'm often talking *really long*.

It is not uncommon to see a maturity date on a preferred stock as far in the future as the year 2095. With these very long maturity dates that some preferred stocks have, chances are decent that the maturity dates aren't going to mean a whole heck of a lot, given that they probably exceed the investor's lifetime.

Therefore, in the absence of a shorter maturity date, when it comes to safety of our principal, this leaves our investment at the mercy of rising and falling interest rates that will constantly affect the value of our preferred stock.

Remember the two kids on the seesaw named Value and Interest Rate? As one goes up, the other goes down. And, you might also recall that in general, the longer the seesaw, the greater the fluctuations in value. Lastly, when it comes to the direction interest rates are moving, just remember this: No one really knows. It is very hard to predict the direction of interest rates.

Understanding that many preferred stocks have long maturity dates, let's return to the "heads I win, tails you lose" game. In this game, generally, three possible things can happen: Interest rates can stay the same, they can go up, or they can go down.

If interest rates stay the same, the value of a preferred stock won't fluctuate much. But let's take a look at what would happen if interest rates go up or go down—and why investing in preferred stocks can sometimes be construed as a "heads I win, tails you lose" type of game.

Scenario One: Interest Rates Go Up.   If interest rates go up, what happens to value? (Think: seesaw.)

Value goes down, and in the case of long-term maturities, value can potentially go *way* down.

So, let's suppose when you invested in a preferred stock you received a 7 percent yield.

Now, interest rates go up. And as a result of the rates going up, the value of your long-term preferred will very likely go down.

Given higher interest rates, you notice that you can now invest in new preferred stocks that offer, as an example, 9 percent.

Sounds good, right? But if you sold your preferred stock that was paying 7 percent, you're likely to sell it at a loss, given that its value went down. And looking to replace the lower-yielding preferred stock with one providing a higher yield typically wouldn't make any sense given you would now be investing in it with less money.

Therefore, in this case, when interest rates went up and you were in long-term preferred stocks, the loss would likely be far too great to sell and reinvest in the higher-returning preferred stock.

So you're stuck. Painted in the corner. You lose.

Okay, next possible scenario:

Scenario Two: Interest Rates Go Down.   This time, interest rates go down. What happens to value?

Value goes up, right? Right.

So, suppose you invested in a preferred stock that pays 7 percent.

Interest rates go down, so, value starts to go up.

You're happy because you presumably aren't losing any money—the underlying value of your preferred stock is trending up, and, better yet, you locked in a 7 percent rate of return on what could be a very long-term investment.

So far, so good, right? Well, here's where the "tails you lose" scenario *could* come into play:

Just when you're celebrating that you apparently locked in a 7 percent long-term rate of reliable return, all of a sudden something not so good happens, and that "something not so good" is known as a "call." A call simply means the company issuing the preferred stock is going to refinance its debt. Because interest rates went *down* and the company can now offer new preferred stock at a lower rate, it calls, or takes back the 7 percent preferred stock and gives you your money back.

You get your money out of the investment (more, less, or the same as the amount you put in, depending on a variety of circumstances). But now, with your money out of the preferred stock due to the call, can you get the same 7 percent return you just had? Chances are you won't be able to, because what happened to interest rates in this scenario? They went down, leaving you stuck in a lower interest rate environment without being able to reproduce the reliable return you just had.

Certainly, there are many factors that can lead to deviation from the two scenarios. They are certainly not set in stone. Some preferred stocks are issued without having the possibility of a call, and a variety of other circumstances can very well make the two scenarios differ from the outcomes I outlined.

That said, these possibilities could very well occur, and in many cases are *likely* to occur. Recognizing that the maturity dates are typically very long on preferred stocks, my personal preference is to generate reliable returns by using other investment strategies, such as bond ladders and a variety of other instruments I haven't yet addressed.

But no doubt preferred stock does have its time and place in many investment portfolios, and it's for this reason I felt compelled to try to shed at least some light on what these are, how they work, and the pitfalls that could possibly exist.

Let's move on to another type of stock that has a reliable return aspect to it. Unquestionably, it's one of my favorites, especially for the baby boomers out there seeking reliable returns for income *and* the possibility of getting some growth from their investments.

Dividend Stocks

Most people would be inclined to think the following scenario cannot be possible, but by the end of this section, I'll show you how it's done. No, it's not one of David Copperfield's magic tricks. The only magic is what dividend stocks can do for you.

Suppose I invest $100,000 in a diversified portfolio of dividend stocks.

From the outset, the dividend stock portfolio generates $7,000 per year in reliable income (that's a 7 percent return, and yes, it can be done—I'll show you where in a little while).

Every investor's worst fear comes true: The stock markets get hit real hard; the value of the dividend stock portfolio goes down 30 percent and is now worth $70,000.

With the portfolio of stocks now worth far less of what it was worth when I started, how much income can the portfolio reliably produce now?

Answer: the *same* $7,000 the portfolio produced before the value went down.

Strange? Absolutely. True? Without a doubt. Guaranteed? Not at all, but I will show you how to reduce the risk.

During the rest of this very important section, we'll learn many of the ins and outs of dividend stocks, the risks and the rewards as to how in the worst-case scenario, your portfolio can still potentially produce a highly attractive and reliable rate of return.

When it comes to generating reliable returns from your money, especially for the baby boomers out there, discussing dividend stocks is often my favorite subject of all.

For those of you who have not heard of these things call dividends, some stocks pay dividends, and the ones that do offer the best of many possible worlds:

- Possibility of growth
- Income
- Free stocks

Regardless of whether you are investing for growth, for income, or to receive free stocks, here's a quote that does a pretty good job of summarizing just how important dividend stocks are to every investor: "Dividends have accounted for well over half of the long-term real return on big-company stocks."—*Forbes*, June 7, 2004.

Take dividends out of the equation, and the growth one can potentially receive in the stock markets doesn't look as appealing as it once did.

Dividends Defined

In its most simplistic form, a dividend is a cash payment made to the shareholder of a company. As an example, if I own one share of stock of ABC Company and ABC pays a cash dividend of $1 for each share I own, then logically, when ABC pays a cash dividend to its shareholders I would get $1.

Now, here is a very crucial point that we will be exploring in greater detail:

The $1 cash dividend I receive from owning my one share is totally *independent* from the *market value* of the stock itself. For purposes of this section, this is such an important point that I need to repeat it: *The $1 dividend I receive from owning my one share is independent from its value.*

Let's make sure you understand it by way of an example:

Assume I own one share of ABC Company stock.

- If ABC Company stock is valued at $10 per share and ABC pays a dividend of $1 per share, how much cash do I receive? $1, right? Right!
- If ABC Company stock goes *down* in value from $10 to $5 per share, and ABC pays a dividend of $1 per share, how much cash do I receive? $1, right? Right!
- What happens if my one share of ABC Company goes *up* in value, and what once was worth $10 per share turns into another Berkshire Hathaway? If ABC stock is valued at $100,000 per share and ABC pays a dividend of $1 per share, how much income do I receive? $1, right? Right!

As you can see in these examples, the amount of income (dividend) the company pays per share has nothing to do with the market value of the share. Therefore, the cash I receive is based on the *amount* or the *quantity* of shares I own, *not* the value of them.

Bottom line: When it comes to generating reliable returns from stocks that pay dividends, the value of the stock is totally independent from the dividend I receive.

You may want to read the preceding paragraph a few times until it sticks with you. If you remember and understand it, "magic" will happen. This magic is most valuable when you need to generate *income* and the possibility of *growth* from your portfolio.

To see how powerful this can be, let's start by taking one big step back.

A Closer Look at Dividends

Most investors are somewhat familiar with stock market investing. Each share of stock you hold represents a portion of actual owner-ship in a company. As a large or even small stockholder, you stand to gain or lose money based on how that company performs.

But when it comes to understanding the value of dividends, one of the first things you need to completely understand is that a stock can make you money one of two possible ways: by appreciating in value or by generating cash in the form of dividends.

Most people are only familiar with making money in stocks when they go up in value. But that only represents one way returns can be generated. On the other side of the fence, generating cash in the form of dividends tends to be vastly underrated. After all, when a dividend is paid, you literally get *cash* paid into your account, and that's obviously not such a bad thing. Given how attractive this could be, I'd like to take some time to discuss this very important area of investing to build wealth or to generate reliable returns for income from this type of stock.

When a company makes a profit, at the company's discretion, a portion of the earnings can be distributed to its stockholders in the form of cash. The distribution is called a dividend. Although there are many reasons a company might distribute a dividend, one of the main reasons is that it's a way for the company to reduce taxes.

Dividends are typically paid by large companies that generate regular profits but are too mature to grow significantly. Examples of such companies are General Electric and Coca-Cola. Fast-growing companies in new industries such as telecommunications and bio-technology seldom pay dividends. Instead, they reinvest their profits to help grow the company.

Prior to the bull market of the 1990s, the average dividend yield on stocks in the Standard & Poor's (S&P) 500 index was about 4 percent. During the 1990s, however, dividends declined as many companies reinvested their profits in an attempt to generate much-desired growth. By the time the bull market ended in 2000, according to *SmartMoney* magazine (October 7, 2002, Internet edition), the average dividend yield on stocks in the S&P 500 had declined to 1.5 percent. In 2003, thanks to something called the Jobs and Growth Tax Relief Reconciliation Act, special tax incentives for corporations made distributing dividends quite attractive.

In the past, dividends were taxed more heavily, much to the disappointment of many investors, who argued that this amounted to double taxation—a company was taxed on its profits and then shareholders receiving dividends were taxed on those same profits as well. The Jobs and Growth Tax Relief Reconciliation Act dramatically cut the federal tax rate on stock dividends from a maximum of 38.6 percent down to 15 percent, and as a result many companies began increasing their dividends. For example, in 2004, Microsoft made a special $32 billion one-time dividend payment of $3 per share and doubled its regular dividend to 32 cents per share.

This change in the tax law makes dividend-paying stocks particularly attractive to income-seeking investors as an income-producing option, as well as to growth investors looking to ensure a portion of their individual stocks have something to show for taking risk via receiving the cash these stocks produce.

In addition, dividends paid to an investor can also be reinvested to acquire more shares of the company that just issued the dividend itself. Instead of receiving the dividend as cash, the dividend is reinvested to purchase more shares. Some refer to this as "receiving free shares of stock," given that you are using the cash the company pays in the form of a dividend to buy additional shares.

Contrary to some opinions, you don't need to always worry that dividend-paying stocks produce cash but have little chance for appreciation. If you take a look at the dividend-paying stocks in the S&P 500, they had an average return of 28 percent in 2003, the year the Jobs and Growth Tax Relief Reconciliation Act was introduced. By no means does the fact a company pays dividends mean the growth will always be stagnant when compared to companies that pay no dividends.

With dividend stocks, you get the best of both possible worlds: income *and* growth. However, while this all may sound good, there are most certainly risks. A company can *cut* a dividend at any time. While some companies have long track records of rarely, if ever, missing a dividend payment, it could happen without notice. And when relying on the dividends being paid for income, a missing dividend would not be a very reliable thing, would it?

To minimize the risk, when needing to rely on dividends for income, I often recommend staying away from investing in individual dividend-paying stocks. Relying on individual stocks to pay dividends can be a dangerous and unreliable proposition, something we definitely want to avoid as much as possible.

Let's take a closer look.

The Danger of Individual Dividend Stocks

Recently, a company known as NovaStar has not performed well. I don't mean to pick on NovaStar, but what happened to this company demonstrates the danger of relying on individual stocks to pay dividends, especially for those looking to generate reliable returns for income, such as a retired investor who needs a predictable cash flow.

For the past several years, NovaStar was a bright, shining star of the dividend world, paying an attractive dividend. One day, however, NovaStar announced the company was having problems and needed to retain more of its capital. So what did it do? It made an unexpected decision to no longer pay dividends to its shareholders.

What do you think happened to the value of the stock? As soon as the announcement came out, the value of the stock tanked. Investors not only lost their shirts, but some lost their pants, shoes, and underwear as well.

The same thing happened to a company known as Impac Holdings. For years, it paid an attractive dividend as well. It was the staple and mainstay of many investment portfolios looking to generate income from dividend stocks, and for quite a while, it was doing really well for its investors. Then, one dark, unpleasant day, the dividend was drastically reduced. As a result, the value of the stock dropped considerably. Not only was the once reliable income cut, but the value of the stock went way down.

Not good.

Because companies can cut or even eliminate the dividends (income) they pay to the stockholders at any time, receiving dividend income from individual stocks cannot be considered highly reliable by any means. There are some companies out there that over the course of decades have not missed a dividend payment, but this does not mean that they never will.

As with any investment, as I've mentioned many times before, one must always ask the question, "What's the worst thing that could happen here?" With dividend stocks, the worst thing that can happen is what happened to those who owned stock in NovaStar or Impac; the dividend is eliminated, the stock loses a great deal of value, and someone starts tossing unreliable financial advisors out windows.

That's a pretty bad worst-case scenario.

But wait . . . haven't I introduced you to dividend stocks as a *reliable* way to produce *consistent* returns? Yes, I have. So let's explore the way to minimize the risks I've just mentioned.

Avoiding the Pitfalls of Individual Dividend Stocks

The best way to protect against the type of disaster where a company cuts a dividend and its stock value plummets is, as always, *diversify*. When investing in dividend stocks for reliable returns and the possibility for growth, one can purchase many dividend stocks in a variety of diversified market sectors. That is one way of creating reliable returns.

If one of your many dividend stocks suddenly stops paying a dividend, you are reducing risk by the fact that in a diversified dividend stock portfolio, you wouldn't have a large percentage of your overall investment in any one place.

Sounds good, but we're not out of the woods yet. Diversification among many dividend-paying stocks certainly helps, but there are still a few problems we need to address.

First is the expense of diversifying. If you wanted to diversify your portfolio by purchasing a large number of individual dividend-paying stocks, the trading costs alone would not be attractive and would reduce your overall return.

Second, having to keep track of all of these stocks can be quite cumbersome.

Third, and most important, having to choose which dividend stocks to invest in can be very time-consuming.

There is a better answer, and the answer is to consider diversifying your money in a mutual fund, an exchange-traded fund, or something called a "closed-end mutual fund."

Using Closed-End Funds to Generate Dividends

One possibility to create a portfolio of diversified dividend stocks is by investing in exchange-traded funds or closed-end mutual funds.

Given I spent significant time discussing exchange-traded funds in the previous chapter, I'll focus my attention here on the closed-end mutual fund. For simplicity, a closed-end mutual fund on a brokerage statement at first appears to trade and act similar to the way an individual stock does. But although on a brokerage statement it might at first look like it's one stock, in reality it's not even close.

That "one stock" (the closed-end fund) can easily have hundreds if not thousands of stocks inside it. Furthermore, the value of a closed-end fund is based on supply and demand, whereas its closely related cousin, the open-ended mutual fund, determines its value based on what is known as the net asset value, which simply means the value of the stocks in the fund.

Let's imagine we're back at the casino I described earlier, and let's return to a roulette table where the numbers on the table all represent stocks that pay dividends. Instead of picking one number such as black 25 (an individual dividend stock), through a closed-end fund you are automatically invested in *many* numbers on the table. On this "dividend stock roulette table," all of the numbers pay dividends, so if one number winds up not performing well like NovaStar, you're not going to be hurt as much as you would be if you owned it individually. NovaStar might have stopped paying a dividend, potentially sending the value of the company's stock into the toilet, but the damage to your game is considerably less, given that this stock is just one of many other stocks that can much better sustain the overall dividend payments, therefore making the income much more reliable.

Some roulette tables consisting of dividend stocks inside a closed-end fund pay attractive dividends—in some cases anywhere from 4 to 10 percent, sometimes even higher. Furthermore, many closed-end funds pay these dividends consistently, typically on a monthly basis.

The risk of these funds is that while the *income* may be generally reliable, it's possible for the *value* of the portfolio to not only go up, but to possibly go down as well. After all, these are stocks we're talking about, not CDs. This brings us to a very important point. Investors who cannot stomach fluctuation of principal but need high rates of return for income may want to pay extra careful attention here: When it comes to the mentality that "I don't want to lose my principal," a lot of the time (but by no means all of the time), people worry about losing principal in the markets because if they lose money, then they are losing income. When you play the Most Dangerous Game as Dave and Donna's advisor did, then this is an unequivocal truth and a very understandable reason why so many people fear the markets. (As an important reminder, the Most Dangerous Game is when someone is relying on the speculative possibility that the value of their stocks will increase enough in value to give them the income they need. In a dividend strategy, remember: The value of the stocks is *separate* from the income the stocks produce.) When using the reliable returns that dividends generally provide for income, then the risk of playing the Most Dangerous Game is significantly reduced.

Here's an example that demonstrates why . . .

Suppose I have $100,000 to invest, and for purposes of diversifying an income-producing portfolio for possible growth and income, I like the idea of including dividend stocks as part of my investment engine. Instead of investing in individual stocks that pay dividends, I invest in closed-end funds that contain hundreds of stocks paying dividends. And instead of investing in one closed-end fund, I spread out my risk and purchase, as an example, 10 closed-end funds, investing $10,000 into each. The total dividend (or, more simply) *the income* the portfolio produces through all the closed-end funds can be as high as 7 percent or in some cases, even much higher. In dollars, and as an example, that translates into $7,000 per year being generated from this hypothetical $100,000 investment.

Now, certainly, the initial $100,000 I invested can go up or down in value. After all, I'm investing in closed-end funds that contain stocks. As such, maybe a year later the value of my initial $100,000 investment is up 10 percent, for a total value of $110,000. Maybe it falls the other way; collectively, the account is no longer worth $100,000, but went down to $80,000.

As the underlying value of my stocks within the closed-end funds goes up or down, what is the one thing that generally remains consistent? The income of $7,000, that's what. The dividends, or income, the portfolio of closed-end funds produces is in many ways more reliable than the value of the fund itself.

Why? Because remember the critical point reviewed at the beginning of this section: the *value* of the stock is *totally separate* from the *income* it produces. And as for the reliability of this income, if you have a handful of closed-end funds, and each fund likely has hundreds of individual stocks nested within it that are all working to generate income, then you can easily have a grand total of a few thousand stocks collectively paying all the dividends. A few individual stocks within the closed-end fund may very well cut their dividend or eliminate it, but with this strategy, you could have thousands of other dividend-paying stocks working to maintain the income.

Simplifying the Concept of Dividend Stocks

Because this can get confusing, I'm going to walk you through an analogy I often use to help make the point a bit clearer.

Imagine you and I invest in real estate, purchasing a house today for $100,000 (with no mortgage). Because this is an investment, to cover our monthly expenses we rent it out to a guy named Jack. We researched Jack's track record in other properties he's rented in the past and it appears that he has never missed a payment. We have a strong belief that Jack will be a good, reliable tenant, providing us with a monthly income to cover our expenses.

Jack pays us a total annual rent (our income, otherwise known as a dividend) of, as an example, $7,000. From our original investment of $100,000, we are therefore receiving a 7 percent rate of return. If the house increases in value to $150,000, would that change our income? Not at all. We would still get our $7,000 from Jack, which continues to represent a 7 percent return on our original investment of $100,000 even though the house has gone up in value.

What if our house goes *down* in value to $80,000? Would our income being received from Jack change? Not at all. As before, we would still get our $7,000 from Jack, which continues to represent a 7 percent return on our original investment of $100,000 even though the house in this case has gone *down* in value.

So, regardless of whether the value of the house goes up, declines, or remains the same, we are still getting our $7,000 from our original investment of $100,000. This $7,000 represents a 7 percent return, which stays the same regardless of the value of the house. Better stated, *the rent we are receiving is totally independent from the value of the house itself.* Just like a dividend-paying stock, this allows us to generate reliable cash flow from the original investment while we likely ride out the ups and downs, in this case, of the real estate market.

Therefore, we can safely conclude that the income (dividend) Jack pays us is totally independent from the value of the house. This same principle applies with the dividends (income) we can get from stocks. If the value goes down, Jack is still paying the rent, making the bad market years much more tolerable given the income is still there.

Now, let's take things a step further. Let's discuss some of the risk: Jack is the only guy paying us rent. He lives in the house himself. So, what's the risk here? The risk is obvious: Even though Jack has a strong history of being very reliable, maybe for whatever reason, one day Jack gets laid off from his job and stops paying the rent.

This can happen as easily with a tenant paying rent as it can with a company paying a dividend. And if it does happen, you and I are in trouble. We need that $7,000 to cover our expenses. If Jack stops paying, we aren't receiving anything. Without any backup plan in place, we might be playing the Most Dangerous Game: relying on the *speculative, possible* appreciation of our initial investment to give us the income we need; and that's not the game we ever want to be playing, because that is much more of a *gambler's game* and we are *investors.*

So, you come up with a great idea. You tell me, "Listen, instead of having *only* Jack pay the $7,000, why don't we rent the house out by the room, to *dozens* of people with great track records who *collectively* pay us an annual total of $7,000 in rental income? That way, if Jack unexpectedly falls on hard times and cuts or eliminates his rent check, we would still have many other people paying us their portion of the total income. Certainly, this would minimize the risk compared to renting only to Jack."

Therefore, *diversifying* the tenants and adding many more of them into our house makes this rental income much more reliable than if we rented the house to only Jack. This is exactly what I'm talking about when discussing the critical need to have as many dividend stocks as possible "paying you the rent." The more tenants there are paying their rent, the less likely we'll get ourselves into trouble and fall short on expenses should a few of them fail to pay. Each tenant represents a mere sliver of the engine that is producing our monthly income, thereby reducing our risk and creating a more reliable rate of return.

When you invest in dividend stocks through a portfolio of closed-end funds, there are potentially thousands of "tenants" paying you the income you count on.

Remember:

The income (dividend) a stock pays is separate from its value.

- Regardless of whether the value of the stock goes up or down, our income (dividend) generally remains the same.
- The income *might* change. Even if the company has a highly impressive track record of always paying dividends to its shareholders, there are certainly no guarantees it will always remain the same; it can even get cut entirely.
- To minimize this risk, we don't invest in only a few stocks that pay dividends; we invest in *thousands of stocks* so that if any one company reduces the dividend or eliminates it, there are many other dividend-paying stocks to help cushion such a possible fall.
- And one of the instruments we can use to diversify into dividend stocks is a closed-end fund.

The Power of Dividend Stocks

A real-world example of this concept in action will help you better understand just how powerful this can be. I'll use Dave and Donna from back in the beginning of this chapter to illustrate the point.

If you recall, at the time Dave and Donna retired, they had $2 million and needed to generate income from their nest egg that required a 7 percent needed rate of return.

Do you remember why they got into so much trouble?

They got into trouble because the advisor they were working with was dangerously *speculating* that the *value* of their stocks would grow enough to give them the income they needed. And unless you have a crystal ball all shined up and ready to go, there is no possible way of knowing if the stocks will consistently appreciate by 7 percent year after year.

So what happened?

In Dave and Donna's case, the value of the stocks didn't go up 7 percent; the value went down 15 percent. So, the 15 percent loss of value *in addition to* the 7 percent they were withdrawing for income really got them into hot water. The total loss for the year was 22 percent, making it much more difficult the following year for their portfolio to provide them with the income they needed. And if you recall, the following year, the account value went down even more while they continued drawing their income from it. What game were they playing? They were playing the Most Dangerous Game.

If at the time they needed to generate income from their portfolio the advisor had repositioned their investments so that they included dividend stocks through instruments such as closed-end funds, Dave and Donna would have likely fared much better. In the dividend-paying portfolio of stocks, as we've learned, they would have continued receiving 7 percent from the dividends without having to draw from the stocks at the same time they were going down in value.

Again, how does this happen? How could they have invested their money into a highly diversified portfolio of closed-end dividend funds paying 7 percent, then see a drop in value but still receive income of the same amount?

Because of the important point many people aren't aware of that I brought up several times before: The amount of income you receive is not based on the *value* of the shares, but the *quantity* of shares purchased.

So, suppose Dave and Donna invested $2 million into a well-diversified portfolio of many closed-end funds paying 7 percent dividends (this would certainly *not* be prudent, because diversification into other investments would absolutely be essential for a number of reasons. I'm using this merely to illustrate the concept).

Suppose when they invested their $2 million, that amount purchased a total of 10,000 shares. The dividends (or income) they would have received would be based on the *quantity* of these 10,000 shares, *not* the market value of them. If those shares were later worth more or less than the initial $2 million investment, it likely wouldn't matter in regards to the *income* the portfolio produces. As long as the *quantity* of shares doesn't change, when thousands of stocks inside a portfolio of closed-end funds are paying the dividends, the income generally remains the same.

This is so often overlooked, and I can't emphasize enough its importance and the value of knowing this.

Buying and Selling the Dividend Stock Portfolio

When a portfolio such as this is established, if the value of the portfolio goes down, you should generally *not* sell off any positions. Selling off shares of a closed-end fund that is producing income will reduce the number of shares in the portfolio and therefore reduce the amount of income one receives.

Selling off positions when they are down in value will recognize the loss. To understand why this can hurt you more than you may think, let's get back to Dave and Donna.

Suppose Dave and Donna's initial $2 million account was generating 7 percent for income. A year later, the value of their portfolio goes down. Let's use a very steep drop as an example. Let's say terrible things happen in the market and their overall account loses 20 percent of its value and is now worth only $1.6 million.

If Dave and Donna hold the portfolio, they should generally maintain the *same* income as when they *first* invested. They continue living off their income and, while they are certainly aware of the paper loss, they understand they are still invested in the same *amount* of shares that could go back up in value at any time.

If they panic and sell the portfolio when it is down, in this case they would then be left with $1.6 million in cash. With the cash in hand, the next question would likely be, "Where can I now invest $1.6 million to generate the same income I need?"

Answer: most likely by having to invest in stocks for speculative growth that *could* and *might possibly* get them the return they now need. With less cash on hand, the rate of return required to produce the same amount of income they need would be much higher. A higher rate of return would require riskier investments, whereby someone would very likely have little choice but to play, as we well learned before, the Most Dangerous Game.

It's for this reason an income-producing portfolio of high quality closed-end funds should generally be considered a "buy and hold" portfolio, especially if the account goes down in value. If Dave and Donna's portfolio was set up properly in the first place—in a *highly* diversified portfolio *with small amounts of money allocated to a large variety of closed-end funds*—unless there is a major problem within the portfolio, they should infrequently need to change any part of these holdings.

If the portfolio goes down in value and the income it generates is satisfying to the investor, then one would very likely want to hold the portfolio until it potentially increases back in value. Chances are you might be thinking, "What if it never comes back? What if the value stays down?"

But the *greater risk* would be the Most Dangerous Game Dave and Donna already played: In their world, when the value of the portfolio was going down, they were pulling income from the same pot of money, thereby *accelerating* the loss. Remember the bathtub analogy: They were taking water out of the tub while some of it was going down the drain at the same time.

In the case of dividends being produced through the closed-end funds, if the portfolio goes down in value, Dave and Donna would *not* be taking money from the declining value. They would be generating income from the dividends paid based on the *number of shares* that have *remained the same.* That's why it is so critical to remember that the value of the shares has little to do with the income they produce.

One of the main risks of a closed-end portfolio generating income is if dividends get cut or eliminated. It is therefore the reason why the only way anyone should ever rely on income being produced from this area of their diversified portfolio is to invest in *many* closed-end funds so that many companies are collectively paying the income, not just a few.

Furthermore, even though at the time of this writing an investor can receive dividend income as high as 10 percent (or more) from a portfolio such as this, one must not rely on this type of strategy alone. Prudent investment engines should never be constructed with one product, no matter how good it appears to be. One must always consider diversifying into bonds, stocks, CDs, and so on to prevent unforeseen problems. In this type of portfolio, if emergency cash were needed from the portfolio, it would be a disaster to pull money out of a closed-end fund if it was down in value (because, as mentioned, doing so would reduce the income). You absolutely need other areas to take money from just in case the value of this type of portfolio goes down.

Again, always ask yourself and your advisor: "What is the worst thing that can go wrong here?"

If someone cannot stomach *any* possibility that a portfolio like this can go down in value even though, presumably, the income is still being produced, then one should explore other strategies, some of which I discuss during the course of this book.

That said, there are plenty of people I have worked with over the years who need to generate high returns for income from their investments. Even though many of us would prefer to produce the income in something as completely safe as a CD, the low returns these safe instruments offer often don't provide the income we need, nor will they provide potential for growth many Baby Boomers and retirees generally require while receiving income.

This is why educating yourself on a closed-end fund portfolio could wind up playing an important role alongside other parts of a diversified investment engine.

Ten Percent Dividends: Is That Really Possible?

When I mentioned closed-end funds that pay high dividends such 8 percent or even higher, I'm sure some of you might be thinking, "How can a stock pay that high a dividend, when most stocks pay dividends of 1 percent to as high as 6 percent?"

It would be difficult to summarize every type of closed-end fund available, but in general, the closed-end funds that pay high monthly dividends, such as ones that pay 8 percent or more, can often be categorized into a few possible areas including, but not limited to: leveraged funds and covered call funds.

Leveraged Funds.   One of the advantages closed-end funds have over their close cousin, the open-ended mutual fund, is that a closed-end fund is legally allowed to use something called leverage. When you invest $1 into a closed-end fund that permits leveraging, the manager does something open-ended funds cannot do: The closed-end fund reserves the right to borrow against this $1 and invest the additional amount. For simplicity, the fund might be able to borrow 10 percent on that amount, so your $1 investment is actually purchasing roughly $1.10 of dividend-paying stocks (less the cost of the borrowed money). Add this up for the many dollars the fund collects, and you'll see that when leveraging, the fund purchases an enormous amount of additional stocks with the added borrowed money.

With more stocks purchased as a result of the borrowing, investors have more stocks working for them to produce the dividends and therefore get a higher dividend.

The danger of the leveraged funds is that their value is more volatile than that of funds that do not use leverage. The higher the leverage, the greater the dividend and the greater the risk that the value will go down. For those who don't need the higher income, I would recommend you invest in funds that do not leverage and therefore tend to be less volatile (than leveraged funds). But for those who need to count on the higher dividends for income, you may very well need to invest in leveraged funds.

Covered Call Funds.   A covered call is a conservative option strategy that is specifically designed to generate income. This is *not* a dividend, but some of the higher-income closed-end funds out there produce the income by doing something called "writing" covered calls against a stock index.

One covered call fund I have invested in generates an estimated income of approximately 1 percent per *month*. The underlying index the fund writes calls against is the S&P 500, and although it generates a very high income, it is still considered to be within the realm of a conservative investment. It is therefore something that could potentially be a worthy fit inside a diversified portfolio of closed-end funds.

Adding It All Up

Many investors I work with need high rates of return to generate the income they need. By "high rates of return," I'm referring to returns of 7 percent or greater. With such a need, which would you rather rely on?

Like Dave and Donna, the *possibility* that the *value* of the stocks in your portfolio will go up 7 percent year after year to provide the income you need?

Or,

Thousands of stocks within a well-diversified portfolio of closed-end mutual funds producing *dividend income* of 7 percent—income that does not rely on the speculative appreciation of stocks to generate it?

The closed-end fund is certainly not without risk, but when comparing it to playing the Most Dangerous Game, for those that don't have time to make up potential losses, it would not be hard to argue that this is the Less Dangerous Game of the two. As you dive in to explore concepts such as this for *portions* of your money, perhaps you'll feel the same way.

Final Thoughts on Closed-End Funds

When evaluating closed-end funds (www.etfconnect.com is a great resource), be sure to check if the fund is trading at a "premium" or a "discount." These concepts are important when evaluating which fund to invest in for your diversified portfolio.

In general, when you have a choice between funds, you should typically invest in the fund that is trading at a discount rather than at a premium.

Without going into too much detail about the technical reasons and what this means, just know that when you are purchasing a fund trading at a discount, you are buying the stocks in the fund for *less* than what they are currently worth. You're buying them on sale, and that is obviously a good thing. The belief here is that because you are buying the stocks on sale, the value of the portfolio is more likely to increase (something that is certainly not guaranteed).

Conversely, purchasing closed-end funds trading at premium simply means you are paying *more* than the underlying stocks are currently worth. You are *overpaying* for the stocks. While this is not desirable, on occasion you may very well choose to invest in a closed-end fund trading at a premium as a result of the attractive income the fund produces.

In addition, closed-end funds are offered either as new issues or for purchase in the secondary market.

- A new issue is a closed-end fund that is coming out on the market and is being offered to investors for the first time. Here, the price of a new issue is fixed by the issuer.
- A secondary market closed-end fund is one that has already come out into the market. The basic laws of supply and demand establish the price of a closed-end fund offered in the secondary market.

In general, I recommend purchasing closed-end funds in the secondary market. Why? Because when you purchase new issue closed-end funds, you are going to pay loads (fees and commissions) on the issue that are built into the purchase price.

Just recently, someone asked my opinion on a closed-end fund about to be issued. On the front page of the prospectus, I showed her that the share price was $18.75, but the offering price was $20. That spread of $1.25 per share was simply the fees and commissions built into the sale of the new issue. Certainly, there are going to be times when purchasing a closed-end fund "at issue" makes much sense, so by no means take my preference as an absolute.

Ideally, an investor should first look into the secondary market before purchasing a newly issued closed-end fund. Chances are there are some quality buys out there that will cost less in fees and commissions and still satisfy the reasons for investing in a closed-end fund in the first place.

There are other factors not mentioned here to consider before investing in a closed-end fund designed to generate dividends. As with any other investment strategy discussed in this book, careful consideration should always be given before an investment is made, and it's therefore advisable to seek the assistance of a qualified advisor.

The Great Wallendas Teach Us a Lesson

Ever hear of the Great Wallendas?

For many years, and even today, the legendary Great Wallendas (otherwise known as the Flying Wallendas) have astounded audiences with their incredible tightrope-walking talents. For decades, everything went just fine, but according to the web site devoted to their history (www.wallenda.com), "it was during a promotional walk in San Juan, Puerto Rico, in March 1978, that the patriarch of the Great Wallendas fell to his death at age 73. Not because of his age or capabilities, not because of the wind, but because of several misconnected ropes along the wire."

All it took was one bad moment for Karl to go spiraling down to his unfortunate death. Years and years of perfection, and all it took was one moment of mishap to end his career and life.

The tragic event reminds mc of the stock markets. For many investors I have met, life in the markets was going along just fine. But all it took was one bad moment to get wiped out.

As a result of tragic market stories, many investors understandably fear the markets, especially those like Dave and Donna who have had some really bad experiences. People like the Dave and Donnas of the world understandably fear going out on the tightrope without any safety nets underneath them, and no matter how much a well-diversified portfolio of low-cost and tax-efficient stock indexes can help buffer a bad market fall, no matter how good the track records might look, they have a tough time trusting not only the markets, but the advisors who accompany them.

People of this mind-set might be interested in:

- Investing in the stock markets to try to make as much money as possible.
- The opportunity to lock in the account value every year, and use this account value as a base to draw income from.

- If the value of the account later goes down, the ability to look back to the highest account value and *draw income from that amount for the rest of life.*

If these features sound interesting, then this section is for you.

Investing in the Markets with Safety Nets Beneath You

Before I let the cat out of the bag and reveal how the preceding scenario could be done, I want to describe another scenario I see quite a bit, especially with the baby boomers out there who are just getting started in retirement or are moving closer to it. Perhaps their situation is something you can relate to.

Mark and Rhonda started investing late in the game. With little in savings, just as they cleared their 50s they suddenly realized they would have to either work longer or get serious about investing.

Their situation is not uncommon.

Meeting with them, I gave them an honest assessment of where they were at and what they could expect for retirement income. The result was not pretty. In fact, based on the way they were doing things and their desired income at retirement, it looked as though they wouldn't even come close to making it to where they wanted to go. Their nest egg wasn't much, the amount they were saving wasn't enough, and with retirement nearing on the horizon, they understandably didn't want to take big risks with their money to try to earn higher returns.

In addition, they also well understood that because they feared loss, their conservative nature of investing greatly reduced the chances of making significant returns in the market.

A few years back, they tried their hand with an advisor who managed to lose them a lot of their money. Not surprisingly, this was simply because he wasn't investing through diversification; he was trying to time the market by trading individual stocks, chasing horses, and trying to predict the next winner of the next race, which is something I hope we've learned not to do with the majority of our money.

Afraid of losing more, they pulled their money away from the advisor and ever since have been investing in an overly diversified portfolio consisting primarily of highly conservative bond mutual funds. Over the past few years, they've seen lower rates of return on their money and they have been a little uneasy knowing the returns aren't going to get them where they need to go. After their bad experience, however, they just can't muster up enough courage to venture back into the stock markets.

With retirement approaching, their biggest, understandable fear is losing money again. Quite simply, if they lose money, they won't have time to make up the loss. When it comes time to generate income from their nest egg, they understandably fear there will be less money to produce it from.

Their choices to ease the pain are primarily:

- Inject more money into their highly conservative investments, which they don't really have.
- Make significant cuts to their budget or downsize their home, which they would rather not do.
- Extend their age of retirement, which they'd prefer not to do not only because of lifestyle reasons, but also because of some health problems that might wind up forcing Mark into an earlier retirement than expected.
- Invest their current nest egg more aggressively, which they don't want to do.

Mark and Rhonda's concerns are not uncommon and cause a paradox of sorts. Ideally, they'd invest in the markets to go after higher rates of return, but they don't want to take risks whereby losing money would adversely affect their potential to generate income down the road.

For an advisor, this is somewhat challenging to solve. I can talk to them about how a well-diversified stock and bond portfolio should minimize their concern. It might sound good, but there is obviously risk and no guarantees that success will be achieved. No matter how much I discuss diversification and review portfolios with years of attractive returns with minimal loss, investing in the markets does have risk.

As much as I believe in diversification through index exchange-traded funds and taking some additional risk with the "flavors of the day" portion of a portfolio outside the core holdings, people such as Mark and Rhonda who have had bad experiences might have a hard time accepting suggestions such as this.

What they were looking for is something the stock markets alone cannot do: guarantee them protection on their income if their stock account goes down in value.

But there is one investment that can guarantee such a request. And that investment, in this particular case, is something called a variable annuity.

Annuities: Aren't They Bad?

When hearing the term *variable annuity*, some of you may very well be thinking:

- "I've never heard of those before."
- "I've heard bad things about them."
- "I don't really understand them."

As far as I am concerned, annuities are without a doubt one of the least understood products in the investment universe simply because there are so many different kinds that do so many different things. They are so often generalized, mislabeled, and misunderstood, that for better or worse, they have either completely saved someone's life or totally and completely destroyed it.

Before discussing the variable annuity that could help solve Mark and Rhonda's concerns, I ask you for the moment to try to erase everything you might have heard about them—not just the bad, but the good things you may have heard as well. If you think you understand annuities, you may really only have an understanding of one very specific type, and for better or worse that could definitely cloud your thoughts.

Annuities Defined

Bad stories abound about annuities being a vehicle used to take advantage of investors. Of course, there are unscrupulous people in every profession. After all, most doctors improve and save people's lives, but there are also a few who unfortunately ruin them. The same applies with financial advisors. Some have saved lives and greatly improved them, but there are undoubtedly others who have ruined them as well.

When it comes to getting clear information on an annuity, you can easily wind up getting quite dizzy, to say the least. Take, for example, *Money* magazine. A few years ago, *Money* had a cover story entitled "Inc($)me for Life" (Walter Updegrave, July 2002). This well-written article discussed various strategies available to produce quality retirement income. Much of the article focused on the use of annuities in an investment portfolio, specifically immediate and variable annuities. Updegrave basically summed up his opinion by stating he believed a significant portion (25 to 50 percent) of a retirement account should be invested in an annuity.

Then, a few years later, within a month of one another, two more stories about annuities from the same author came out in *Money*'s paper and Internet editions. One story issued a dire warning that investing in an annuity was probably the worst thing you could ever do ("Three Retirement Deals You Can Do Without," August 30, 2006). Then, a few weeks later, another article appeared that praised the annuity ("An Income Plan That's Built to Last," September 12, 2006).

Unless someone had working knowledge of annuities and did a close comparison of the articles, most people would not have known the differences between the annuities discussed that did far different things for different people. Many investors came away with confusion; annuities are sometimes great and sometimes not so great, but who knows how to tell the difference, and how do you know when and if you should consider using one?

Here's another example of how confusing annuities can sometimes get: For many, many years, highly praised nationally syndicated newspaper columnist Humberto Cruz trashed variable annuities. And even more than variable annuities themselves, he despised people that recommended them. This well-known columnist could not have said worse things about these products.

Then, seemingly out of nowhere, more surprisingly than if my New York Islanders actually won another Stanley Cup, he wrote a column that stated he invested his wife's *entire IRA* in a variable annuity ("New Benefit Could Be the Next Big Thing in Annuities," June 22, 2006). In his follow-up articles, he stated how much this shocked his readers: Not only did he invest in something that for years he had completely trashed, but making matters worse, he used money from an IRA to do it, which is something that is scorned upon by various experts.

Of any investment product I have ever come across, I don't think there is anything that causes a more bipolar reaction and hot debate than using, or not using, an annuity in your portfolio.

I firmly believe that many of the misunderstandings come about due to the frequent mixing and matching of one annuity's features with another's. In many cases, it would be like saying, "I'll never vacation in the Bahamas because I hear the lines for the ski lifts are way too long."

Mixing and matching one feature with another causes nothing but confusion, so before moving on to discuss the features of a variable annuity that could very well satisfy Mark and Rhonda's precise concerns, here's a quick breakdown of the different types of annuities. I'll keep it real short and, I hope, sweet.

- *Immediate annuity.* An immediate annuity is similar to a pension. You make a one-time deposit into this contract with an insurance company, and in exchange for the deposit, you get an income stream for life. The income stream runs out when you do, and you only have access to the income during your life, not your original investment. If someone has ever said to you, "Don't invest money in an annuity, because you will never see your principal again," this is the type of annuity they were talking about. While to "never see your principal again" might seem like a bad thing, there are many positive benefits of including an immediate annuity in a retirement income plan, one of which I'll be discussing a bit little later in the book.
- *Fixed annuity.* The fixed annuity is sometimes referred to as a "tax-deferred CD." In this annuity, your money is safe from loss. You invest money into an account for a certain number of years, and while you are invested, you typically get a fixed rate of return. The interest earned is not reported to the Internal Revenue Service (IRS) until you withdraw money, and at the end of the term, you can typically take all your money out, leave it in, or *convert* it to an immediate annuity.
- *Index annuity.* The index annuity is similar to a fixed annuity except that the interest you receive is linked to the performance of a stock market index. If the index goes up, you earn interest and lock it in (once the interest is credited to the account, it cannot be lost). If the index goes down, you may not earn anything, but your original investment and any prior-year earnings are protected from loss. At the end of the contract term, just like a fixed annuity, you can typically withdraw

all your money, leave it in, or convert it to an immediate annuity. I'll have a few more things to say about the index annuity later in this chapter.

- *Variable annuity.* The variable annuity is far different from the aforementioned types. In its utmost simplest form, when investing in a variable annuity, you are making direct investments into stock market subaccounts, a term closely associated with stock mutual funds or indexes. As with the fixed annuity and index annuity, any earnings are tax-deferred until money is withdrawn, but unlike any of the other annuities, this type of investment incorporates actual investments into the stock market. I'll go into more detail on this type of annuity in a few moments.

As you can see, the significant differences between all these annuities can often lead to gross misunderstandings. Because the variable annuity best matches Mark and Rhonda's needs, let's continue and take a closer look at how this VA works.

Variable Annuities

A few pages back, I mentioned that a variable annuity provides investors with:

- Investments in the stock markets to try to make as much money as possible.
- The opportunity to lock in the account value every year, and use this account value as a base to draw income from.
- If the value of the account goes down, the ability to look back to the highest account value and *draw income from that amount for the rest of life.*

How does a VA do this? Stay tuned. Before we get there, I want to clear some more potential bad air here.

If you read a lot of financial magazines and the business sections of newspapers, you might very well have heard some negative things about variable annuities (for short, I'll call them VAs).

For every bad article I have read on VAs, I have read others that are positive. Sometimes, the good article and the bad article are from the same publication over a very short period of time (like the ones I mentioned earlier from *Money* magazine). Up until recently, many advisors I know seldom believed in using VAs. They felt the guarantees offered were not worth the extra fees, and more important, the guarantees should not be needed at all, especially if the investment portfolio was properly well-diversified.

But things have changed, and the changes are worth mentioning here. Because of various new features offered, for the same reason that Humberto Cruz invested his wife's entire IRA into one, many advisors I know are discussing VAs with investors more often than before. For certain investors, especially those who want to grow their money in the markets but fear losses would adversely affect their income, using a VA for a portion of one's money could be a worthy consideration.

Just recently, the *Wall Street Journal* published an interesting article entitled "Investing with a Safety Net" that highlighted some of these interesting features VAs now offer (April 18, 2007, "Getting Going" column by Jonathan Clements). The article highlighted these new features that offer "a no-lose proposition, so you might as well gun for the big win," suggesting to "buy variable annuities with part of your nest egg—and then wring maximum advantage out of the guarantees."

In fact, one person who used to openly trash the VA has recently come forward with some updated thoughts worth mentioning.

In an interesting, widely quoted article entitled "Confessions of a VA Critic," author and PhD Moshe Milevsky tells an interesting story. A few years ago, he and co-author Dr. Steven Posner, who was at the time working as a derivatives analyst for Goldman Sachs, conducted an exhaustive study to try to determine if the fees in a VA were justified by the benefits they provided.

Not surprisingly, back then the conclusion was an emphatic no; the fees in a VA were definitely not worth it, especially when it came to the fees for something called the death benefits (which I'll describe shortly).

As a result of their findings, a long list of top news organizations such as the *Wall Street Journal, Reader's Digest, Money*, and *Newsweek* carried stories about their findings, trashing the VA and driving home the belief that variable annuities were "overpriced, oversold, and unsuitable." Their research was published all over the press and caused all sorts of fear about ever investing in one.

However, that was a few years ago, and new features and cost structures within a VA led Milevsky to take a second look and proclaim in his recent article, "This (the new VA) isn't your grand-mother's variable annuity."

What this one-time critic of VAs basically concluded is that since his study was conducted, fees and benefits within many VAs have really changed. Quite simply, the bad press stung many of the insurance companies offering variable annuities. As a result, money started to flow out of VAs, the amount of new money being invested into them went down, and to attract new business, many of the companies offering VAs started to clean up their acts. Although many (but certainly not all) of the companies cleaned up their acts, much of the press has unfortunately been quite slow to react.

This is why the updated study by Milevsky is important to recognize. Some worthwhile excerpts from his findings follow.

The living benefits of a VA (which I'm about to discuss), according to Milevsky,

> . . . protect the owner in the event that something goes awfully wrong during the early part of their retirement or when they start generating income. And, after the market meltdown earlier this decade, this so-called "sequence of returns" risk might not seem as remote as during the euphoria of the late '90s. Indeed, markets don't have to go down and stay down to ruin your retirement. All you need is a bear market at the wrong time, and the sustainability of your income can be cut in half.

This risk, the risk that drawing income from a portfolio while it is going down in value, especially in the early stages of retirement, is exactly what happened to Dave and Donna, discussed earlier, whose advisor was playing the Most Dangerous Game.

Milevsky continues:

> After spending quite a bit of time poring over some of the more recent designs as well as talking to actuaries, regulators, and advisors, I'm not even sure these instruments deserve the old and maligned name of variable annuities.
>
> I can no longer claim that you are being overcharged for these guarantees or that you can achieve similar goals at a lower cost.
>
> After some careful analysis, the same mathematical models that told us a decade ago that basic death benefit guarantees were overpriced are now telling us that many living benefits are *underpriced*.

The reason I'm spending a few moments here discussing press reports is merely because what you may have heard about the VA *was* most likely absolutely true, and in quite a few cases *is* still true. However, times have greatly changed, but mind-sets have not. And while I am here neither to defend nor to recommend a VA, the updated features some VAs offer I believe are worth an objective look, especially if the information you are receiving is either generalized, not updated, or, at worst, mixing one annuity with another.

So, with the understanding there is bad press and good press, as with anything *anyone* recommends, that leaves only one person who can truly make a decision as to whether you should invest some of your money in a VA: you.

After learning some facts on VAs, by the end of this chapter *you* and only *you* should be able to make a better-educated decision as to whether a VA (or any other investment, for that matter) should ever be considered to play a role within your diversified investment portfolio.

Out of all annuities, I'm going to spend the most amount of time discussing the VA simply because, as the title of this book says, you can never be too rich. If you want to invest for growth, the stock market historically offers the highest rates of return, and the VA provides this opportunity with some interesting safety nets underneath the stock investments.

Let's start with some of the basics:

All money invested in a VA grows tax deferred. When you decide to take money out, you pay ordinary income tax on the withdrawal. For those who don't know what this means, just know that ordinary income tax is the worst of all taxes and is one of the well-deserved reasons that when focusing on taxes alone, some media or advisors find reason to trash the VA. If you are investing in a VA, you are exchanging the more favorable long-term capital gains tax rate (currently 15 percent) with the worst tax rate, that of ordinary income (your tax bracket that can be much higher than 15 percent). That said, the guarantees you cannot find anywhere else except in a VA might outweigh the tax disadvantages. Again, this is something only you can decide once you understand the benefits found in a VA and judge whether they are worth the potentially higher taxes and fees commonly associated with them.

Money invested in a VA goes into what are legally known as "subaccounts." Subaccounts are very close in structure to mutual funds, but for reasons I won't get into at the moment, the regulators want advisors to refer to them as such. Also, know that many VAs also offer stock market indexes as investment choices, not just managed funds.

Money in the subaccounts is kept separate from the insurance company. The money invested in a variable annuity typically resides with the fund or index chosen as an investment. If there's a problem with the insurance company your money is with, your money is legally with the investment company, not the insurance company. This differs from fixed, index, and immediate annuities. With those annuities, your money remains with the insurance company and is not segregated somewhere else, such as with the fund companies found inside the VA.

The rate of return you receive on a VA is determined by how well (or not so well) the subaccounts perform. These are direct stock market investments we're talking about, not linking returns to the market as you find with an index annuity.

If you invest in a VA, or in any annuity for that matter, you should not plan on withdrawing any money until you reach the age of 59½. Why? Because if you do, the money you withdraw will not only be taxed at ordinary income rates, but the IRS will also charge you with a 10 percent early withdrawal penalty as well.

So far, investing in a VA is really all about investing directly in the stock markets and deferring the tax until later on when you decide to make a withdrawal.

That's all the plain-vanilla stuff. But let's get into some of the benefits that could make investing in a VA satisfying to people such as Mark and Rhonda who are fundamentally concerned that the loss of value in their stock accounts would result in a loss of income.

Death Benefits

Many people investing in a VA do it because of the death benefit feature. Think of a death benefit as a life insurance policy wrapped around your stock market investments (for the record, however, the death benefit of a VA is *not* an actual life insurance policy). For an additional fee, the insurance company promises the investor that when you die, your family receives *at least* the amount originally invested, less any withdrawals.

Suppose I invest $100,000 in my VA. But after I invest, awful things happen: The value of my contract goes all the way down, and down, and down, to $70,000.

In this case, the death benefit feature of my VA guarantees that when I die, the insurance company will return the amount I originally invested to my family. So, because I invested $100,000, although the account is now worth only $70,000, the death benefit returns the original investment to my family (less withdrawals).

While death benefits can certainly provide some attractive guarantees, they offer no value to people while they are alive. During the crash of 2002, many people lost their shirts, pants, and wallets and said, "The heck with the death benefits. I'm getting out of this deal."

So they took their money out of the VAs and went elsewhere.

That left a slight problem for the insurance companies that offer VAs. There was so much money leaving the VAs that they had to find a way to attract people back in. That's when they came up with a fascinating concept known as the "living benefit."

Living benefits are one reason people such as Humberto Cruz invested his wife's entire IRA in a VA. Simply put, these living benefits provide a solution for people such as Mark and Rhonda who are looking for maximum growth on their investments but don't want any risk to their income.

Let's take a look at how they work.

Living Benefits

What is a living benefit? A living benefit is the safety net under your stock market investments that protects your *income*. And let me be really clear here—the living benefit protects your *income*, not your cash value (or principal).

To illustrate the benefit, I'll use an example of how this could work. Follow me here—if at first it sounds confusing, I promise I'll clear it all up.

Suppose I invest $100,000 into regular stock market investments. By "regular" I mean money *not* invested in a VA, but rather, an investment into plain-vanilla individual stocks, mutual funds, and/or index funds. Five years later, the value of my account has grown to $200,000 (a very attractive return, but I'm using this for the concept only, and the more extreme round numbers here and coming up will help convey the point).

All of a sudden the market crashes. Ridiculous losses take place, and in a short period of time the account that was once worth $200,000 is now worth $100,000.

To make matters worse, I *just* retired and I now want to use my account to draw income from. Chances are if this really happened (as it did to many people who retired in 2001 or 2002), I'd likely have to keep working to make that money back. And if I didn't go back to work, I'd have to draw my income from the current account value—the $100,000.

This would certainly not be good, and while I'm doing that, I can't help but wish I could turn back the clock and draw my income off the once highest value, the $200,000.

Sorry. We can't go back in time. In this regular stock market account, I'm out of luck. No magic here, I can only draw my income off the $100,000, not the $200,000 that my portfolio was once worth.

That is . . . unless I had the living benefit of the VA.

Up until recently, VAs only had death benefits, but because of this living benefit option, I now find more advisors discussing them with more people, such as a Mark and Rhonda, who want a guarantee that if they lose money in the markets, their *income* will not be adversely affected.

Let's recap this scenario, using Mark and Rhonda as the example.

Mark and Rhonda's $100,000 grows to $200,000 in a VA. Then, just as Mark and Rhonda are ready to retire and draw income from their account, the market completely crashes, leaving the value at $100,000 (again, a somewhat extreme scenario that merely helps to convey the concept).

The living benefit option locks in the highest contract value and uses this high value as the *base* to draw their income from. Some contracts lock in this high value once a year, whereas others do it once every three months; and there's even one on the market now that locks in the high value *once a day*.

In this scenario, although the *cash value* of their account is only $100,000, their *income* is drawn off the account as if it was still worth its highest value of $200,000.

In this bad scenario—where Mark and Rhonda once made a lot of money, then lost it—they would be allowed to turn back the clock and draw their income off the highest amount. Most companies will allow them to draw income off that $200,000 for the rest of *both* of their lives. Furthermore, if the $100,000 cash value ever grows back above the once-highest value of $200,000, this even *higher* value then becomes the base their income is drawn from.

So, follow me here; because this can get a bit confusing, I'm going to go through the example step by step:

- Mark and Rhonda's VA account is originally worth $100,000.
- Years later, thanks to a good market, it's worth $200,000.
- The market tanks; value is back down to $100,000.
- Just their bad luck—now they want to draw income from the account.
- The living benefit allows them to look back to the highest value, the $200,000. This becomes the amount they are now drawing their income from—and if need be, they can continue doing so for the rest of their lives. The amount of income one can draw off this amount will vary from company to company, but the amount generally resides within the 5 to 7 percent range.
- The cash value is $100,000 (if they want to take all their money out of the contract, the cash value is the amount they would withdraw as a lump sum). Suppose while they're drawing income off the $200,000 income base, the $100,000 in cash value grows . . . and grows and grows, all the way to an amount that *exceeds* the $200,000 highest value the account was once worth. Suppose the account grows back to a value of $250,000.
- The new highest value of $250,000 now becomes the *new* base Mark and Rhonda's income is drawn from.

That's a scenario of things starting off well, and then turning real bad. Let's look at another scenario where things are *never* good. It would be every investor's worst fear: Things start out bad, and then get worse:

- Mark and Rhonda invest their $100,000 into the VA with the living benefit.
- The account never goes up. In fact, due to a horrific stock market and a portfolio that was not diversified, the value drops to $50,000.
- Several years go by and the value never changes; it remains steady at $50,000.

- Now, they need to draw income from the account.
- If they were invested in a regular stock market account, they'd be drawing income from the $50,000 value.
- But in this bad-case scenario, many living benefits offer a minimum guaranteed rate of return. To keep this simple, I'm not going to get into detailed math here. I'm just going to say that for every year Mark and Rhonda are in the contract, the living benefit guarantee will add a *minimum* return to the amount originally invested.
- So, although the VA's *cash value* is only $50,000, the amount they can draw *income* from might be (for example only) $125,000 (the original $100,000 invested plus a minimum rate of return applied to that amount for every year they are invested).

As a reminder, they would *not* be able to withdraw the full $125,000 in cash. The $125,000 merely represents the *base* their income is drawn from. Again, if it was a regular stock market account without any living benefit protection, their income would be drawn from the $50,000 cash value, not the $125,000 income base the living benefit of a VA provides.

No doubt, if market losses occur early in retirement, an immediate loss can have drastic effects on a portfolio, making it very difficult to recover (the story of Dave and Donna, whose advisor was playing the Most Dangerous Game).

Scenarios such as what happened to Dave and Donna are exactly what living benefits protect against. Living benefits are a feature that allows an otherwise conservative or fearful market investor such as Mark and Rhonda some peace of mind. It allows a person to invest for growth while not sacrificing income.

Therefore, the living benefit could be especially attractive for those people who are getting closer to retirement (or in the early stages of it) and are looking to generate market returns with protection on their income.

Living benefits for most variable annuities can be summarized this way: *While trying to grow your money in the markets, the first check for income you receive will be the worst one you'll ever get.* If the markets go up, you'll lock in a higher amount of income and retain that increased amount for as long as you need to, presumably even for the rest of your life.

As with any investment, just be sure you take a close look at the fees and other important elements not detailed here. With some VAs that offer living and death benefits, the benefits can get complicated. It's quite important to understand all aspects of the contract before investing, including, but not limited to, the cost of these benefits, surrender fees, and the length of time one needs to keep their money with the company before the contractual term is complete.

Variable Annuities and Aggressive Investing

A by-product of the living benefit is the opportunity for people to get more aggressive with their investments than they normally would without the VA's safety nets underneath them.

Take, for example, Henry, who was one of the first investors I met to invest in a VA due to the living benefit. Henry is a conservative guy, and when he showed me his accounts, I was surprised to see his entire VA invested in the most aggressive funds.

The funds were doing quite well. The returns were way up and still climbing. But why would a conservative investor like Henry invest in aggressive funds? His answer was that he was a few months away from locking in the value of his living benefit, and his attitude was, "If I can catch that high and lock it in, then worst case, if the account dips, I get the benefit of drawing my income off that high for the rest of my life, or until it reaches a new plateau."

The living benefit had turned this once-conservative investor into someone who was swinging for the fences by getting more aggressive with his investments.

Henry wasn't the last to do this. Over the past few years, I've seen quite a few people invest more aggressively then they normally would have simply because of the income protection VAs offer.

So, for those who want to invest a bit more aggressive in the markets and swing for the fences, investing in a VA with a living and/or death benefit might very well be a viable consideration for a portion of your money, given the various safety nets available.

If it sounds interesting, then just be sure to discuss the details with a qualified advisor before making an investment. There are many companies out there offering VAs with living and death benefits, and the guarantees each company provides can be considerably different from one another. I've only skimmed the surface with concepts here, and, as mentioned, be sure to understand all the details before diving in.

Certificates of Deposit: When 6 Percent = 0 Percent

Investing for reliable returns can take many shapes and forms. We've covered bonds, preferred stocks, dividend stocks, and variable annuities. Another investment people can consider for the slice of their portfolio they want to keep safe and earn a reliable return on is, of course, a certificate of deposit (CD).

When striving for reliable rates of return on your investments, CDs are an obvious choice. While many investment portfolios are quite deserving of having one or many CDs within their presence, surprisingly, a CD isn't always a riskless investment.

To illustrate, consider the following question: "How is it possible to earn a 6 percent return on an investment but actually wind up making 0 percent?" When it comes to investing in CDs, it may be a bit easier than you might think.

Sheila is a friend of mine from Southern California. Years ago, Sheila got divorced and ended up with a few hundred thousand dollars. Having little experience in the stock markets, she recruited an advisor, who invested her money in various individual stocks. Within a year or two, although the advisor was doing a pretty good job diversifying the account, the markets got the best of many investors and Sheila's account wound up losing a moderate amount of money. Having a very low tolerance for risk, Sheila panicked and pulled all of her money out of the market, placed it in CDs, and vowed to never invest in anything but CDs ever again.

For safety of principal, there's no doubt that CDs offer peace of mind. But is a CD really safe? When it comes to Sheila's situation, not exactly. In fact, it can easily be argued that she's actually *losing* money in her CDs every year.

By the time Sheila caught up to me, most of her CDs were paying right around 6 percent. For simplicity, for every $100,000 invested, she was earning her $6,000 per year. That sounds like a decent return, but hold on a second. It's not as great as you may think. Sheila saw the guaranteed rate of return, but did not see the whole picture.

First of all, that $6,000 is going to show up on page 1 of her tax return as income that will be reported on Schedule B in the Part I section entitled "Interest." Sheila was in the 28 percent tax bracket. So, in the 28 percent tax bracket, Sheila will pay over a thousand dollars in tax on the $6,000, reducing her real return to just over $4,000. All of a sudden, her 6 percent CD is now really paying her approximately 4 percent. But it's not over yet.

Next up is what many commonly refer to as the "hidden tax"—
the one we all pay, otherwise known as inflation. Depending on the
source you listen to, inflation typically runs at around 3 percent.
Many say it's considerably higher, but the government doesn't want
to agree. Why? Well, many of the government entitlement programs
are pegged to the inflation rate. If inflation is reported too high,
then guess what happens? Uncle Sam has to raise the amount it pays
to all people in various entitlement programs. Can the government
afford to raise the income for these programs? Not quite. Not only is
the federal deficit high enough as it is and only getting worse, but
there are significant problems within the under funded Social Security system itself. Having to pay out more money due to higher
reported inflation would only make things worse.

Let's get back to Sheila's CD. So far, we have learned that, no
thanks to taxes owed on her CD interest, she may have *believed* she
was earning 6 percent, but in reality, because she pays tax on that interest, she's really earning just over 4 percent. Factoring in inflation,
which I will moderately assume runs at 3 percent, Sheila's real rate
of return on that CD is actually not much more than 1 percent.

As if that's not bad enough, the situation for those in retirement
could be even worse. For those in retirement collecting Social Security benefits, the interest generated from CDs could easily cause the
investor to pay more taxes on their Social Security benefits.

When factoring in the additional tax one could be paying on
Social Security as a result of interest being earned on a CD, it's sad,
but true: The actual return on a CD paying 6 percent can easily be
0 percent, meaning a certificate of deposit can sometimes be more
appropriately deemed a "certificate of *depreciation*."

Am I saying that one shouldn't invest in CDs? Not at all. In fact,
I would venture to say *more* people should be investing in them (as I
discussed earlier with investors such as Stock Market Stan, who
I believed had far too much money in the stock markets). I can think
of plenty of reasons why someone should consider having CDs in
their portfolio, including:

- *Diversification.* As much as the argument could hold true that
  6 percent can actually equal 0 percent, there are situations
  that still make investing some money in CDs a perfectly prudent investment. For example, I can think of several clients
  of mine who have quite a bit of money in stocks, real estate,

and so on, and for them, having some money in CDs is most certainly not a bad choice.

- *An elderly person deep into retirement.* Someone late in the retirement years should not be overly concerned with inflation and taxes eroding their returns. For many late in retirement, preservation of capital should usually be the number-one consideration for their money, and CDs are a highly worthy consideration to achieve that.
- *Short-term investing.* The need to keep your money liquid for use in the near future certainly makes investing in a CD completely justifiable.

Sheila, however, didn't fall into any of those categories. She was young; she needed higher returns for income, but solving her desire to get a higher return while keeping her money safe posed its own unique set of challenges. No matter how much I educated her on the value of dividend stocks or how a well diversified investment portfolio of stock indexes and individual bonds via a ladder would ease her concern, she just couldn't stomach any part of investing into *anything* that could cause harm to her money.

Any good advisor should naturally take this acute fear into strong consideration. Why talk about the value of diversification in a stock portfolio when the end result is going to be a person who either would ultimately never do such a thing or, if they did do such a thing, would end up being, quite frankly, a nervous wreck at the very first sign of any bump in the market?

Unfortunately, when it comes to trying to get higher rates of return while keeping an eye on complete safety, there are not many options to consider. The short list is:

- Bond ladders consisting of corporate, municipal, or government bonds, which we've discussed.
- Index annuities.
- Structured products, such as one type of structured product often referred to as a "growth CD."

We have already spent quite a bit of time exploring bonds. Let's now spend a few moments taking a closer look at the index annuity and then something few people are aware of, something that is occasionally referred to as a growth CD.

Index Annuities

As mentioned earlier, an index annuity is a deviation from its close cousin, the fixed annuity. To remind you, a fixed annuity is sometimes referred to as a tax-deferred CD. For the safety-conscious investor who refuses to have any risk to principal *and* is looking to defer taxes, the fixed annuity could be a good choice.

But for those that want a chance at potentially receiving higher returns than the "bird in the hand" interest rate CDs or fixed annuities offer, this is where an index annuity might be worthy of consideration for a small portion of someone's money.

An index annuity is a version of a fixed annuity that links its returns to market indexes such as the Standard & Poor's 500, NAS-DAQ-100, and Dow Jones Industrial Average. If the index your money is linked to goes up, you make money. If the index goes down, you won't lose your principal or any prior-year earnings, and many companies offer a minimum rate of return.

Any prior-year earnings are typically locked in automatically on your contract's anniversary date, which is an attractive feature of most accounts. If you made money as a result of the stock market index going up, once it's locked in on the anniversary date of your account, the earnings can never be lost.

For these guarantees, however, you will give up two key things:

1. *Liquidity.* Typically, during the length of time that you are in the contract, you'll have access to only a small portion of your money each year. Withdraw any more than the penalty-free amount and the fees could get quite steep. When you enter into an index annuity contract, you are locking yourself into a term, which are typically seven years or longer.
2. *Limited growth potential.* You also won't get the full return of the index your returns are linked to. Annuity companies use different methods of calculating your return such as "averaging," "point to point," "monthly caps," and other possibilities. As an investor, you need to well understand how the various crediting methods work before investing your money. These calculations can get confusing and typically lead to one thing: a lower rate of return than the true growth of the index.

So now you may be thinking, "If index annuities limit my access to my money and growth, why would I want to invest in them?"

While those limits may not sound appealing, for a small portion of your money earmarked for growth that you greatly fear losing, I would not discount the peace of mind the few quality index annuities available on the market can offer.

So, is an index annuity a good investment? My simple answer is "it depends." Every investor is different and for some, exploring one of the few index annuities out there that have favorable terms could make an investment into this type of annuity worthy of consideration for a small portion of your money. As with any investment, just make sure you thoroughly understand all the details before investing.

CDs That Pay 10 Percent

Back in the bad market years of 2001–2002, many people pulled their money out of the markets and placed it in cash. Afraid of investing in the markets again, they went searching for new products, one of which was the index annuity, which attracted quite a few risk-adverse investors for reasons previously discussed.

As investors started pulling their money out of cash and investing it with insurance companies offering index annuities, many banks scratched their heads, wondering how they were going to attract this money back into their pockets.

In some cases, the answer led the banks to essentially replicate the concept of an index annuity, but within the framework of a CD.

This brings up an interesting area of the CD market that many investors have never heard about. The area of the market I am referring to is technically entitled "structured products." Many people, however, refer to one area of them as "growth CDs." For purposes of clarity, I'm going to use this latter name instead of the more technical "structured product" counterpart.

A so-called growth CD offers the same safety as a regular bank CD: safety, Federal Deposit Insurance Corporation (FDIC) protection, and a predetermined length of time until maturity.

The big difference is that in a regular bank CD, you know exactly how much interest you're going to earn before investing in it. It's a "bird in the hand" investment. Regardless of whether it's a three-month or five-year CD, you know exactly what you're going to get: maybe it's 5 percent for one year, 7 percent for seven years, and so on.

The interest you receive on a growth CD, however, is not determined by interest rates. Similar to the way index annuities calculate their rate of return, the potential earnings on a growth CD is determined by a stock market index, such as the S&P 500 or various foreign indexes.

If the S&P 500 goes up, then you will presumably earn more interest than the "bird in the hand" bank CD. But if the S&P 500 goes down in value *and* you hold your CD until maturity (typically three to five years on average), you at least get your money back. Some growth CDs not only guarantee you'll get your money back, but they also provide a small amount of interest even if the market goes down.

Keep in mind: If you break the growth CD prior to maturity, you will get fair market value for it, which could be less than the amount you invested. But again, if held to maturity, the assurance you have in these CDs is that in the worst-case scenario, you will at least get your money back.

As for taxes, the interest on a growth CD is still taxable, just like on a bank CD. But let's assume Sheila invests in a growth CD and because of a strong stock market, she hypothetically receives 10 percent per year for the three years she is invested in it. With these types of earnings, no one would be able to rightfully call these CDs "certificates of *depreciation.*"

Don't expect to go into your local bank and ask about growth CDs or structured products. Ask someone at the bank for these types of CDs and they will likely not have any idea what you are talking about. These types of CDs are offered by some of the most reputable banks in the world but are available only through various brokerage accounts. Structured products or growth CDs are a highly specialized area of the market, and many financial advisors and brokers have not heard of these investments. Unfortunately, many people are missing out on what could be a worthy inclusion in their diversified portfolios, especially those who are still young like Sheila and want to keep their money safe but also want the possibility of earning more interest than the conventional bank CDs offer.

At the time of this writing, some growth CDs have yielded impressive returns over these past few years, posting gains of well over 10 percent due to an attractive market. Needless to say, as with any stock market–driven investment, there are no guarantees that these gains will continue for any length of time, if at all. But if the concept sounds interesting to you, be sure to consult your advisor to get some more information to determine whether growth CDs make sense for a portion of your money.

Real Estate

The final area of investment that could deliver some measure of reliable returns is, of course, real estate.

Many investors want to participate in the real estate market—and with good reason. Complementary to the other reliable return investments we've discussed during the course of this chapter, real estate can produce reliable rates of return as well.

Real estate undoubtedly diversifies a portfolio of stocks, bonds, and cash. Although past performance is no guarantee of future results, over many years, the real estate sector has traditionally performed quite well.

How well? After 2001, low mortgage rates fueled a boom in the real estate market. Unless you've been hiding for the past five years or so, you might have heard of many self-made millionaire real estate investors who were popping up all around the country.

With this explosion of growth and speculation, it should come as no surprise that at the time of this writing, the "irrational exuberance" of the residential real estate market has quickly gone belly-up in many areas of the country.

Does that mean one should stay out of this sector?

No way. Remember: Unless we're referring to the "flavors of the day" sector of our diversified portfolio, we are not trying to time the markets with our money, we are *investing* it. With this, diversification combined with the art of rebalancing contains the fundamental assumption that there is never really such thing as a bad market sector. Quite the contrary; diversifying and rebalancing a portfolio recognizes that every "bad child" is destined to awaken into a "good child"; we just aren't sure exactly when that's going to happen.

Even with the downturn of the residential real estate sector, real estate in general will likely always remain a fundamental ingredient of many diversified portfolios. It is for that reason, along with the art of rebalancing, that even at the time of this writing where residential real estate is generally believed to be a cold sector, it should certainly not be ignored.

Furthermore, as a reminder, remember something very important: At the time of this writing, the residential real estate sector is going through a pronounced downturn. But does that assume *all* real estate sectors are bad? Not even close. Recall the Bloomingdale's analogy from an earlier chapter: Real estate is merely the department in the store, while subsections within the real estate department most certainly exist.

With that, even during this bad downturn of the residential housing sub sector within the real estate asset class, there are still many other subsections that are doing quite well, such as commercial real estate properties.

Does that mean you should try to go out to buy a piece of real property? Not exactly, although needless to say, you most certainly could (even with your IRA money, which I'll be discussing later on). But real estate certainly isn't easy to invest in; analyzing the market can be quite tricky. Furthermore, purchasing investment properties yourself usually requires significant capital, time, money, and the possible frustration of having to deal with fixing someone's hair clogged sink.

While you might very well wind up purchasing a property to represent the real estate slice of a diversified portfolio, investing in real estate is an entire subject unto itself. Many investors find it difficult to understand real estate investing, and as such, the difficulty of investing in the real estate market in part led Congress to enact a law in 1960 providing for the creation of real estate investment trusts (REITs).

Real Estate Investment Trusts

REITs are companies dedicated to owning and sometimes operating income-producing real estate such as apartments, shopping centers, offices, and warehouses. Essentially, REITs allow investors to participate in the benefits of owning larger-scale real estate—often high-quality commercial properties—which tend to be less volatile than the residential real estate market, especially during a tricky time period such as the one we're now in at the time of this writing.

There are two basic types of REITs: public and private. The major difference is that public REITs are just that, publicly owned and traded on the major exchanges; one can buy and sell at any time. Not so with private REITs. Let's look at what this means in more detail.

Regulation: Public REITs must comply with the requirements of the Sarbanes-Oxley Act, including quarterly financial reporting. This leads to a certain degree of financial transparency that some investors feel adds security to the investment. Private REITs, by contrast, are required to do little in the way of disclosure, other than file an initial offering registration with the Securities and Exchange Commission.

Here is a summary of REIT characteristics:

- *Volatility.* Because they aren't exchange-traded, private REITs aren't subject to the daily fluctuations of the market as public REITs are. Typically, a private REIT intends on either going public one day or selling off its properties. Either way, at the time the shares go public (get listed and offered on the stock market exchanges for trading) or the properties within the REIT are sold off, at some point in time, the intention of a private REIT is for the investors to have an exit strategy that will allow them to cash out at some point in the future.
- *Liquidity.* Investors can readily buy and sell public REITs over the exchanges, which is not the case with private REITs. Redemptions for a private REIT are generally not permitted until two or three years after the date of the initial investment, if at all, and are usually offered at the par price (the price at which the security was issued). Private REITs may even restrict investor redemptions.
- *Dividends.* Private REITs have historically yielded dividends of 7 percent to 8 percent, compared with only 5 percent to 6 percent for public REITs.
- *Purchases.* Private REITS are purchased via a private offering memorandum through a licensed securities broker. Public REITs can be purchased through your broker or direct through any number of discount brokerages. You can invest directly in REITs or buy shares of a fund that invests in REITs. It is a good idea, however, to engage a financial advisor to help with the purchasing decision. Factors that should be evaluated when investing in REITs include:
  - The geography and type of properties the REIT holds.
  - The economics of those properties.
  - The experience and expertise of the management team.
  - The financial terms of the REIT investment.
  - Your individual financial circumstances and goals.
  - Fees and redemption clauses.

Like most securities, public REITs have historically experienced cyclical ups and downs. Typically, they have performed poorly when interest rates have gone up, but that is most certainly not always the case.

A dip in the market shouldn't necessarily worry potential investors. You can still reap the benefits of REITs while minimizing your risk in a number of ways. First, you can invest in REITs in certain sectors. There is an enormous variety of REITs available of all different flavors—there are REITs for prison properties, government properties, apartments, trailer parks, leisure properties, resorts, or even regional REITs (a good resource on investing in REITs is located at www.nareit.com, the National Association of Real Estate Investment Trusts web site).

It is also important to consider the quality of a REIT's management, tenants, and underlying properties. BioMed Realty Trust, for instance, specializes in leasing laboratory space to tenants such as biotechnology and pharmaceutical companies. If you believe that there will be growth in the health care sector, which many people do, it may make sense to complement that belief with a REIT such as BioMed Realty Trust that could possibly also do well (please don't take this is as recommendation—I use BioMed merely as an example).

As with all asset classes you are considering as part of your diversified portfolio, I typically recommend you use an *index* to represent the asset class or subclass, and not an individual company—no matter how strong it appears.

Is That All?

You may be asking if this completes the discussion on the ingredients to a diversified investment portfolio striving for reliable rates of return.

Not quite. I have one final sector that I have not yet addressed. Although I briefly mentioned it a while back, I didn't go into much detail.

The final slice of a diversified portfolio that I feel is strongly worthy of consideration is something that most people have never seen as an *investment.* Rather, they've seen it only as a *cost.* But by the time I'm done discussing it, perhaps you'll feel it *is* an investment, especially since it offers some interesting benefits that no other investment provides.

Lastly, even if you don't agree with me, then at least by reading the next chapter you just might find a way to get yourself a free million dollars.

Sound good?

Let's continue to explore one final sector that you may want to consider for your diversified investment portfolio.

CHAPTER 4

Adding a Little Life to Your Life

Here's a good travel tip: The next time you want to stretch out on a crowded flight, tell everyone around you that you sell life insurance. As you entertain your fellow passengers with wonderful tales of insurance, they'll quietly plot their escape, donning their parachutes and inching toward the exits. One guy might even wind up easing the pain by tossing himself out of the plane. Did he have life insurance? Maybe you sold him a policy and his family is in luck. Regardless, chances are you'll get an entire row of seats to yourself.

Dramatic? Sure. But the subject of life insurance often raises fears and stereotypes. After all, when thinking of life insurance, the two most common images that come to mind are death and pushy salespeople, both of which many of us would prefer not to deal with.

Now, if this entire chapter seems out of place, it may be because you are thinking, "Just how the *heck* does something that *costs* money make *me* rich?" The first time someone recommended I include life insurance as part of my diversified portfolio, I absolutely asked the same question.

However, after years of evaluating all different kinds of investment strategies, I can honestly say that I see life insurance not as a *cost* but as just another *investment* within my diversified portfolio that sits right alongside stocks, bonds, and other investments previously discussed. When used correctly, as you'll soon find out, an investment into a life insurance policy merely offers me multiple unique options that none of my other investments discussed in the prior chapters could ever provide. I know right now this might sound strange, but after this section is complete, I'm confident you'll wind up feeling the same way.

So, before you give up your seat or toss me out of the plane, stick with me for a moment. You might find yourself pleasantly surprised. And if at the end of my discussion you don't agree, I certainly won't be offended. As with anything I discuss in the book, I am not here to try and *convince* anyone to do anything—it's the same mentality I have when I'm at the office, where I sometimes consider myself the concierge at the Bloomingdale's department store of investments. Give me an idea what you want, and I'll take you around the store to show you what's available in the marketplace. Don't like what you're seeing? No problem. We'll just keep shopping until we find you the best possible match.

Even if you don't wind up considering adding life insurance to your diversified portfolio, do yourself a big favor. Spend a few minutes reading this chapter. While I can't guarantee you'll wind up with life insurance within your diversified portfolio, I can say with great confidence that after I'm done you won't ever look at life insurance the same way again.

So, if you're on an airplane reading this, before we begin, tell those around you that you absolutely love life insurance and plan on talking about it for the next few hours. Chances are, you just might be able to get an entire row for yourself. If you're lucky enough to clear everyone away, stretch out, get comfortable, grab a drink, skip the in-house movie, and let's get started.

Why Would I Buy Life Insurance?

We'll start with the obvious reason why most people would ever consider getting a life insurance policy: I die, it pays; and in almost every case, it pays my heirs a lot more than what I put into it. For this reason, especially during the working years while you are most likely taking care of a family, many people include at least some type of life insurance in their planning. If something happens, the policy pays the spouse, kids, business, or a partner a bunch of money. Simple and basic stuff.

Within this mind-set often lies the unfortunate belief that paying for the cheapest insurance is the best way to go. True, whenever you pay for something, it is often construed as a cost. I couldn't agree more. However, when it comes to getting life insurance, if you view it as a cost, chances are that can mean only one thing: You bought it the wrong way. If you absolutely, positively cannot afford anything else but the cheapest, though, then buying life insurance in the least expensive manner is completely understandable. After all, if someone dies, leaving *more* behind is certainly much better than leaving less.

However, any time you buy something the way the insurance companies *want* you to purchase it, chances are it's not in *your* best interest, but in *their* best interest. And when it comes to paying for life insurance by buying it the cheapest way possible, congratulations—you are buying it exactly how the insurance companies want you to. Here's why.

Term versus Permanent Life Insurance

The least costly life insurance policy is known as term insurance. Simply put, a term insurance policy is the least expensive insurance for the highest possible death benefit. But if I purchase, for example, a 20-year term policy, how long is the policy good for? That may sound like the old riddle, "Guess who's buried in Grant's Tomb?" The answer may seem completely obvious, but when it comes to life insurance, sometimes it's really not.

When asking the question "How long is a 20-year term policy good for?," most people would simply reply, "Twenty years." That's not exactly correct. In nearly all cases, in fact, that would be *incorrect*. Most term policies could be maintained until you turn 100 years old.

Odd? To most people it is. But in reality, the only thing the "term" in a term policy refers to is the number of years the cost of insurance (otherwise known as the premiums) will remain the same. In term life insurance, the premiums are lowest *during* the "term." After the term is complete, the insurance company is free to raise the premiums to a predetermined rate that is buried deep inside the contract that barely anyone ever reads. And when it is allowed to raise these premiums after the term is complete, how much do you think it raises them to? Answer: *More than you'll ever humanly want to pay.*

Once the term is complete, the premiums skyrocket through the roof. Sure, you can pay them, and you are welcome to pay them until you are 100 years old, but who would? The annual premiums after the term is complete are astronomical. The only time I'd ever consider paying the premiums on a term policy after the term runs out is if I am going to die the day after the term is complete.

As an example, suppose my premiums on my term policy are $1,000 a year. At the end of the 20-year term, my premiums may skyrocket to a ridiculous $10,000 for the same policy. Obviously, at that point, the insurance company wants to do only one thing: get rid of me as soon as possible. And to ensure that happens, it is going to raise the premiums to make absolutely sure it gets what it wants—and that's get me the heck out of the policy.

All of this may seem obvious, but why is this important? It's important because as in the preceding chapters where we were once perhaps *gamblers* and now we are hopefully *investors*, this is the first step in making you see life insurance not as a *cost* but as an *investment*.

Recognizing how term insurance works is also important because you need to realize that the insurance companies love people that buy term policies simply because (1) so few of the people paying for term policies ever die within the term, (2) when the term runs out, barely anyone ever continues paying for them, and (3) as a result, the insurance companies make fortunes from collecting the premiums on term policies they never have to pay death benefits on.

Bottom line: The insurance companies want you to buy a term policy. It's a great deal for them, but if you see life insurance as an investment, you'll realize a term policy is rarely the most efficient way to go. In fact, as far as I'm concerned, when compared to other types of life insurance policies, it's often a waste of money—not only because you will typically pay premiums and rarely have a death benefit paid, but because of one very important point: When the term ends, if for any reason you want to take out a *new* policy, you are going to pay a much higher rate, given that you will be older and perhaps in worse health.

As far as I'm concerned, the only reason to ever consider term insurance is if you cannot afford anything else. But can you really not afford anything else? The only way you likely cannot afford anything else is if you view life insurance as a cost, not as an investment.

I don't *pay for* term, because I know I'll very likely outlive the term. I know paying for term is the way the life insurance companies want me to purchase it. And, for a variety of reasons I'll soon be discussing, I also know I'll want to keep the policy for most likely a very long time, presumably for the rest of my life. Therefore, I *invest* in a different type of life insurance known as "permanent life" (universal or whole life insurance).

The major differences between term and permanent life are that (1) in many cases, permanent life's premiums are guaranteed to remain the same *for the rest of my life* (not just a term), and (2) I can accumulate *cash value* in the permanent life policy for reasons I'll soon suggest.

True, the annual premiums for permanent life are going to be higher than if I had paid for term. But again, I am an investor. And I know that investing in permanent life is going to provide me with a wide variety of options that I simply cannot get anywhere else.

Term Conversions

Some term life policies can be converted to permanent life. The term portion of the life policy can keep costs down for a number of years. Then, as the term ends, should one want to keep the policy beyond the term, they have the right to *convert* the term policy into permanent life (at a higher premium). In some cases, term policies that contain conversion privileges are a worthy consideration when designing a life insurance strategy that best meets one's unique situation. Given there are so many different ways to design life insurance policies, for the purposes of this book, I'm going to stick with just the basics, but it is important that when and if you consider investing in life insurance, you look into term life with conversion privileges.

Some benefits permanent life offers you may be aware of, while others are going to be surprising. With that, here are a few reasons why investing in permanent life could be a great addition to a diversified investment portfolio:

- The most obvious: If I die, a permanent life policy will give my heirs more money than I invested into the policy (in most cases, *much more money*).
- If I don't want it later in life, I can potentially profit from selling it.
- It offers the ability to create a Private Pension for myself that provides a highly attractive, tax-friendly income stream that I cannot outlive.

- By investing in permanent life insurance, I can also give myself the opportunity to receive tax-free income at retirement.
- If I need long-term care assistance, some permanent life policies give me the option of using my policy to pay for such a need.
- With a little permanent life in my investment portfolio, if I choose to, I can later spend all of my money and "still leave it all behind."
- With permanent life, I can have the insurance company pay for taxes upon my demise.
- And finally, adding permanent life into my investment portfolio can also give me the opportunity to get my family or me a "free million dollars."

Let's take a closer look at these points.

Adding Instant Wealth to Your Estate

This is the most obvious benefit. If you have life insurance and you die, the policy's death benefit is paid to your heirs, and this can be helpful for many reasons. This is why 99 percent of people pay for life insurance. You certainly didn't need to buy this book to learn this, so let's quickly move to more interesting concepts.

Profiting from Selling Your Life Insurance Policy

I currently pay several thousand dollars a year for a multimillion-dollar death benefit. If something happens to me, my family gets a few million. That's a good thing in what I would personally consider a bad situation.

However, most people believe they won't die and "the few thousand dollars a year it costs me to pay for life insurance" will have been a total waste of money.

Is it? Not to me it isn't. As mentioned, I view life insurance in my diversified investment portfolio as just another "child" of mine that I don't ever plan on getting rid of.

So, with my permanent life policy in hand, suppose something decent happens to me—namely, I live for a long time. I don't die, and later in life I no longer have any need for the policy. I can assure you that many people wind up feeling the same way about their life insurance policies.

If I did what many others do with their policies, I would let it lapse, which simply means I would stop paying the premiums and the insurance coverage would fade away.

A lapsed permanent life policy is often a complete and total waste of money. You paid the premiums for all of those years just to throw it all away? It's important you see a permanent life policy as an investment, not a cost. And when it comes to an investment, there should always be a payoff or an exit strategy, correct? Absolutely. Otherwise, it's not an investment; it's a cost, or even worse, a total loss. With permanent life, however, if there comes a time later in life when I no longer need the policy, this is when I plan on beating the insurance company at its own game.

Instead of letting the policy lapse, I *sell* the policy to someone else. Yes, sell it, which is a completely legal strategy often referred to as "life settlements" that many people aren't aware of. It's also something the insurance companies would rather you not know about.

As an example, suppose I invest a few thousand dollars a year into a permanent life policy that has a death benefit of a few million dollars. Over a long period of time, suppose I don't die and the grand total of what I invested into the policy is, as an example, $100,000. *Selling* the policy into what's commonly referred to as life insurance's "secondary market" when in my 70s will potentially put *several* hundred thousand dollars in my pocket.

One hundred thousand dollars invested into a life policy that has a strong possibility of paying me several hundred thousand dollars— and I didn't need to die to get that money? This is one of many reasons why I view including life insurance in my diversified portfolio an investment and not a cost.

Some people will make an understandable comparison: They'll figure out how much money I would have hypothetically made if I had invested that same few thousand dollars a year into a stock market portfolio. Regardless of what the results are, there are some very obvious benefits to a life policy that traditional stock market investments don't offer, many of which I haven't even discussed yet. Because of life insurance's unique benefits you cannot get from other investments such as stocks, I don't agree with the comparisons. I just don't see it as comparing apples to apples.

If I had merely paid for term life because it's the least expensive, I would most likely not have the opportunity to sell and profit from keeping the policy. Therefore, term would not be an investment; it would be a cost, and that is something that could be a good reason to throw myself out of the plane.

With permanent life I most certainly have an investment, mainly because there is an *exit strategy* to permanent life policies. The exit will most often be selling it to one of the many financial institutions purchasing these policies in the secondary life insurance markets. In my hypothetical example, a financial institution potentially pays me a few hundred thousand dollars because it knows I invested in a permanent life policy, the type of policy where my annual premiums generally remain the same for the rest of my life. Once it assumes responsibility for the payments on my policy, the institution that purchased my policy has a much better chance of *predicting* the risk because the premiums for a permanent life policy generally do not change for the rest of my life. With term life, it can't measure the risk: What happens if the term ends, I didn't die, and the premiums skyrocket through the roof? Few financial institutions would ever take that risk, and as a result, not many companies in the secondary market would ever buy my policy if it's term.

> If you are currently in retirement and have a permanent life insurance policy that you no longer have any need for, *don't* let the policy lapse. If you are over the age of 70, a little research into the life settlement market will likely offer you the opportunity to sell your policy for a potential profit as well.

The Secondary Life Insurance Market

Let's take a step back for a moment. If you've never heard of this secondary market for life insurance, just know that it is a very, very large industry. There's a massive secondary market out there that wants to buy permanent life policies from those who are typically over the age of 70.

Who are these buyers in the secondary market? They aren't Don Corleone or the Sopranos. They're places such as Lehman Brothers, UBS, Berkshire Hathaway, hedge funds, and private funds that want to pay for the right to own and become the beneficiary of your policy. Once they own it, they assume full responsibility to pay the annual premiums and ultimately receive the death benefits once you're gone.

The reason these companies want your policies is simple: As morbid as it may sound, they will continue paying as little as possible to maintain the policy in hopes that you die as soon as possible. Needless to say, when you die, they collect the death benefit. After paying you for the right to take over the policy, they own it, they pay for it, and they get the death benefit. Some policies they purchase will pay death benefits within a few years, while others will pay many years later, but when the policies are all pooled together, the law of averages says the companies buying these policies will make tremendous profits, just like most insurance companies have for hundreds of years.

I go into more detail about the secondary market later in this chapter, but for now, let's take a step back and summarize this discussion on selling your policy. Then we'll move on.

The insurance companies want me to buy a term policy because most of them never pay out. Once the term is up, the premiums skyrocket. When this happens, in almost every case, the policy will terminate or lapse. I won't continue it, and with rare exceptions, no one in the secondary market will buy it from me because of the very high premiums they'd have to pay to continue the policy.

Knowing there are many benefits to including a life policy in my diversified portfolio, I'm willing to invest in a policy called permanent life. Investing in permanent life will give me plenty of options, one of which was discussed here: to sell it for a potential profit when later on I no longer have a need for it.

Tax-Free Retirement Income

Another potential benefit of adding some life insurance to my diversified investment portfolio is that I can also give myself the opportunity to generate tax-free income in retirement.

To begin with, first understand there are many ways to design a permanent policy, and I won't take you through all of them. For the sole purpose of this particular benefit, I'll briefly discuss two ways to do it:

1. *No cash savings, highest possible death benefit*: as an example, $2,000 investment per year, no cash accumulation and a $2 million death benefit.
2. *Accumulate cash savings, lower death benefit*: as an example, $2,000 investment per year, accumulate cash and a $1.5 million death benefit.

Why would one ever want to consider #2? Doesn't everyone want their death benefit to be as high as possible for the lowest premiums? In some cases the answer would be most certainly "yes," but in other cases the answer would be "no." Here's why:

The reason it might make sense to design a permanent life policy to accumulate cash savings is because the cash inside a life insurance policy provides two distinct benefits: (1) tax-deferred earnings on my investment and (2) when properly done, withdrawing the accumulated cash can be done tax free.

The only other vehicle that allows me to do something like this is a Roth IRA. As discussed later in this book, a Roth IRA provides similar features: tax-deferred growth and tax-free withdrawals. However, there are plenty of restrictions to a Roth, including, but not limited to a maximum limit to the annual contributions one can make and the possibility that one cannot make *any* contribution at all given various restrictions I detail later on.

Therefore, investing in a permanent life policy with cash value accumulation could be a strong consideration for the following reasons:

- It can be used by those who cannot contribute to a Roth IRA or want to contribute more than current Roth contributions allow.
- Tax-deferred investing.
- Tax-free income during retirement.
- Access to your investment: The cash value within a permanent life policy can be withdrawn at any time without penalty (taxes may apply, though).
- A tax-free death benefit that will most often be worth far more than the cash value.

As for term insurance? Term has no cash value, which is another reason it's not the type of insurance I would typically suggest.

As mentioned before, because I have *invested* in permanent life, if I discover in the future that I no longer want the policy for tax-free retirement income, what do I do with it? In this case, I would withdraw the cash I accumulated, and then sell the policy for a profit.

Long-Term Care Benefits

Many, but certainly not all, permanent life policies offer the insured the opportunity to draw money from the death benefit for various long-term care needs should they arise. One particular policy allows the insured to use over 50 percent of the death benefits for long-term care needs. In most cases, certain restrictions apply; just be sure you are well aware of them before this benefit becomes an ancillary reason to invest in a permanent life policy.

In the scope of benefits being discussed, this is a minor point, but for some, it could wind up becoming one of the most compelling benefits of investing in a permanent life policy in the first place.

Spend All Your Money and Still Leave It All Behind

If you are still in the accumulation, working years of your life, I'll ask you to fast-forward to retirement for a moment. While this most certainly does not apply to everyone in retirement, we come across many retired people who have a strong, noble desire to save as much of their money as possible to pass on to their families. Although this is immensely heroic, it often pains us to see retirees who have spent a lifetime to save money, only to sacrifice certain things for themselves for the betterment of their children.

As an example, a few years back I met a real nice woman named Kate who had done a great job saving up a sizable nest egg. She had accumulated well over a million dollars, very respectable for a woman who was widowed at a young age and heroically managed to work three jobs to put her daughter through an Ivy League school.

At the time I met Kate, her daughter was unfortunately having a few problems including a nasty divorce, a deadbeat husband, and a floundering career. As a result, Kate was being as frugal as possible with her money. Although her daughter felt strongly she wanted her mom to spend more money, Kate felt differently; behind closed doors, she was really worried about her daughter, and with the exception of an occasional no-frills trip every now and then, she felt tremendously guilty spending money on herself.

I first met Kate when she came to me looking for a few stock market tips. Her plan was to take a small portion of her nest egg and invest it in the markets. Her hope was that over time, the money would grow as much as possible so she could leave "a little more" to her daughter.

After I had walked Kate around the Bloomingdale's department store of investments, she was having a hard time deciding where to invest. We looked at investing in stocks, bonds, and a variety of other investments, some of which looked good, but she just couldn't make up her mind.

No problem. We just kept walking around Bloomingdale's, where I introduced her to a handful of other choices. At the far end of the store was the permanent life insurance department. As we passed it, I recommended we at least take a look, but at first glance Kate thought I was crazy. "Why would someone my age ever get life insurance?" I shared a few concepts as to why it might make sense, but she wasn't convinced.

Again, no problem. So we once again took the escalator back down to the more popular stock market department. Here, I introduced her to the laws of diversification, rebalancing, and indexing that could serve her daughter quite well. Feeling more comfortable with this strategy than anything else in Bloomingdale's, she finally decided to jump in.

Around six months later, however, the markets got a bit wobbly, and although the portfolio was well diversified, Kate's venture into the stock market was making her a bit uneasy, so she asked me to meet her back over at the Bloomingdale's department store of investment choices.

On the higher floors, she wanted to take another look at the permanent life insurance department. After pondering all options, she decided it made the most sense for the following reasons:

- High tax-free death benefit for her daughter—an amount that would have taken many, many years to accumulate if she had remained invested in the stock markets. With the permanent life policy, she completely eliminated both the time and risk it *could have* taken her stock investments to equal the life insurance's immediate death benefit amount.
- High liquidity: Although she had plenty of money *outside* the cash value of the permanent life policy, she felt comfort knowing she could withdraw the cash value with no penalty at any time if she needed it.
- Tax-deferred earnings on her money.
- Long-term care provisions nested within the policy: If she ever needed to, subject to certain limitations, she could withdraw money from the death benefit to help subsidize long-term care needs.
- And finally, if for any reason her daughter didn't need the policy's death benefit, because the insurance was permanent life, Kate would have the ability to *sell* the policy to someone else.

While these were all valid reasons for Kate to invest in the permanent life policy, as far as I was concerned, none of them was the *best* reason.

Because Kate's daughter was now guaranteed to receive a high death benefit, about a year after the policy was issued a magical thing started to happen. Over time, Kate started spending more money. She did a little shopping here and there, had a nice meal out once in a while, and, instead of those no-frills trips, Kate started taking advantage of fancier fare. Why? Because even if she wound up spending "*all* her money," the permanent life policy would still pass the current value of her estate to her daughter through the death benefit.

There is one final benefit worth mentioning: Before investing in the life policy, much of Kate's money was invested in taxable CDs. Investing some of her CD money into the permanent life policy kept her cash value safe, earned her a higher rate of return than her CDs were providing, high liquidity, tax-deferred accumulation, and the ability to withdraw money tax free in case she needed it. Not only did this tax deferral reduce the income tax she was paying on her CDs, but it also reduced the tax on her Social Security benefits as well.

Have Someone Else Pay the Tax

Jack was a successful guy. As a career meter-reader for the electric company, his travels through small towns over many years inspired him to invest in real estate. When I first met Jack, the value of his apartment buildings was somewhere around $9 million, and he also had around $1 million in various cash accounts. As successful as Jack was, he had what he called "his one bad trait"—he called himself "the world's most stubborn guy." A few people, including his CPA, his attorney, and myself tried talking to him about various taxation and estate issues, but time and time again he put things off.

Then, disaster struck. Seemingly out of nowhere, cancer got the best of Jack, and a few short years later he was unfortunately gone. When the kids inherited the $10 million estate, was it really worth $10 million? Not quite. Because very little planning had been done, the estate wasn't worth $10 million; it was really worth just over $5 million due to a nasty thing called the estate tax. See, if dying isn't bad enough, at death, Uncle Sam wants one last chance at collecting taxes from your assets. In Jack's particular situation, his kids had to find a way to pay just under $5 million in estate taxes.

Where did they get that money? They had no other choice but to sell some of the real estate properties Jack had worked so hard to accumulate and that they so desperately wanted to keep. The simple solution his CPA and attorney had been trying to convince him of was to use a fraction of the real estate's equity to invest in a permanent life policy. Doing so would have provided the kids with a death benefit that would have paid the estate taxes due upon his death.

But due to a problem he had many years earlier, Jack disliked insurance companies. He saw life insurance as nothing but a cost, not as an investment that he could do so many things with, even selling it at a profit if he eventually wanted to.

Having to sell off properties created major frustration for Jack's kids. Aside from their desire to keep the properties, the sheer amount of time they had to dedicate to traveling, meeting with advisors, real estate agents, and attorneys caused a great deal of stress.

Think estate taxes can't happen to you? Due to ever-increasing life expectancies and the magic of compounding interest, it doesn't take much for your family to potentially get hit with estate tax upon your demise. Investing in a life insurance policy is by no means the only solution to reduce or eliminate estate tax, nor is it always the best choice. But it is certainly one possible option that often deserves very strong consideration, especially for larger estates.

Taxes on Inherited Individual Retirement Accounts

The estate tax isn't the only thing that can become a potential problem. What about IRAs and annuities? Due to possible double taxation on accounts such as IRAs and annuities, these can be one of the worst investments to pass on to beneficiaries.

Let's take the example of an IRA. Suppose I am a recently retired baby boomer. I'm in my early 60s and my company 401(k) is worth around $200,000. I transfer the 401(k) into a self-directed IRA and start investing in my diversified portfolio of stock market indexes, with a small portion reserved for some flavors of the day. Beautiful. Everything is going really well.

Suppose I live another 20 years. To keep things simple and rounded off, let's assume that at my death, my IRA is worth somewhere around $800,000.

In this example, I pass the IRA to my wife. At her hypothetical age of 80, suppose she combines my IRA with hers (which all spouses can do). Now, the total of *both* IRAs is $1 million. She lives another 10 years, and by the time she's gone, the IRA is now worth approximately $2 million.

She passes away and our children inherit it. True, the children can "stretch" the IRA, which simply means they can keep it as their own and take out nothing but their required minimum distributions based on their age (something I'll discuss in more detail later on). But how many children really stretch the IRA, taking out tiny portions instead of cashing out the entire thing?

In my experience, very few. While there are some children who do stretch IRAs, many children simply cash them out and therefore have to pay the tax. In this all-too-frequent case, here's what could happen:

- The $2 million IRA is inherited by the kids.
- They don't stretch it; they cash it out.
- As a result of cashing out, they owe income tax at *their* tax rate. Assume state and federal taxes, rounded off for sheer simplicity to 35 percent.
- That means $700,000 in taxes is paid to the IRS.
- . . . Leaving $1.3 million for the kids.

Consider: $700,000 to the IRS, $1.3 million to the kids. Not good. If that isn't bad enough, it can get worse. In addition to the income taxes, there could also be estate taxes due as well. In such a case, the $1.3 million left over after the income tax is paid can easily lose another 30 to 50 percent to estate taxes, leaving as little as $700,000 to the kids.

The estate tax and income tax situations can certainly change over the next few decades. No doubt about that, and they most likely will. But will there be no taxes owed? That's highly improbable. Could it be a higher or a lower tax? It's possible. Quite simply, no one knows. But especially with the federal deficit soaring beyond comprehension, I think it's a pretty safe bet that there will always be *some* tax owed on the transfer of tax-deferred assets such as an IRA or annuity.

As mentioned, using the death benefit from a permanent life insurance policy is *one* way for an estate to pay the estate or income tax owed. I am not saying someone should go out and purchase a very large life insurance policy to cover *all* possible taxes. There are other options to consider.

What I am saying is that prudent planning strongly suggests taxation issues such as this should absolutely be addressed in every financial plan. For a number of reasons we're discussing, adding a little life insurance to your diversified investment portfolio to help pay some taxes could very well be just another reason to consider investing in a permanent life policy.

I should also mention that when it comes to IRAs, many retirees ask me what they should do with their required minimum distributions (the amount the IRS requires someone to withdraw on an annual basis from their IRA after they turn age 70½). Many people I meet in retirement don't need this money and are forced to take it every year. Instead of investing it into the markets or in something such as a taxable CD, it might make sense to consider investing the required minimum distribution in a permanent life policy that will help pay at least some of the taxes that will likely be owed upon inheritance.

And, as I've mentioned more than a few times, if you invest in a permanent life policy and later on decide you no longer want it to help heirs pay taxes upon your death, what can you do with the policy? You guessed it—you can likely *sell it for a profit*.

Doubling Your Income at Retirement: The Private Pension

If you are reading this and are not yet in retirement, or you are far away from it, just know this: If there is *one* strategy in this book that will benefit from planning *as early as possible*, for reasons I'll soon discuss, this one is it.

At the moment, some people I meet in retirement have the luxury of a company or government pension. Unfortunately, these plans are very quickly becoming a thing of the past. According to the *Wall Street Journal* (March 18, 2007, "Getting Going" column by Jonathan Clements, "Principles Remain, Methods Must Change"), "Among workers with retirement benefits, 83% had traditional company pensions in 1980, according to Boston College's Center for Retirement Research. By 2004, that figure had shrunk to 39%, as companies shifted to 401(k) plans instead." Now, in 2007, it's estimated that percentage has shrunk down to less than 25 percent.

So much for pensions. By the time many baby boomers retire, a good, solid, and reliable pension could be an ancient artifact of the past.

But are pensions really a thing of the past? Not with what we call "the Private Pension" they aren't.

If you are already in retirement, there's a possibility you can still create a Private Pension for yourself. Doing so could be one of the most simplest and reliable income concepts you'll ever come across; and for those of you that are still in the accumulation stage, understanding how this strategy works could be a significant benefit for you further down the road.

Regardless of where you are—whether you are in the accumulation stage of life or in retirement—imagine this:

At retirement, you can generate an attractive fixed income for the rest of your life. No matter how long you live, the income is guaranteed never to run out, eliminating the common concern, "Will I ever outlive my money?"

In most cases, the Private Pension typically returns *at least* 7 percent on the amount invested. When planned early on, one can create returns as high as 10 to 15 percent for the rest of your life.

Once the return is locked into place, the income the Private Pension produces is not subject to market or interest rate risk. The returns are truly locked in from the start and will never change.

The income continues for the rest of your life, and when you die, the amount used to fund the Private Pension is returned to your heirs *tax-free.*

Sound interesting? To many people, it truly is.

Let's begin with an overview of how this works for someone already in retirement. After I finish discussing the strategy for a retiree, I'll then discuss why you might want to plan for this while in the accumulation stage.

The Private Pension and the Genius Behind a Peanut Butter and Jelly Sandwich

You may find this a bit "nutty," but to begin the discussion of the Private Pension, I can't help but compare it to what I truly believe is one of mankind's greatest creations; yes, the one, the only . . . peanut butter and jelly sandwich.

Who was the person—as bold as Einstein, as clever as Da Vinci—to invent the legendary PB&J? What forward-thinking genius brought us this delicious treat, this ingenious sandwich that also serves as a great example of why "the whole is often far greater than the sum of its parts"? A history lesson about the visionary who invented the PB&J is unfortunately far beyond the premise of this book, so for now let's focus on the sandwich itself and what it means in terms of generating highly attractive reliable returns when in retirement.

Alone, peanut butter and jelly are merely two separate jars of everyday, somewhat ordinary food products. But together in a sandwich, they are eternal soul mates, a true match made in heaven.

Similarly, for those of you currently in retirement, there are two investment products you most likely have not ever considered for yourself. But just like PB&J, together these investments could create the greatest income sandwich an income-hungry belly has ever had.

Before I tell you more about the Private Pension, let's briefly recap some of the places where someone in retirement might consider getting reliable income while keeping their money generally safe.

- *Certificates of deposit.* CDs certainly are safe. But between a CD's typical low interest rates and taxes on the earnings, you'll protect your principal, but you might starve while doing so. If you invest $100,000 in a five-year CD, at the time of this writing, you'll earn around 5 percent, or $5,000 a year. But if you're in the 28 percent tax bracket, after taxes you'll net only around $3,600. Furthermore, the increased taxable income could push someone in retirement into a higher tax bracket and possibly affect his or her Social Security taxation as well.
- *Bonds.* Sure, you'll likely get your money back at the maturity date, but to get any reasonable rate of return, you might have to hold some bonds longer than you'd want. A bond ladder might be an excellent consideration, but sometimes, especially at the time of this writing, the yield on many good credit quality bonds remains quite low.
- *The stock market.* While dividends, preferred stocks, real estate investment trusts (REITs), and other investments can indeed offer attractive reliable returns, these are not considered to be completely safe investments. Furthermore, many people in retirement are looking for the simplest, safest, and the most effortless way to generate reliable returns, especially when it comes to generating retirement income.

Therefore, to get reliable returns, you sometimes need to be creative. Think outside the box. Be imaginative. And that's where the Private Pension comes into play.

The peanut butter side of the Private Pension is something called an *immediate annuity*. To remind you, an immediate annuity is essentially an investment contract with an insurance company that provides you with a guaranteed pension for the rest of your life.

Consider, for example, my friend Bill, who is 77 years young. The laws of probability say he can easily live another 10+ years, and when I first met him, Bill's belly was hungry, really hungry, for reliable, attractive and effortless income. After we explored various options inside the Bloomingdale's department store of investments, Bill fell in love with the Private Pension and decided it was what he wanted, so he invested his $100,000 in an immediate annuity.

In exchange for this one-time deposit, Bill gets a lifetime income stream of $12,000 per year. Throughout the remainder of Bill's life, most of the income is tax free thanks to the Internal Revenue Service (IRS) gift to investors when investing in an immediate annuity known as the "annuity exclusion ratio rule." The problem is that if Bill dies tomorrow, the income stops and his original $100,000 investment is gone, which could provide a nice return for the insurance company . . . but such an event would certainly not be so good for Bill's wife, Francine.

To solve the problem of Francine tossing me out a window when the income stops, let's switch to the other side of Bill's Private Pension. For the jelly, every year Bill removes $5,000 from the $12,000 annual income stream he receives from the immediate annuity and invests it in a life insurance policy *with a death benefit equal to the amount he used to fund the immediate annuity*. With the life insurance policy in place, Francine is assured that she'll get the $100,000 back when Bill dies and the income stops.

The difference, or in technical terms, the arbitrage, between the income the immediate annuity pays ($12,000) and the cost of the life insurance policy ($5,000) equals the amount of money Bill gets to spend for his income ($7,000).

Where else could Bill get a 7 percent return for income that's mostly tax free, never to change regardless of market conditions, with a guarantee that the original investment returns to his heirs tax-free upon his death?

We've worked with many Bills, especially during times of ultra-low interest rate environments. Some have invested thousands to create their Private Pensions, while others have done it with millions. Needless to say, you must have ample savings outside the Private Pension for various needs, especially for protection against inflation and health care considerations.

Keep in mind that age, health, and other factors will ultimately determine your bottom line and whether or not this strategy makes any sense for you. In general, the older you are or the earlier you plan it, the tastier this sandwich gets. As long as you can qualify for at least some level of permanent life insurance (some people simply cannot), the numbers could work out quite well for you and your heirs.

Bonds? CDs? Stock market?

Creamy? Crunchy? Super-chunky or reduced fat?

Everyone has their own taste, but one thing is for sure: In the complex world of investments and considering the fear many have about outliving their money, this Private Pension sandwich could be one well worth sinking your teeth into.

The Private Pension in Action

Before taking a closer look at the many ways one can design a Private Pension, let's recap Bill's plan. Remember, the math that follows is not accurate for everyone and should therefore be considered hypothetical. Exact numbers for any one person will depend on a variety of factors including, but not limited to, age, health, and the current interest rate environment. That said, before any money is ever invested into a Private Pension, all returns and insurance costs must always be well documented, guaranteed in print by the insurance companies, and, of course, well understood by the investor considering a Private Pension.

In Bill's case, the structure of his Private Pension was:

First, he invested $100,000 into an immediate annuity. This provides lifetime income of $12,000 per year, mostly tax-free. The income is locked in, never to change, and will continue for the rest of life.

For many people, the understandable concern of an immediate annuity is that there is no access to the invested amount; there is only access to the income it provides. Furthermore, when the person receiving the income dies, the income ends with them and there is nothing left for heirs.

To counter that risk: First of all, one would never invest *all* their money into a Private Pension. There must be ample savings outside the plan for a wide variety of reasons (inflation and unforeseen emergencies are at the top of the list).

Next: in his case, Bill removes $5,000 a year from the $12,000 yearly income and invests it into a life insurance policy worth the same amount he used to fund his Private Pension ($100,000).

The difference between the income the immediate annuity produces and the amount that needs to be invested into the life insurance policy represents the dollars that's left for Bill to spend. This is otherwise known as an arbitrage.

In his case, this leaves Bill with a locked-in 7 percent rate of return for income that will last the rest of his life. This amount is mostly tax-free (a tax-equivalent return of most likely over 9 percent, depending on one's tax bracket); it will never change regardless of what happens to the markets or interest rates.

When he dies, the income stops *and* the $100,000 he used to fund his Private Pension is returned to his heirs through the life insurance.

Customizing the Private Pension

Let's look at a few examples on how the Private Pension can be customized to meet different desires. We'll then take a look as to why planning for this early on while in the accumulation stage can make the Private Pension much more compelling.

Scenario #1: More Income, Leave Less Money to Heirs.   To increase Bill's income, he can consider leaving less money to heirs. Instead of leaving Bill's family $100,000 tax free as in the preceding example, to increase his income, he can leave them *less* death benefit:

> Bill invests $100,000 in an immediate annuity that produces a 12 percent return, providing him with a guaranteed lifetime income of $12,000 a year.
>
> He then uses some of this income to purchase a life insurance policy not worth $100,000 as earlier, but less—for example, $75,000—upon his death. Because he is leaving less death benefit, the amount invested into the insurance will also be less. As an example, leaving $75,000 would require not $5,000, but $3,500 per year.
>
> With less money invested in his insurance, Bill then is left with a higher amount of spendable income. In this case, the guaranteed income for the rest of his life would not be 7 percent as earlier, but 8.5 percent, or $8,500 a year, mostly tax free.

By lowering the amount he leaves to his family, he increases his income.

Scenario #2: Less Income, Leave More Money to Heirs. What if Bill doesn't need as much income and wants to leave *more* money to heirs? In this case, he can *raise* the amount of life insurance he leaves and thereby *lower* his income.

Instead of leaving heirs $100,000 as in the original example, Bill wants to leave them more.

Bill invests $100,000 in an immediate annuity that produces a 12 percent return, providing him with a guaranteed lifetime income of $12,000 a year, mostly tax-free.

He then uses some of this income to invest in a life insurance policy worth more than $100,000. To leave heirs $125,000, he would have to spend $7,500 per year.

Bill is then left with a guaranteed income of $4,500 a year (4.5 percent return) that is mostly tax-free. This is less income than the other examples because Bill chooses to leave more money to heirs.

As you can see, there is no science to the Private Pension. The numbers are completely flexible according to one's desires. We have designed Private Pensions for people who received income (after the cost of the life insurance) of anywhere between 5 and 15 percent. It all starts with an understanding of a person's exact needs and investments and whether or not they can qualify for a permanent life insurance policy at all, which brings up another important point.

Scenario #3: Bad Health. We often hear people in retirement say, "I'm not in good health. The cost of insurance would be *way* too high to make the Private Pension work."

As long as someone can qualify for *some* life insurance, the Private Pension can still work out just fine. True, bad health will cause the required investment into the insurance to be higher, but the income being produced from the immediate annuity will be higher as well. Remember:

- The *immediate annuity company* wants Bill to die right away (he gives the insurance company $100,000 and, as morbid as it sounds, the company hopes he dies immediately).

- The *life insurance company* wants Bill to live a very long time (he keeps investing money into the insurance policy every year, and the more years he invests, the more attractive it is for the life insurance company).

So if Bill placed $100,000 into an immediate annuity, the annuity company would certainly appreciate it if they paid him income for a few short years and then died. Why? Because remember: Once he dies, the income stops and the annuity company keeps the amount originally invested.

But if Bill is in bad health, to entice him to invest, what will the insurance company do? The annuity company will *increase* the amount of income he receives. In this case, let's look at another example of how this could work:

Let's suppose Bill's health isn't good, but he still wants to create a Private Pension for himself. In case of bad health, here's what the Private Pension may look like:

Bill invests $100,000 in an immediate annuity. Because he's in poor health, the annuity provides him not with a 12 percent rate of return (as in the healthy scenarios above), but, as a hypothetical example, a 15 percent rate of return, which gives him a guaranteed lifetime income of $16,000 a year. Remember: He's getting a much higher income because he's sick and the annuity company would like to think they will be paying Bill for a short period of time.

Because he's ill, the investment into his insurance will also be higher. From the higher amount of income coming from the immediate annuity, he removes the amount necessary to replace the $100,000 upon his death. In this case, the investment into the life insurance policy will be higher than $5,000 (in the scenarios when he was healthy). In this example, maybe he'll have to remove an amount as high as $9,000.

In this hypothetical example, Bill is still left with a guaranteed income of $7,000 (7 percent) a year, mostly tax free, which in this example is the same amount of income received when he was healthy. So, even if someone is not in good health, as long as they can qualify for some life insurance, the Private Pension can still possibly work in their favor.

To summarize, the Private Pension creates what's called an "arbitrage" (a spread) between the investment into the life insurance and the income the immediate annuity produces. The difference or spread between the investment into the life insurance and the income the immediate annuity generates is the Private Pension, the amount one gets to spend for the rest of their life.

Scenario #4: Benefits of Planning Early.   For those in the accumulation stage, you may be asking, "Why plan it now?"

When discussing the Private Pension with those in the accumulation stage, some will quickly dismiss it due to their young age. This is entirely true for the immediate annuity side of the Private Pension sandwich. For many reasons, it typically makes no sense at all to ever invest in an immediate annuity until you are past the age of 70.

But if the concept sounds like something you'd consider when in retirement, then along with the other benefits discussed earlier, this could be a strong reason to consider adding some life insurance to your diversified investment portfolio.

Why do it now? It's simple: The younger you are when initiating the life insurance policy, the higher the income from the Private Pension will be. For those concerned about whether they will have enough income at retirement or whether they will outlive it, this is truly one of the most powerful strategies to help minimize both concerns.

Let's look at an example as to why the Private Pension can be such a powerful strategy *the earlier you plan for it* by first recapping Bill's original plan:

In his 70s, Bill invests $100,000 in an immediate annuity that produces a 12 percent return, providing him with a guaranteed lifetime income of $12,000 a year.

He then uses a portion of this income to invest in a life insurance policy to replace the $100,000 upon his death. At the age he created the Private Pension (mid-70s), this requires an investment of $5,000 per year.

He then has a guaranteed net income of $7,000 (7 percent) a year, mostly tax-free.

Suppose Bill read this book while he was in the accumulation stage of his life and the concept sounded interesting. If he took out the $100,000 life insurance policy when he was in his 50s, the Private Pension later on would look much more attractive at retirement.

Fast forward to Bill now in his 70s when he's ready to begin his Private Pension. With the permanent life policy in place since his 50s, he removes (in this example) $100,000 from his savings and makes a one-time deposit to fund the immediate annuity.

Having preplanned for this to happen, Bill's Private Pension may now look something like this:

> Now in his 70s, Bill invests $100,000 in an immediate annuity that produces a 12 percent return, providing him with a guaranteed lifetime income of $12,000 a year, mostly tax-free.
>
> He then uses some of this income to *continue* investing in the permanent life insurance policy. Because the life insurance was initiated when he was in his 50s, the annual investment to continue the policy could be a mere 1 percent. Remember: The earlier you take out the insurance, the less investment it will require.
>
> In this example, Bill would only have to remove 1 percent from the immediate annuity to keep the permanent life policy in force.
>
> He is then left with a guaranteed income not of 7 percent but of 11 percent, or $11,000 per year, mostly tax-free.

By planning for the Private Pension much earlier, Bill vastly increased his annual income *for the rest of his life.* In this example, he will receive an 11 percent rate of return, mostly tax free, locked in for the rest of his life and guaranteed never to run out. If that sounds good, be sure to remember that an 11 percent mostly tax-free rate of return is equivalent to a *taxable* return of 13 to 14 percent.

If you can plan now to give yourself such a high rate of return for the rest of your life and never outlive the income, wouldn't it make sense to plan for this now? If there's ever a strategy to plan for as early as possible, I hope you can see that the Private Pension is usually at the top of the list.

Double My Income at Retirement? How?

This brings me to a key point. Earlier, I claimed the Private Pension can often more than *double your income* when in retirement. How can I make that claim?

At some point in the past, you may have heard or been advised about the withdrawal rate from a retirement portfolio. As mentioned at the end of the preceding chapter, many advisors will prudently tell you that when you retire and start using your investments for income, you should not withdraw more than 4 to 5 percent of your portfolio per year. If you can keep your withdrawals to within these percentages, then given all historical stock and bond market data available, prudent planning says these withdrawal rates will provide you with the best chance of not outliving your money.

If you understand the concept of the Private Pension, then you understand that this strategy will not only greatly increase your income, but it will also give you the assurance you won't ever out-live it.

The Private Pension is an *insurance-based* strategy that is *guaranteed* to produce the results. And, if planned for early, the amount of reliable income that can be safely produced from the Private Pension when you reach retirement years can easily be as high as 10 percent or in many cases, even higher.

Therefore, that is how adding life insurance to your diversified investment portfolio *as soon as possible* can potentially better than double your income at retirement.

The power of this strategy cannot be emphasized enough. The Private Pension offers:

- Highly attractive income (that typically far exceeds the recommended withdrawal rate).
- Mostly tax-free income.
- Income that you will not outlive.
- Income that is not subject to any stock market or interest rate risk.
- The assurance that the amount used to fund your Private Pension will be returned to heirs tax-free.

Who says there will no longer be such things as reliable pensions when we retire? With a Private Pension in place, that will never be the case.

Did I Waste My Money?

When discussing the Private Pension with someone in the accumulation stage we'll often hear the comment, "But what happens if I never wind up initiating a Private Pension? If I don't do it later on, I wasted my money on the insurance!" That's the person speaking who sees life insurance as a *cost*. I hope by now you see it as we do, as an *investment* that has many possible benefits and exit strategies including giving yourself the opportunity to *sell it at a profit* if you later have no use for it.

Many people in their 50s start to actively plan for retirement. Would it not be smart at such an age to also start planning how one is going to get the most amount of reliable income in retirement with the least amount of risk *and* the assurance that you will never outlive your money?

The Private Pension and IRAs

Until now, the income the Private Pension generates is mostly tax free, and that's certainly an attractive benefit. This assumes the Private Pension is funded with after-tax dollars outside a qualified account such as an IRA.

But designing a Private Pension using IRA money could make sense as well. Here's why:

When an IRA was originally conceived, what was it designed to do? Be used for income in retirement, correct? For various reasons, using your IRA money to create a Private Pension could very well be the best of all alternatives.

Imagine for a moment that you are in your 70s and in retirement. Now it's time to use your IRA for the reason it was created in the first place: to give you income. After many years of accumulating money in their IRAs, many retirees we meet are looking for a simple and safe way to generate reliable income, especially the kind they cannot outlive.

Many people we meet in retirement withdraw only the required minimum distributions from of their IRAs. When an IRA is passed to the next generation, as mentioned earlier, many heirs cash out the IRA and as a result would very likely wind up paying a lot of tax.

So, if generating an attractive income stream you cannot outlive *and* passing the value of your IRA tax free to heirs both sound interesting, you may want to consider using all or a portion of your IRA money to create the Private Pension.

Here's a hypothetical example:

Suppose I have an IRA worth $100,000. Also assume I have plenty of money outside the IRA. With the IRA money, I invest in an immediate annuity that provides a lifetime income of $13,000 a year.

I use some of this income to invest in a life insurance policy that provides $100,000 at death. Hypothetically, suppose a $100,000 death benefit requires an annual investment of $6,000. Removing this amount from the yearly income leaves me with a guaranteed $7,000 per year.

Now, for the rest of my life, I have an income stream of 7 percent being generated from my original investment of $100,000.

At death, the income dies with me and there's nothing left to heirs.

Except, however, remember: I was removing $6,000 per year to invest in the life insurance policy worth $100,000 when I die.

Therefore, when I die, the heirs get the $100,000 value of my IRA *not* fully taxable, but *tax-free*. This is because the *value* of my IRA is inherited in the form of a life insurance policy's tax-free death benefit.

With this planning, I receive a guaranteed income that I cannot outlive and my heirs receive the full value of my IRA not taxable, but tax-free.

Needless to say, taxes and a variety of other issues have to be factored in to determine whether or not using IRA money to fund a Private Pension would make sense given your own personal needs.

One Million Dollars—For Free?

At the time of this writing, the following is a very hot topic for people in retirement. In places such as Southern California, Arizona, Las Vegas, Florida, and various other densely populated retirement spots around the country, the concept is truly spreading like wildfire. After all, if structured and planned correctly, what I'm about to discuss could possibly give you and/or your parent(s) a million dollars for free (for reasons you'll soon realize, the actual amount, if any, can be much more or less).

Let's quickly summarize how getting a free million dollars for free could come true:

- Regardless of the insurance concepts I've described, let's suppose hypothetical Sam, who is over the age of 70, has no desire to ever add *any* life insurance to his diversified portfolio.
- For reasons you'll soon understand, let's suppose Sam gets himself qualified for a life insurance policy. Although qualified, he never has any intention to personally pay for it.
- Therefore, in this concept, Sam *borrows* the first two years of premiums from a financial institution. As with any borrowed money, Sam is charged interest on this loan.

During the two-year period of the loan, any one of the following three scenarios can transpire:

1. *Sam dies.* In this scenario, Sam's family would receive the full death benefit of the insurance policy less the loan and interest accrued.
2. *Sam's health deteriorates.* Suppose Sam's health takes a turn for the worse and the life insurance policy that once seemed like something he'd never want is now something that makes total sense for the family to keep. After all, if he knows he doesn't have much life left in him, the insurance would provide a significant return for the family. In this scenario, to keep the policy in his family, someone—Sam, his wife, children, whoever—needs to pay off the loan. Once the loan is paid off, the family would then be required to pay the premiums until Sam dies in order to receive the death benefit.
3. *Sam lives and doesn't want the policy.* And finally, the scenario that is compelling to many: At the two-year mark when the loan is due, Sam raises the money to pay it off by *selling* the policy into life insurance's secondary marketplace. A financial institution in the secondary marketplace pays Sam cash for the right to own, pay the premiums, and eventually receive the death benefit.

    Continuing with this last scenario, Sam pays off the loan from the proceeds of the sale, and he keeps over the amount left over for himself. How much is leftover varies. After paying off the loan, we've seen people keep anywhere from as little as

$50,000 up to millions of dollars. The net amount depends on a variety of factors, some of which I'll be covering shortly.

The process can end there. Sam sells the policy, pays off the loan, pockets the difference, and does whatever he wants with the money, which could very well be the "free million dollars" itself.

But the process does not have to end there. Let's take it one step further. Let's suppose Sam wants to *leverage* the money he made from the sale of his policy into even more money for his heirs.

With the money Sam received from the sale of his policy, he can then invest in a *new* life insurance policy on himself, or perhaps someone such as his wife.

With this new life insurance policy in place and paid for by the proceeds from selling his policy, the amount passed to heirs through the death benefit can far exceed the amount Sam received from the sale.

Not to complicate things, but there could be several creative variations: At the outset of the plan, *both* Sam and his wife could have taken out policies, or Sam could have split his original policy into two. In either case, the proceeds from the sale of *one* policy into the secondary market could have been used to pay off the loan on both policies. In this case, one policy is sold, and the proceeds from selling the first policy pay off the loan on the second policy. The second policy is then kept in the family, thereby creating "free" life insurance for heirs out of thin air. I won't get into too many mind-twisting scenarios here, but there are a few creative possibilities that could be quite interesting when more than one policy are initiated from the start.

Sound interesting? To many, it certainly is. But there are a few things you must know. First of all, to qualify for this strategy, three key requirements have to be in place:

1. A person over the age of 70 has to be insurable. We've seen people anywhere from "poor health" to "excellent health" qualify, but many people simply cannot. By a wide margin, there are many more people wanting to take advantage of this strategy than can qualify for it.

2. The person also has to have a minimum net worth typically of $1 million or more.

3. The person needs to have "capacity" for insurance remaining on their lives. Capacity, in the world of life insurance, basically

means that you cannot insure yourself for more than your net worth (subject to certain factors, working people can typically insure themselves for an amount up to 25 times their annual incomes). So, as an example, if my net worth is $1 million and I have a life insurance policy currently in place for $1 million, then I have reached my maximum capacity and cannot apply for additional insurance. However, if I have a net worth of $1 million and have an insurance policy in place with a death benefit of $250,000, then I still have the capacity to add an additional $750,000 of insurance on my life.

Assuming the person applies for the life insurance and gets qualified, the next step is to secure a loan to finance it, bringing up the next likely question, "Why would anyone want to lend me money on a life insurance policy?"

First off, the financial institution is lending money to generate interest, which is why *any* lender loans money.

The next likely question is, "Who are the lenders and purchasers of the policies in the secondary market?" As reported in sources such as the *Wall Street Journal* (February 21, 2007, "A Lively Market in Death Bonds") and the *New York Times* (December 17, 2006, "Late in Life, Finding a Bonanza in Life Insurance"), it is not the Sicilian Mafia who are doing this. As the *Times* article reported, it is typically entities such as Credit Suisse, Deutsche Bank, Berkshire Hathaway, and large hedge funds. Due to the low risk the lenders have, many financial entities are eager to get into the game that is often referred to as "life settlement," "premium financing," or "spin life" market.

To understand why the lender doesn't have much risk and why lenders want to finance these policies, let's return to Sam's three scenarios and view the risk from the lender's perspective:

1. *If Sam dies within the first two years*, the *guaranteed* death benefit gets paid and from it the lender is contractually paid back the premiums it paid plus accrued interest. The only risk to the lender here is that if the insurance company discovers any type of fraud on the original application (material omissions such as health- or net-worth-related issues), the insurance company would not have to pay the death benefit; rather, it would be required to return the premiums paid.

In this worst-case scenario, the lender would get its money back but not the interest it was supposed to receive.

2. *If Sam wants to keep the policy after two years,* for him to continue ownership of the policy, he'll simply have to pay the lender back the premiums paid plus accrued interest. There's no risk to the lender here, either.

3. *If Sam doesn't die and doesn't want the policy,* he sells the policy into the secondary market. From the proceeds of the sale, he pays the lender back the premiums paid plus accrued interest. There's still no risk to the lender.

In all three scenarios, the lender is highly likely to get its money back plus interest at the end of two years. At this point, you might ask, "What if the policy cannot be sold into the secondary market?" However unlikely this would be, if the policy could not be sold into the secondary market, Sam would *not* be responsible for paying back the loan. These loans are known as *nonrecourse;* they do not have to get paid back. In fact, most lenders out there *hope* they don't get paid back.

Why?

Because in the event the loan is not paid back, the lender would keep the policy for itself and assume the financial responsibility from there. After all, the policy acts as collateral for the loan, and this type of collateral is arguably the best type of collateral—everyone is going to die at some point, and not only is the death benefit on the policy guaranteed by the insurance company, but it is also guaranteed not to go down in value.

Think about it: When someone lends money to purchase a house, what's their biggest risk? The biggest risk is that the value of the house will go down, the borrower will default, and the bank could very well be stuck holding a house worth less money.

In a life insurance policy, however, the collateral *never* goes down because of the guaranteed death benefit on the permanent life policy. In the event the borrower (Sam) doesn't pay off the loan, the lender will simply keep the policy for itself, bringing up an important question from the lender's perspective: How much life does someone in their mid-70s have left in them? In most cases, the answer is, "not much." In most cases, the lender or purchaser of the policy in the secondary market will likely have to pay the premiums for only a few years in order to collect much more money through the death benefit than it paid out in premiums.

Some death benefits will pay off right away, providing an astronomical return for the lender or purchaser, and some will take many years to pay off. But when it's all averaged together, the lenders and/or purchasers of the policies know they'll make plenty of money and are very willing to take the risk to get it.

Selling the Policy

Questions about selling the policy into the secondary marketplace often come up, in particular, "How much can I expect to sell the policy for after the two-year period is up?" The only answer is "It depends." That's frustrating, I know, but there is no way for anyone to tell you how much it will sell for. When the policy is offered into the secondary market, the amount received depends on one primary thing: the health and life expectancy of the insured.

On one extreme end of the spectrum, suppose the insured's life expectancy is very short. In this case, the secondary market would likely offer a high purchase price. As a hypothetical example, if the death benefit of a policy is $5 million, someone in the secondary market might offer as much as $2.5 million (remember, from that $2.5 million the initial loan would have to be paid off). Why $2.5 million? Because why *not* pay someone $2.5 million for a $5 million death benefit that, according to updated health records of the insured, will likely pay off very soon? (If this is the case, however, the insured should likely pay off the loan and keep the policy for the family.)

On the other extreme end of the spectrum, suppose the insured's life expectancy is very long. In this case, the secondary market would likely offer a *lower* purchase price. As an example, if the death benefit of a policy is $5 million, someone in the secondary market might offer only $1 million or even less. Why? Because in the case of a long life expectancy based on updated health records at the time of the offering, the purchaser of the policy might end up paying premiums for a long time until the death benefit is paid.

As you can see, determining an exact amount of what the policy will sell for in the secondary market is difficult. Most likely, someone *will* buy it, but at what price? While there are certainly industry averages (currently, approximately 25 percent of the death benefit), there's just no way of knowing the exact amount until two years goes by and the insured's life expectancy in the secondary market is determined by a purchaser.

All that said, there are many companies in the secondary market that would be willing to buy the policy *as soon as it is issued* (whereby there is never any money borrowed to pay the premiums; the policy is bought outright and the insured receives money right away without having to wait two years). In most cases we've seen, however, it usually makes little sense to sell the policy outright, so I won't bother discussing the details of such an offer here.

Regulation

What is the one entity that does not want these types of arrangements to transpire? As you may have guessed, it's the insurance companies themselves. Historically, many insurance policies lapse, meaning they are issued, paid for, then terminated before the death benefits are paid. Insurance companies love policies that lapse. It's their very own version of free money.

However, policies that are purchased by the financial institutions will *never* lapse. The entity in the secondary market that purchases the policy *will* pay the premiums until death, leaving the insurance companies on the hook to pay death benefits on every one of these policies.

Needless to say, the insurance companies don't exactly like this. It messes up their profit margins. As a result, many companies are making it much more difficult for people over the age of 70 to get policies issued, knowing that many of those insured will likely wind up selling their policies later on. In fact, many companies are now starting to slow down the process of issuing policies until they presumably raise the insurance premiums to offset the cost of policies that won't lapse. There is also a chance that by the time this book is in your hands, although I would say it's unlikely given recent legislation, this entire concept can be terminated altogether.

Risks

One risk of selling your policy is that once a policy is sold into the secondary marketplace, you cannot get it back. It's an irrevocable sale, and this should not be taken lightly. For various reasons, some of which I mentioned in the prior sections, a life insurance policy can be a very valuable asset to the heirs of one's estate.

Additionally, selling the policy into the secondary market requires an intermediary. If the intermediary, or broker, generates an offer from the secondary market, make sure you receive competitive quotes from a number of buying sources, and get it in writing. Due to lax oversight of these transactions, there have been cases where the broker takes a higher than usual commission from the sale of the policy into the secondary marketplace, leaving the insured with considerably lower profits after the loan is paid off.

Lastly, if the loan does not get paid off, some sources claim the IRS won't forgive the loan, and this could be another risk. Although most of the policies that get sold are owned by a *trust*, some ponder that the IRS will treat the unpaid loan as a taxable event if it doesn't get paid off. Would the trust be responsible for paying the tax? Probably, but then who's really liable? The trust? The lender? The insured? Because the tax code on these dealings is murky, if the loan doesn't get paid back, just know this is another risk that should be addressed before venturing into this area.

In summary, the "premium financing" and "life settlement" offerings remain quite topical in today's marketplace; people later in retirement are selling the asset of their insurability and making quite a bit of money from the sale. This doesn't mean you should do it. But at least you understand one interesting area of the life insurance world that you may want to further investigate.

Life Insurance: Conclusion

We've talked about quite a few concepts, and I'd like to summarize some of the thoughts for you here.

In almost all cases, term insurance is not the most efficient way to buy life insurance. Term insurance is hopefully nothing but a cost, and it's also the type of insurance the life insurance companies want you to buy. Most people outlive the term and then let the policy lapse due to the high cost of continuing the policy after the term is complete. Most term policies are not an investment, they are a *cost;* and because of that, it makes little sense to ever consider term insurance.

Instead of acquiring insurance the way the life insurance companies want us to, I discussed a much smarter way: *invest* in something called permanent life insurance, which could represent just another sector within our diversified investment portfolio. Including this within the buy-and-hold diversified investment portfolio gives us the

opportunity to take advantage of benefits none of our other investments can offer us, including:

- The necessary ingredient to a Private Pension that could bet-
  ter than double our income at retirement and guarantee it
  never runs out for the rest of our lives.
- The opportunity to generate tax-free income at retirement.
- The opportunity to "spend all our money" and still "leave it all
  behind."
- Potential long-term care benefits.
- An opportunity to get a "free" million dollars.
- Instant wealth creation through a tax-free death benefit.
- Money for our heirs to pay possible estate and/or income
  taxes due upon our demise.
- If further down the road none of these benefits are of any
  interest to us, we have a possible exit strategy to sell the pol-
  icy into the secondary life settlement market for a potential
  profit.

Perhaps you, too, will see a benefit to including permanent life
insurance as just another sector within your diversified investment
portfolio. If you have any interest in any of the concepts presented in
this chapter, speaking with a qualified advisor to assess your personal
situation is certainly necessary before anything is implemented.

Okay, enough about investments and death. Let's move on.

CHAPTER 5

A Break in the Action

We're making good progress here, and I hope you've learned a few interesting things. Because this movie's plot is about to take a turn in a different direction, let's quickly recap a broad summary of what we have just covered.

Diversification among the fundamental asset classes is the golden key to investment success. It takes the guesswork out of investing and provides us with the greatest chances of sustained and consistent success. For maximum diversification, low fees, control of our taxes, and historically attractive performance, I strongly recommend using stock indexes to represent each asset class within a diversified portfolio.

To invest in the indexes, consider using index exchange-traded funds (ETFs). If, however, you plan on making frequent contributions to your investment portfolio, to keep transaction fees to a minimum use an index *mutual* fund instead.

Each index within the buy-and-hold diversified portfolio is like a newborn child: While at various times we like one more than others, we should *love* them all the same. At any given time, without any notice, we fully realize that as one child starts acting up, another is due to be really kind to us. These are natural *cycles* that no one can predict. It's for this reason we should rarely, if ever, consider giving one up. Therefore, we can conclude that our diversified portfolio of stock market indexes should serve as a buy-and-hold foundation for our investments intended for accumulating wealth.

To take advantage of unique opportunities in the marketplace, we should consider reserving a small portion of our money outside the buy-and-hold diversified portfolio of indexes. Because we should plan on holding our diversified portfolio presumably for a long time, there are going to be times when various opportunities evolve that we will want to take advantage of. An individual stock, a unique stock index, or any number of other investment opportunities might come up. I refer to this portion of the diversified portfolio as the flavors of the day.

Once the diversified portfolio is established, the management of the buy-and-hold portfolio is done through the simple, mechanical, and *un*emotional act of rebalancing preferably once a year or more, depending on various market circumstances. Rebalancing a portfolio provides us with the greatest chance of achieving every investor's dream: buying low and selling high.

What often prevents us from achieving every investor's "buy low and sell high" dream is our *emotions*. To overcome this, we need to remember the World's Most Difficult Investment Formula: Investing − Emotion = Success.

The first step in actually building our diversified portfolio is to follow the Rule of 120 (120 minus your age equals the percentage of stocks that should be in your portfolio).

As time goes by and we edge toward retirement, the Rule of 120 helps ensure we shift from the accumulation stage to the reliable returns stage of our lives; as we inch closer to retirement, it is highly advisable to start moving a greater percentage of growth investments to investments that produce reliable returns, especially when we need to ensure our income is maximized and produced as safely and efficiently as possible.

Shifting into investments that produce reliable returns will help us avoid playing the Most Dangerous Game: the game that relies on the *un*reliable, speculative, potential growth of stocks to produce the income we need.

Investments that generally provide reliable returns for income include but are not limited to:

- *Bonds.* As much as possible, using bond ladders is more desirable than using bond mutual funds. Ladders generally provide stable rates of return with maturity dates that give us peace of mind knowing the date when our principal will be returned to us even if the value of the bond goes down.
- *Preferred stocks.* Preferreds are a hybrid of bonds and stocks. While the underlying instrument is a stock, there is also a

stated rate of interest similar to a bond that can provide us with reliable income.

- *Dividend stocks.* Dividend stocks offer the best of both possible worlds: potential for growth *and* income. It is important to remember the key concept of dividend stocks: that the market value of the stock is completely independent and separate from the dividend (income) it produces.

- *Closed-end or exchange-traded funds.* For more consistent and reliable income, consider using exchange-traded funds or closed-end mutual funds; within a well-diversified portfolio of these funds, there are potentially *thousands* of dividend-paying stocks that produce the income one needs. Having many stocks paying us dividends helps ensure that if a few reduce dividends or even eliminate them, there are many others helping buffer a potential fall.

- *Variable annuities.* The living benefit of a variable annuity provides the opportunity to try to grow our money as much as possible without risking our income. The living benefit also allows us to look back to our highest account value and draw income from that amount even if the account later goes down in value. Furthermore, in the event of a bad market where the account has lost value, the death benefit generally returns the amount we originally invested to our heirs.

- *Certificates of deposit.* CDs also provide reliable rates of return. However, the low rate of return and taxable interest might not deliver the higher returns for income some might need. Those of us who are looking to a CD for total safety but are in need of higher rates of return might consider a *growth CD* or an *index annuity.* Both investments typically offer a minimum rate of return and safety of principal with the potential for higher rates of return as determined by the performance of various stock market indexes.

- *Real estate.* For reliable rates of return, real estate is also worthy of consideration. While purchasing actual real estate properties might very well be an option, doing so can be complicated and time-consuming. To simplify an investment into real estate, one might consider a real estate investment trust (REIT) that is either listed on the public exchanges or privately held.

- *Life insurance.* Permanent life insurance could represent just another slice of our diversified portfolio, given that it offers us

options and benefits no other slice of the portfolio can provide. This includes, but is certainly not limited to, The Private
Pension, which can likely better than double our income at
retirement and make sure we won't outlive it.

That's certainly a lot of ground covered, and I hope you are
keeping up with this film.

It's especially important to recap the preceding chapters at this
point, because this is the part of the movie where the plot takes a
sudden turn. As if James Bond just got knocked out by a tall, sultry
woman only to awaken somewhere deep in the Amazon rain forest,
it's time for us to move to a new location. While this new location
isn't as scenic as the Amazon, it no doubt plays an important role in
the movie we are busy producing.

So, fasten your seatbelts and hold on tight, because we're about
to race off to an important location in the near distance commonly
referred to as individual retirement accounts (IRAs).

CHAPTER 6

Individual Retirement Accounts (IRAs)

A "first time" event sticks with us for a long while, presumably for the rest of our life. When I recall various "first times" I've had, a few things immediately come to mind:

- My first kiss (sixth grade, back of the school bus. Name of girl withheld to protect her reputation).
- The first time I saw Springsteen in concert (Nassau Coliseum, The River Tour).
- The first time I got into a car accident (smashed my dad's car in front of Carvel).
- The first time I got into a fistfight (against my older sister back in first grade; I lost *real* bad).
- The first time I got a base hit in Little League (a lucky shot over the second baseman's head).

And, of course, the first time no one will *ever* forget, the one that typically tops *everyone's* list: the first time someone told me I should invest in something called an individual retirement account (IRA).

Ah, yes. The first time someone told us we should invest in an IRA. Who can ever forget that magical moment?

A long time ago it may have been, but I inexplicably still remember it well. Tired from staying up late at a Saturday night high school gathering, I do have a minor recollection of the event. A nice, crisp Sunday morning I'm sure it was, and while everyone else was most likely out enjoying the perfect day, I was busy relaxing on the family couch watching a good Clint Eastwood movie or something of the sort.

And while relaxing on a Sunday morning, what would be the best thing that could have topped off the moment? Any ideas? Of course—you guessed it—having your mother come into the room to discuss what an IRA is and why you want to invest in it. Yes, at that moment, my financial planner mom truly delivered the goods. And all I can recall from the conversation is pain, confusion, frustration, and the feeling of "can we get this over with as fast as possible?"

Back then, I really had no idea what an IRA was or why I should pay the slightest attention to it. Even the words "tax deduction" didn't mean much to me. Although it may have been a long time ago, perhaps you can recall your first time being introduced to an IRA as well.

Most of us end up with at least one IRA, but many people don't truly understand what they are, why they are helpful, and how they work.

IRAs Defined

To start with, an individual retirement account is not really an individual retirement *account;* according to the IRS, it's really an "individual retirement *arrangement.*" But, other than being the life of the next New Year's Eve party, when it's discovered you're the only person who knows that, this information alone won't do you much good in the long run. Investing in one most likely will, though, and it is for this reason you should have at least a basic understanding what it is in order to ensure your long-term success.

In its simplest form, an IRA is an investment vehicle designed with the specific purpose of helping us save for retirement. To motivate us to save, Uncle Sam offers us something called a *tax deduction.* While our money is invested and (we hope) growing in this slice of our diversified, rebalanced portfolio, we pay no tax until we start taking money out. "Paying no tax until we take money out" is otherwise known as *tax deferral.*

Tax deduction *and* tax deferral is a powerful combination that can really help us accumulate quite a few dollars toward our retirement.

Combining them is just like mixing liquid hydrogen and nitrogen. Those two compounds mixed together have launched space shuttles into orbit, and there's no doubt mixing tax deferral and tax deductions can do the same for your money.

Individual retirement accounts are an essential part of most financial plans. You can open an IRA on your own and start contributing directly into it, or you can set up an IRA to *receive* funds from a previous employer's qualified employer-sponsored plan such as a 401(k), 403(b), or any number of other qualified plans that generally fall under the same umbrella of an IRA.

IRAs: Frequently Asked Questions

IRAs can be quite a complex subject—so complex, in fact, that many books have been written about this one subject alone. Because I can't possibly cover all aspects of the IRA in a book about many different subjects, I figured I'd stick with some of the most common questions that I've heard over the years. I suggest reading through the following frequently asked questions to find subjects that are of interest to your particular situation. As best I could, I've tried to keep the questions in a progressive order, starting with the most basic and then advancing to questions that often come up after one retires.

The Basics

Q. What exactly is an IRA, and how can it benefit me?
A. Many people don't truly understand what an IRA is and why it can be helpful toward their retirement. For this reason, I'm starting with this question, the most basic of all. If you don't exactly understand what an IRA is and why it's valuable for your long-term success, then why pay any attention to it in the first place?

Let's take it from the top, and I'm going to keep it really simple. I'm going to stick with the very basic concept and eliminate what can sometimes be very long-winded technical details.

Let's suppose you have a job where you earn an annual salary of $33,000. This places you in the 25 percent tax bracket, meaning you are going to pay a 25 percent tax on the upper portion of your income. I say "upper portion" because, in reality, we live in what's known as a "marginal tax system." If the tax code wasn't complex enough, trying to figure out exactly how much tax you pay on all your income can be a bit frustrating as well. The "marginal tax system" means that you don't pay the same percentage of tax on *all* your income. The first few dollars actually get taxed at a lower rate than the last few dollars. Getting into the complexity of the tax system will only add confusion, so to keep things simple, I'm going to assume for the concept's sake that *all* your income is taxed at 25 percent.

So, in this hypothetical example, if you paid 25 percent tax on your $33,000, at the end of the year you would owe the IRS a total of $8,250. You'd have to write a check for that amount—it's lost money paid to the IRS, something you'll never see again.

But, if you are a savvy investor and want to save for retirement, Uncle Sam is going to give you a break. He tells you this year you can invest up to $4,000 into an IRA (every year the contribution levels will change). The deadline to make the contribution for the *current* tax year is April 15 of *next* year.

But why would you want to do that? Besides investing a few dollars toward retirement, how does a contribution help you in terms of *current* taxes? That's what this thing called a tax deduction is all about.

If you didn't invest in the IRA, you would have to pay tax on the full amount of income, the $33,000. But now that you contributed $4,000 into your IRA, that $4,000 is fully deducted from your earnings of $33,000. The salary you earned now appears on your tax return not as $33,000, but at the *adjusted* amount of $29,000 (you deduct the $4,000 you contributed to the IRA from your $33,000 income).

Instead of paying tax on the $33,000, you pay tax on $29,000 (the $33,000 less the deduction of $4,000). In addition to paying tax on less income, in this hypothetical example, the deduction of $4,000 also dropped you into a lower tax bracket. Now, instead of paying $8,250 in tax, you are paying only $4,350, which represents a savings of $3,900 in taxes.

In this example, to some, a $3,900 tax savings might not appear to mean much. But over time, the tax savings combined with the tax deferral means quite a lot, especially when you make contributions on an annual basis.

Q. Can tax-deferred investing really help me out?
A. It sure can, especially over longer periods of time. Take a look at the hypothetical scenarios in Table 6.1, which for simple math are based on an initial investment of $100,000. Suppose over a 20-year

Table 6.1   Taxable vs. Tax Deferred Investing

	Taxable 8%	Tax Deferred 8%
Year 5	$126,471	$146,935
Year 10	$159,813	$215,892
Year 15	$202,031	$317,216
Year 20	$255,402	$466,095

period of time you had a choice to invest by paying the tax as you go or by deferring the taxes owed. Assuming an 8 percent return for both and that taxes owed in the "Taxable" column are paid from earnings, Table 6.1 shows the results.

Which would you rather have: a nest egg of $466,095 or $255,402?

Now, suppose at the end of 20 years you generate *earnings only* from your nest egg. Assuming a reliable 8 percent return, the taxable account provides annual income of $20,402 and the tax-deferred account provides annual income of $37,287, representing $17,000 more per year thanks to tax-deferred investing.

Q. Is there a downside to tax-deferred investing?
A. Yes. In all cases, withdrawals are typically taxed at the worst tax rate of all, that of ordinary income (something I discuss in greater detail in the chapter on taxes). In general, the more years you have to invest (typically, a minimum of 10 years), the more attractive the benefits of tax-deferred investing become. Furthermore, next-generation beneficiaries such as children could be faced with double taxation of estate and income tax when and if cashing out a tax-deferred investment such as an IRA (and annuities don't fare much better when passed on to heirs).

Q. How much can I contribute to an IRA?
A. The quick answer is up to the maximum contribution for that year, an amount that increases as the years go by. Anyone can contribute to an IRA as long as they have earned income of *at least an amount equal to the contribution itself.*

So, suppose I earned a total income of $4,000 this year. Besides my wife tossing me out of the house, if I wanted to I could invest that entire amount into an IRA and basically wipe out all of my reportable income for that year. While my personal life might be a wreck, when it comes to my investments, the great news is that I saved on my taxes, and this alone might be a good reason to get thrown out of the house.

For tax year 2008, the maximum amount one can contribute to an IRA is $5,000 per person. Anyone over the age of 50 can contribute an extra $1,000 in addition to these limits due to something called the catch-up provision. The contribution limits typically change every year; for a detailed schedule, I would recommend visiting various Internet sites such as www.irs.gov.

Q. Can my wife *and* I both contribute to an IRA?
A. Yes, but only if you like your spouse. All joking aside, you most certainly can. If only one person is working, then a contribution to an IRA can be made for *both* spouses as long as there is enough income reported to equal the combined contribution.

Suppose the annual contribution limit is $5,000 per person. In this case, I can contribute up to $10,000 for my wife and me as long as I have earned income at least equal to the total of both contributions, which in this example would obviously be $10,000.

Q. How do I contribute to an IRA?
A. Historically, you would simply write a check into the IRA you set up at a financial institution. However, starting in 2007, Uncle Sam is trying to make the process of contributing a bit easier by allowing you to make the deposit automatically from your tax refund (if you unfortunately have one; more on this in the tax section coming up).

Suppose that after doing your taxes, you wind up receiving a $2,700 refund. Through IRS Form 8888, when filing your taxes, you can authorize the IRS to automatically transfer that $2,700 directly to the financial institution holding your IRA.

One word of caution: You only have until April 15 to make the contribution for the *previous* year. If you file your taxes close to the April 15 deadline and plan on having the refund automatically transferred to your IRA, you may be out of luck. If the refund is not transferred in time, you'll miss the contribution deadline.

To avoid this problem, I typically recommend you simply write the check for the IRA contribution by April 15 and don't leave room for error.

Q. Does it make a difference *when* I invest in my IRA?
A. It most certainly does. In most cases, it not only makes a difference, but over time it can make a *big* difference. By investing in an IRA earlier

in the year, you gain the full benefit of tax-deferred compounded interest, which is a very good thing. As a hypothetical example, let's assume you invest $3,000 in an IRA each year for the next 10 years. The IRA grows at 8 percent, compounded quarterly. If you make the contribution at the end of each year—in December—you'll end up with $166,385. But if you make the contribution sooner—say, in April—you'll end up with $181,281. That's because by making the contribution earlier in the year, you'll gain a few additional months of compounding. And as with anything else, those "little things" usually mean "big things" over time. This is just a 10-year example; imagine the impact of compounding interest if you take this example out 20 years.

Q. What's the best investment for my IRA?
A. The best investment is what's right for you. Following your Rule of 120 should help guide you along, but in general, Table 6.2 is a summary of investments you may want to consider using both inside and outside of your IRA.

Investments Outside an IRA

Index/Low-Turnover Mutual Funds. As discussed in previous chapters, indexes rarely change the stocks contained within them, making them a good choice for investments outside the IRA. With rare stock trading done inside the index, there is little tax to pay (if any) until *you* decide to sell the index. It's the same thing with mutual funds that have low turnover where infrequent stock trading is done within the fund. A fund with 100 percent turnover means the entire portfolio of stocks is changed *once* during the course of the year; a fund with 200 percent turnover means the entire portfolio of stocks is changed *twice* during the course of the year. And each time the fund is turned over, it's you who's paying the tax, which is why, from

Table 6.2 Tax-Efficient Investing

Inside IRA	Outside IRA
Growth Mutual Funds	Index/Low Turnover Mutual Funds
Short-Term Stocks	Long-Held Stocks
Taxable Bonds	Tax-Free Bonds

Inside or Outside IRA
Annuities and Real Estate

a tax standpoint, a fund with low turnover is typically fine to be placed outside the IRA. If you are not sure of your fund's turnover, I would recommend looking it up on Morningstar.com or having a qualified advisor inspect it for you.

Long-Term Stocks.   If you are investing in individual stocks within the "flavors of the day" slice of your diversified portfolio and plan on holding these stocks for longer than a year, holding these stocks *outside* the IRA is a great place to do it. If you sell the stocks after a year, you'll pay long-term capital gains rates of 15 percent, which is lower when compared to other types of tax.

Tax-Free Bonds.   If there ever was an investment that should *not* be placed inside an IRA, this one is it. There's no reason a municipal bond paying tax-free interest should *ever* be used in an IRA. Changing a *tax-free* return to a *taxable* return when placed inside an IRA would be a very serious blunder.

Investments Inside an IRA

Growth Mutual Funds.   These funds typically trade stocks quite frequently. Buying and selling stocks on a frequent basis can cause all sorts of short-term capital gains that are taxed at ordinary income tax rates (the highest of all possible taxes and something I'll explain in a little more detail later on). If the fund has high turnover, it means there is a lot of trading going on, and it's therefore best to hold this type of fund inside an IRA where the taxes are all deferred.

Short-Term Stocks.   Similar to the high turnover of a mutual fund, if within your "flavors of the day" section you plan on buying and selling individual stocks on a frequent basis, then frequently trading inside an IRA is an ideal place, given all taxes owed will be deferred.

Taxable Bonds.   Taxable bonds are a good place for investments within an IRA because interest being generated is tax deferred. Taxable bonds placed outside an IRA cause taxable income. If you don't need income from your investments, then investing in taxable bonds outside the IRA causes unnecessary taxes.

Investments Inside and Outside an IRA

Annuities.   Some people adamantly believe one should never fund an annuity with money from your IRA. This is often a hot topic of debate. If there were ever a subject where financial advisors get so heated up that they might consider kickboxing to the bloody death, this one is most likely it. I completely agree that you should not use your IRA money to fund an annuity except under *one* very specific circumstance: if the sole reason to invest in an annuity is to defer taxes. Remember, an IRA already has tax deferral, so if the *sole* purpose of investing in an annuity is to get tax deferral on your investments, then using IRA money to fund the annuity is completely invalid and a total waste. However, if the reason for using IRA money to fund an annuity is to get better rates of return than, for example, a fixed annuity might offer over a CD, or to receive certain guarantees that no other investment has (such as living and death benefits a variable annuity offers), then regardless of doubling up on the tax deferral, investing in an annuity both inside *and* outside of an IRA could make sense.

Real Estate.   Surprising to many, subject to certain limitations, people can use money in their IRAs to fund real estate. I'll go into this in greater detail soon.

Q. What if I don't like my investments? Can I change things around inside my IRA without getting taxed?
A. You certainly can. Think of the IRA as the carton that contains a wide variety of eggs (investment choices). You can move your money from egg to egg whenever you want and incur no taxes or IRS penalties. But as soon as you take money *out* of the carton, that's called a *distribution*, and not only will you owe taxes, but subject to various exceptions, if you are under the age of 59½, you'll also pay a 10 percent penalty.

Q. Is there a way to avoid this 10 percent for early withdrawals from an IRA?
A. There sure is, but just know that any withdrawals prior to turning the age of 59½ are always subject to tax. A 10 percent penalty is added *except* in the case of:

- Death.
- Disability.
- Life annuity.
- First home purchase (up to $10,000).
- Educational expenses.
- Medical expenses.
- Health insurance for the unemployed.
- Certain reservists called to active duty.
- IRS levy.

Another exception to early withdrawal penalties is called an IRS Section 72-T. Based on a series of calculations far too complex to explain here, the IRS allows you to take "systematic" withdrawals from your IRA for a period greater than five years or until you reach the age of 59½. "Systematic" means a fixed monthly income that usually cannot change. If it does change before the time requirement is met, the 72-T is deemed invalid and taxable events and penalties will take place. Structuring a 72-T should always be done with the assistance of a tax and financial professional.

Q. Is there anything I *can't* invest in within my IRA?
A. Yes, the IRS does impose some restrictions. Investments into various items such as artwork, rugs, antiques, metals, gems, stamps, most coins, beverages, stock in an S corporation, life insurance, and other tangible personal property specified by the IRS are not allowed in an IRA. Surprising to most people, investing in real estate *is* allowed (with some exceptions, of course).

Q. Can I really buy real estate in my IRA? If so, how?
A. Most investors believe that their only investment options inside IRAs are common investments such as mutual funds, stocks, and bonds. Believe it or not, you can also invest your IRA assets in real estate. Yes, real estate, and I'm not talking about real estate stocks or real estate investment trusts (REITs). I'm talking about the real deal, the kind of stuff you can touch and feel. Whether it's a fixer-upper or a pristine property located on South Beach, within certain limitations, you can typically use your IRA dollars to purchase it.

The investment vehicle that allows this to take place is a known as a "self-directed" IRA. These "self-directed" accounts enable their owners to pursue a wide variety of real estate investments including single-family homes, urban real estate developments, farms, liens, and mortgage notes.

Setting up a self-directed IRA is relatively simple. You open an account with a custodian or administrator that specializes in self-directed IRAs. Two of the largest providers include Entrust Group, Inc., based in Oakland, California, and Pensco Trust Company, based in San Francisco. Once a self-directed IRA is established with one of these or any number of other companies, you would then *transfer* money from your current IRA to the self-directed IRA. Once that is complete, when you're ready to make a purchase you simply notify your custodian to issue the seller a check.

There are a few things to keep in mind and a lack of understanding about certain restrictions could make self-directed IRA accounts accidents waiting to happen, primarily when it comes to a practice known as "self-dealing."

According to IRS regulations, an IRA is supposed to provide for your retirement, not your current well-being. You can't benefit *now* from an investment you make in real estate via a self-directed IRA. That means you can buy property and rent it out to a stranger, but you can't buy property and live in it yourself or rent it out to a family member. If you do, the IRS will likely step in and disqualify the IRA altogether, causing a large tax bill as well as some penalties for account holders who are younger than age 59½. In other words, you could lose your entire IRA.

How do you avoid getting into a mess like that? You can obviously educate yourself, or you can recruit one of the few financial advisors out there who understand how to set up and administer a self-directed IRA.

Q. You just mentioned "transferring" money from one IRA to another. Is a *transfer* the same thing as a *rollover*?
A. No, it's not. Let's go back to the carton of eggs. Suppose your carton of eggs is actually a bank, which we'll call Bank USA. Bank USA offers various IRA eggs inside it—mutual funds, CDs, and maybe a few other things. Moving money *within* Bank USA's IRA is easy. The money *stays* within Bank USA's carton of IRA investments.

But suppose there's a brokerage across the street known as Brokerage XYZ, and this brokerage has better IRA investment eggs to choose from. Moving your money from Bank USA's IRA to Brokerage XYZ's IRA can be done in one of two possible ways: *rolling it over* or *transferring it.*

Rollover. In this method, Bank USA would issue you a check. Once Bank USA hands you the check, that's when the clock starts ticking. You then have 60 days to race across the street and deposit it with Brokerage XYZ. If you miss the 60-day deadline, the IRS deems this a distribution, which will cause a taxable event. Not only will the entire amount of the check become taxable, but if you are under the age of 59½, you will also be hit with a 10 percent penalty for early withdrawal. The IRS allows only one rollover per year.

As you can see, the rollover method could create complications, especially if it's a wide street you have to race across between Bank

USA and Brokerage XYZ within that annoying 60-day deadline. There's room for error and it's for this reason, with very rare exception, I typically tell people to make their lives simple by sticking with the transfer method.

Transfer. Instead of getting a physical check from Bank USA, there is a much more efficient way to move money from Bank USA to Brokerage XYZ, and that's called a transfer. Best of all, the IRS allows as many transfers as you want per year. Unlimited it may be, but it would obviously be a pain in the neck to transfer money all over the place a few times a year. It would certainly be nice to have your money reside with one company and not have to move it around to other places.

To do a transfer, you'd typically *initiate* the process at the place where you want the money to end up. In this case, that's Brokerage XYZ. When opening an IRA account with Brokerage XYZ, a transfer form will simply give this brokerage the authority to contact Bank USA on your behalf.

Bank USA would then be required to transfer the IRA you have with it *directly* to Brokerage XYZ. This leaves much less room for error. Although neither the rollover nor the transfer is a taxable event, with a transfer, there is no 60-day ticking clock to get things done, and no possibility of early withdrawal penalties. How great is that?

Q. I reached the limit on how much I can contribute to my IRA and/or 401(k). Are there any other investments out there that offer tax deferral?

A. There certainly are. With an IRA maxed out, there are two types of investments that provide tax-deferred treatment just like an IRA does: Cash value inside an annuity and life insurance policies both offer tax-deferred earnings, and the amount one can invest in these contracts is generally unlimited. However, investments in an annuity or a life insurance policy are *not* tax-deductible like an IRA is.

Roth IRAs

Q. What's a Roth IRA?

A. A Roth IRA is a version of a traditional IRA with some key differences. To minimize confusion, Table 6.3 highlights the main differences between the two.

Table 6.3   Traditional IRA versus Roth IRA

	Traditional IRA	Roth IRA
Can anyone contribute?	Yes, up to certain limits as long as one has earned income equal to or greater than the contribution itself	Yes, up to certain restrictions
Are contributions tax deductible?	Yes*	No
Are earnings tax deferred?	Yes	Yes
Can earnings be withdrawn tax-free?	No	Yes*
Can I invest in common investments such as stocks, bonds, mutual funds, and CDs?	Yes	Yes
Are distributions required (required minimum distributions)?	Yes, starting at the year you reach age 70½	No
Are contributions after the age of 70½ permitted?	No	Yes

*Certain restrictions apply.

Q. Which one should I contribute to: a Roth IRA or a traditional IRA?
A. While everyone's situation is indeed different and there is no general answer for everyone, I personally believe that if you meet the requirements that enable you to make a contribution to a Roth, you should seriously consider investing in this first. Although there is no tax deduction, the beauty of *tax-free withdrawals* and no required minimum distributions when in retirement are quite compelling features the traditional IRA cannot compete with. But again, everyone's situation is different, and there could be a few reasons to contribute to a traditional IRA over a Roth. Check with a qualified advisor first. Unfortunately, when it comes to planning, there is rarely a perfect answer for everyone.

Q. Can I contribute to *both* a traditional IRA *and* a Roth IRA?
A. Good question. The answer is "yes," as long as the total combined contribution to *both* the Roth and the traditional IRA does not

exceed the combined contribution limit for that particular year. For example, suppose the maximum contribution for an IRA this year is $4,000. If I wanted to contribute to both, I can split the contribution. I can invest $2,000 into the traditional IRA and get the tax deduction. Then, I can contribute the remaining $2,000 into the Roth IRA but *not* get the tax deduction.

Q. I've heard the expression "convert to a Roth." What's that all about?

A. Subject to certain requirements, you can consider converting all or part of your *taxable* IRA to a *tax-free* Roth IRA at any time. While converting an IRA to a tax-free Roth might sound like a good idea, there's no such thing as a free lunch. Converting from a traditional IRA to a Roth IRA causes a taxable event in the year the conversion is made. Whether or not to convert depends on a number of factors, some of which are:

Factor 1: *Can* **you convert?** You may not be eligible to convert a traditional IRA to a Roth IRA. You *cannot* convert it if:

- Your income tax filing status is "married, filing separately."
- You inherited the traditional IRA from a non-spouse.
- Your modified adjusted gross income exceeds $100,000, regardless of your filing status as a single or joint taxpayer. (It should be noted that according to current tax laws, beginning in 2010 anyone can convert all or part of their IRA into a Roth IRA and spread the taxes owed over two years.)

Factor 2: How are you planning to use your IRA? This is another important factor to consider when converting your traditional IRA to a Roth IRA. On the one hand, if you intend to use the funds for your retirement, you may not want to convert, because doing so will cause the traditional IRA to be included in your income for the year of conversion, in which case it will be subject to income tax. You may instead want to keep a traditional IRA and preserve the tax-deferral opportunity, especially if you plan on using the money within a period of a few years.

On the other hand, if you don't need the funds for your retirement and you have sufficient assets to pay the income tax due upon conversion (most efficiently, from sources other than the IRA itself), you may want to convert to a Roth IRA and let the new earnings accumulate tax deferred. This way, your IRA can one day be distributed to your beneficiaries tax free instead of taxable as all IRAs are passed along.

Factor 3: Do you expect your tax bracket to change? Another factor to consider is whether you expect your income tax bracket to change during your lifetime. It may be difficult to see far enough into the future, but an educated guess can help with your decision. If you have low taxable income and are currently in the lowest tax bracket, it may make good sense to convert your traditional IRA to a Roth IRA now, because you will pay taxes on the conversation at a relatively low rate. However, if you have higher taxable income and are in a higher tax bracket, you may want to delay converting until you drop into a lower tax bracket, or not convert at all.

Factor 4: How do RMDs work for a Roth? A traditional IRA owner must take required minimum distributions (RMDs) every year once he or she reaches age 70½. But there is no RMD for a Roth IRA until after the owner's death (nonspouse beneficiaries of a Roth IRA must take RMDs). So, if you don't foresee wanting to take RMDs from an IRA, a Roth IRA may very well wind up being a better choice for you.

Factor 5: Is it likely that you will want or need to withdraw the money? A Roth IRA owner can withdraw all of the funds from the account tax free, for any reason, as long as the account has been held for five years and the IRA owner has reached age 59½, or meets other certain requirements. So, someone who converts a traditional IRA to a Roth IRA at age 40 cannot withdraw the entire converted amount without penalty until age 59½ or five years after the conversion. This may very well still make the Roth IRA more appealing than the traditional IRA. However, if the IRA owner is older than 59½ when the traditional IRA is converted to a Roth IRA, the account owner can withdraw any *earnings* on the account before the five-year waiting period is up (and get taxed on those earnings).

Should you convert your traditional IRA to a Roth IRA? As you can see, the decision to convert involves quite a few factors. There is just no simple answer. Yahoo! Finance offers a free calculator that can help you decide if converting a traditional IRA to a Roth IRA would be in your best interest, and I would very strongly urge you to consult a tax advisor before anything is actually done.

Q. Is there a better time than others to consider converting to a Roth?
A. Absolutely, and it is a consideration many people miss. If you determine converting to a Roth is a good idea, this is the rare moment

in the history of the stock markets that a bear market can be a good thing. Why? Well, consider that an overall bear market will *decrease* the value of stocks within your IRA. If you convert while the value is down, then you'll wind up paying less taxes on the conversion.

Q. Can I change my mind after converting to a Roth?
A. You certainly can. The IRS permits something called a "recharacterization." Simply put, you have until October 15 of the year *following the one when you converted* to turn back the clock and undo the conversion. For various reasons, this is a great safety net for Roth conversions gone wild. If a mistake is made, or you convert and simply later decide you want to turn back the clock and return everything to the traditional IRA, no problem. The IRS lets you do this via a recharacterization.

Q. I just determined converting my traditional IRA to a Roth is a good idea. How do I actually make the conversion?
A. First of all, who was it that determined converting an IRA to a Roth was a good idea? Depending on who that is, I would strongly recommend you double-check with a qualified tax advisor that you are doing the right thing. I've seen quite a few conversions in my lifetime that made little sense and went on to really hurt those doing them. Conversely, I've also seen many IRAs that I strongly believed *should* have been converted.

That said, converting from a traditional IRA to a Roth IRA is actually a very easy task. All it typically takes is a signature on a conversion form from the financial institution holding your IRA. Once the form is processed, voilà! With one wave of the IRS's magic wand, your traditional IRA is now a Roth IRA, with all the investments remaining intact.

The 401(k)

Q. What exactly is a 401(k)?
A. It's an employer-sponsored qualified plan that many companies offer, and it's the type of savings plan that over time often becomes an investor's largest asset. A 401(k) is somewhat similar to a traditional IRA in that the contributions are usually deducted off the top of your earned income. As of this writing, the maximum contribution to a 401(k) is $15,500 (the maximum is projected to increase to $16,000 in 2008). So, as an example, suppose this year my total earnings are

$45,500. Also suppose that during the year, I invested the *maximum* contribution of $15,500. This $15,500 comes right of the top of my earnings, making my total adjusted gross income not $45,500, but $30,000 ($45,500 less the maximum contribution of $15,500 equals $30,000). Many employers match contributions up to a certain limit, and these matching contributions are often done by adding their company stock to your 401(k). Automatic deductions from a paycheck plus matching contributions is hands down one of the most powerful ways to save for retirement and is something few people should ever miss.

Q. Can I contribute to *both* a 401(k) *and* an IRA?
A. You sure can, but there are limitations that may affect your eligibility to get a tax deduction for the IRA contribution and I'll use this current tax year as an example. I can contribute to an IRA and get a tax deduction only if my modified adjusted gross income (MAGI) does not exceed $62,000 if I am single; $103,000 if I am married and file a joint tax return; or $10,000 if I am married and file separately. If my MAGI exceeds these limits, I can still make the contribution to the IRA but I will not get the tax deduction. (A little complicated, I know, and I apologize for getting a bit technical but it's necessary to answer this question properly. To simplify, the answer is typically "yes, you can," but subject to certain restrictions as indicated above, you might not get the tax deduction.)

In this case, if I don't get the deduction from investing in the IRA *and* I meet the Roth IRA contribution requirements, then in almost all cases, I would strongly recommend considering a contribution to the Roth instead (given that one does not get the tax deduction on a Roth in the first place, but does give themselves the ability to take *tax-free* withdrawals after the age of 59½).

Q. I just left the company I was working for and I have a 401(k). What should I do?
A. In most cases, you can leave your money in the 401(k), but that is often not in your best interest. With rare exception, I often suggest someone set up an IRA at a financial institution, and then *transfer* money in the 401(k) into the IRA for any one of the following reasons:

1. *More investment options.* Some people feel that keeping 401(k)s with several different employers is a good way to diversify their

investments. In reality, most employer-sponsored retirement plans offer limited investment options. The limitation could put your retirement savings at risk, particularly if your investments are concentrated in just a few funds or in employer stock.

In contrast, IRAs offer a much larger variety of investment options, allowing you to better allocate your retirement funds in accordance to your Rule of 120.

On the flip side of this, every once in a while I meet a person who has an employer's retirement plan containing an investment that cannot be replicated anywhere else. For example, the New York Teachers' Union (at the time of this writing) maintains a fixed account that pays greater than 7 percent per year. A fixed interest rate such as this, that is not possible to find anywhere else, is great example of an investment that indicates someone should likely *not* transfer his or her money to an IRA.

2. *Efficient management.* If you have more than one qualified account, consolidating your retirement assets into an IRA can make managing and diversifying them much easier. For many people, having everything in one place simplifies the management process—sticking to the rules of diversification, rebalancing, beneficiary designations, and various estate planning needs.

3. *Too many funds?* A small savings of even half a percentage point in mutual fund expenses can mean thousands of dollars more in your pocket over a few years. If you'd like to see a demonstration, try using the mutual fund analyzer available at Morningstar or the Securities and Exchange Commission (SEC). Just go to www.sec.gov and click on "Calculators for Investors" under "Investor Information." When transferring money from the company plan into an IRA, one can take advantage of investments that are not commonly found in most 401(k)s, such as index exchange-traded funds.

4. *Bankruptcies and creditor protection.* Historically, money inside a company qualified plan account has always been protected from creditors and bankruptcies. As a result, many people wanted to leave their money inside the company plan, especially if bankruptcy lurked on the horizon. IRAs were different as their protection was based on state law. That all changed on April 20, 2005, the date when the Bankruptcy Abuse Prevention and Consumer Protection Act of 2005 came into effect. Under this new federal law, up to $1 million of assets held in

a traditional IRA and Roth IRA are now exempt from the IRA owner's bankrupt estate. Given this bankruptcy creditor protection, transferring 401(k) money into an IRA is now even more compelling than ever before.

Minimizing Tax on Withdrawals

Q. Is there any way to reduce taxes on withdrawals from an IRA?
A. Sort of. I know that's not the perfect answer, but when it comes to 401(k) matching contributions, there is one major opportunity many people unfortunately miss out on.

Many companies match your contributions to their 401(k). Often, the matching contributions by the employer are done in the form of company stock. When leaving the company, transferring this company stock into an IRA could potentially be one of the *worst* things you can do. Why? Because of a little-known gift the IRS gives us called net unrealized appreciation (NUA).

NUA is a complex subject, but I'll try to keep it simple and very brief: Suppose you combined your company stock *and* all other monies within your 401(k) to an IRA. Or you simply combined the entire 401(k) with an existing IRA that you spent years contributing to; assuming both the 401(k) and the IRA are in the same name, combining them can most certainly be done but may not be in your best interest for reasons coming up. After this transfer of your entire 401(k) into an IRA is complete, suppose you then sell the company stock your employer contributed. Assuming you are over the age of 59½ and you withdrew the cash from the sale of this stock, you'd pay ordinary income tax on the entire withdrawal, which is the highest of all possible taxes.

In doing this, you just likely paid the IRS much more tax than if you had separated the company stock within the 401(k) from all other IRA assets. By separating the stock within the 401(k) to its own IRA, you retain a very significant tax advantage called NUA: At some point in the future, when you sell the company stock, you will pay that nasty ordinary income tax only on the value of the stock at the time the contribution was made. As for profits above the contributed amount, because you kept the company stock separate from all other IRA money, you will pay long-term capital gains tax, which is currently taxed at 15 percent, an amount that is most often considerably less than ordinary income tax rates (that can be as high as 40 percent). The tax savings can be tremendous when taking advantage of NUA, and many advisors and investors often miss this truly fantastic possible tax break. (Note: To find out if your company stock has NUA nested inside it, I would suggest contacting a qualified tax advisor or your 401(k) plan administrator.)

Q. Are there any other ways to reduce or eliminate tax when taking a withdrawal from an IRA?
A. Not unless you want to flee the country to escape prosecution for tax evasion. Distributions from a traditional IRA are always taxable unless the distribution includes amounts attributed to nondeductible contributions—but there are several deductions or credits that could possibly help. Several tax credit programs are available that might be worthy of consideration, but these programs are rapidly fading away due to the nasty Alternative Minimum Tax (AMT) that often negates the credit. A tax credit is far different from a tax deduction in that the credit allows a dollar-for-dollar offset against taxes owed. The dollar-for-dollar tax reduction as a result of the tax credit can generally be used against any taxes owed, not just taxes from an IRA distribution. Keep in mind that a tax deduction only allows you to deduct an amount that is typically equal to your tax bracket.

After the Age of 70½

Life with an IRA changes quite considerably for those above the age of 70½. Here are a few questions that pertain specifically these people.

Q. Can I contribute to my traditional IRA after I turn 70½?
A. No, but as long as you have earned income, the IRS does allow you to make contributions to the Roth IRA as long as you meet the required guidelines as previously discussed.

Q. What is a required minimum distribution (RMD)?
A. The RMD is the amount you are required to withdraw from your traditional IRA. After many years of allowing tax deferral, the IRS wants to start collecting some taxes and the RMD is how it ensures it will start getting them.

The first distribution does not have to be taken out until April 1 of the year *following* the year in which you turn 70½. Each year following the first RMD, you'll have to continue taking a distribution regardless of whether you want to or not.

To calculate your RMD, you would need to divide the balance of the IRA at the end of the previous year by the number supplied for your age in the IRS' "Uniform Lifetime Table" found in IRS Publication 590 (available at www.irs.gov). However, if your spouse is more than 10 years younger and is the sole beneficiary of the IRA, you would use the IRS' "Joint Life and Last Survivor Expectancy Table."

I would suggest talking to a qualified investment or tax advisor to help provide you with more details on this important subject as well as how to figure out your exact RMD.

Q. If I begin taking distributions from my IRA before I'm 70½, will I still have to take an RMD the year I turn 70½? Or, can I take credit for previous withdrawals?
A. If you withdrew money from your IRA in years prior to reaching age 70½, your current balance might be smaller, but no credit is provided toward your RMDs. In other words, you cannot use an earlier year's *voluntary* distribution as a credit against a future year's *involuntary* distribution.

Q. I have several IRAs, a 401(k) plan, and a 403(b) plan. Do I have to include the 401(k) and 403(b) balances with my IRAs when determining my RMD?
A. Once the RMD is determined, it is most likely best to take the RMD of *each* plan. I mention "most likely" because the laws regarding RMDs are fairly complicated. If all your accounts are traditional IRAs, then technically speaking, you can take the entire RMD out of one account, but if a 401(k) exists, then the RMD from this account cannot be taken from an IRA. Again, this can get complicated, so I often recommend taking the RMD from each account or discussing the matter with a qualified advisor.

Q. I'm over the age of 70½ and am still working. Do I need to withdraw the RMD from my IRA(s) or old 401(k)s?
A. Yes. The only exception is that you would *not* have to withdraw the RMD from the 401(k) plan offered by your current employer (if you own more than 5 percent of the company, then this exception would *not* apply). That can wait until you are retired. Once retired, you'd then have to start taking the RMD from this 401(k) by April 1 of the year following the year you retired.

Q. I've heard of the stretch IRA or multigeneration IRA. What is that?

A. Suppose I pass away with an IRA. If I'm married, in most cases my wife will simply inherit my IRA and combine it with hers. But as soon as the IRA is passed presumably to my children, that's when the problems could really start. At best, my children will inherit my IRA and withdraw only the required minimum distributions based on *their* age, not mine.

Taking the required minimum distributions based on *their* age and not mine is what the stretch IRA or multigeneration IRA is all about. If they *preserve* the IRA as their own and let it continue growing tax deferred while limiting the withdrawals to only their RMDs, that's the "stretch." They are *stretching* the IRA over their lifetimes.

Is there a difference between the stretch IRA and the multigeneration IRA? Not at all. They're both the same thing.

Q. Is a child required to stretch the IRA?

A. In most cases, not at all. A child can decide to cash out the IRA and pay the taxes owed, which, as I reviewed in the chapter on life insurance, can be quite substantial. Not only will the child have to pay income tax, but estate taxes can also apply. It is not uncommon for a cashed-out IRA to lose anywhere from 30 to 70 percent of its value.

Q. Is there a way to prevent a child from cashing out the IRA?

A. Yes, but the subject is beyond the scope of this book. I would strongly advise seeing a qualified *estate* planning attorney to further discuss the different ways in which this can be enforced.

Q. If children cash out an IRA, what's the best way for them to pay the tax?

A. Life insurance is commonly used as a means to help a child to pay the tax upon cashing out an IRA. But there are far too many considerations that need to be factored into what's right for you. A qualified estate planning attorney can be of assistance in helping you determine the most efficient option given your personal situation.

Q. What is the best way for my heirs to inherit my IRA?

A. Similar to the answers provided in the previous questions, there are just far too many variables to consider when determining the best way to pass an IRA on to your heirs. Again, here I would advise seeing an estate planning attorney to help you determine the most efficient way to pass the IRA along.

IRAs are a complex subject. As with all other discussions regarding IRAs in this book, please be sure to consult a qualified tax advisor before any action is taken.

IRAs: Conclusion

Will this chapter on IRAs be included on your all-time list of memorable "first time" events? That's highly doubtful, but I do hope it provides at least some assistance in answering common questions that often arise regarding IRAs and employer-sponsored plans.

Time to take this movie's plot in yet another direction.

Mother Nature calling yet?

Care for another box of Junior Mints?

Someone in the theater snoring nearby?

Take a break, then let's continue to the next part of this movie . . .

CHAPTER 7

A Few Words on Taxes

I admit it. When I graduated from college and first started making some money, I used to go to my accountant's office at the end of each year and simply ask him, "How much do I owe?" He told me what I owed, and I wrote a check and walked out of the office not paying as much attention as I should have. All I knew about taxes was that I had to pay them and that if I didn't, I'd end up in jail or fleeing to Canada. Other than that, I honestly didn't understand much about them or care enough to take the time to learn more. It's not that my accountant didn't do his best to explain the return to me, but back in my early 20s, the story of last night's Jets game typically beat out a discussion about my adjusted gross income, the details of my deductions, or how I could have saved a few dollars in tax.

Shame on me. Back in those early years of investing, if I had paid more attention, I would have obviously had much more money in my savings accounts. If you find your attitude toward taxes similar to how mine once was, do yourself a favor—don't flip to another chapter. Whereas I understand a chapter about taxes could be about as interesting as watching my Pug sleep, no book about investing should be without a basic discussion on taxation and how it affects your investments. Understanding even a few ways to reduce your taxes can make a big difference in how fast you not only accumulate money, but how well you hold on to it.

Sadly, according to the non-profit group, the Tax Foundation, it's estimated that it takes working full-time from January 1 through Tax Freedom Day on April 30 just to pay your annual taxes. I hope

243

shedding some light on a few issues can help reduce the amount of time *you* spend working for the government just to pay your taxes.

Needless to say, the less you pay in taxes, the more you keep. Over the many years that you will most likely work hard to accumulate money, the more you keep obviously makes a big difference in your overall financial picture. After all, if I can give you a few pointers on a *risk-free* way to accumulate additional money at retirement by saving you some taxes, isn't that something you'd be interested in? Who wouldn't?

No one I know likes to pay taxes. While we all understand the need to help fund our government, most of us hope we pay as little as we have to. Prudent investment strategies, such as taking advantage of new tax laws and paying attention to your investment choices, can certainly help lower your tax burden.

If you haven't heard of the term *tax-efficient investing*, it's one that you should become familiar with. A tax-efficient investment is one that produces the least amount of taxable consequences. For example, a municipal bond or fund—whose income is free from federal and state taxes—might be considered tax efficient, whereas a managed mutual fund that is generating high taxes to us every year might be considered tax *inefficient*.

As you prepare for next tax season, you should mentally gear up to keep the tax efficiency of your investments in mind. While your investing decisions should not be solely based on tax ramifications of the investment, it is one more thing to consider when constructing, revising, or reviewing your diversified investment portfolios, especially in light of new tax law changes as they come up.

How Your Investments Are Taxed

No discussion on taxation should start without a review of some of the very basics. The goal of this section is to enable you to ask more informed questions of yourself, your investment choices, and your advisor.

The Different Types of Tax

To begin with, all investments are taxable in one of three ways: dividends, interest, and capital gains. Let's take a closer look at each, then move toward some tangible ideas as to how to keep Uncle Sam from taking more than his fair share during all stages of investing.

Dividend Tax

As we discussed, dividends are income distributions from a company's profits to its shareholders, and every time you receive a dividend, you pay tax. Currently, for most taxpayers, dividends are taxed at the highly desirable rate of 15 percent. For low-income individuals, dividends could be taxed even lower, as low as 5 percent.

Generating dividends is a sound strategy for many investors. Dividends, which were previously taxed at ordinary income rates, are now taxed at this lower rate, which makes them particularly appealing to investors for a variety of reasons we've discussed.

Curious to know how much dividend tax you are paying? Open your 1040 tax return form, look at the first page, Line 9a, entitled "Ordinary Dividends." If there is a number on that line, then yes, you are receiving dividends and paying tax on them. If you specifically told your financial advisor that you wanted to invest for growth and pay the least amount of tax, you may very well want to reevaluate your current investment strategy. I'll provide an example of this coming up.

If you want to know *where* these dividends on Line 9a are coming from, turn to Schedule B of your tax return, Part II, "Ordinary Dividends." The line items on this page will show you the places where you are investing that are generating the dividends being recorded on page 1, line item 9a. Where did the person doing your taxes find these? That's easy. It was summarized from all the 1099-DIV forms your investment company(s) sent to your mailbox during tax season.

As an investor, you have the option of receiving the cash or reinvesting the dividends, otherwise known as a dividend reinvestment plan (DRIP). In this plan, instead of the dividends being paid *to* you in the form of cash, they are used to purchase *additional stock* of the company that just paid the dividend. Some people refer to this as getting "free stock."

Either way you choose, you'll always be taxed on the dividends. When you set up your account, you should have been asked whether you want to reinvest the dividends or receive them as cash. A fair number of people aren't sure which one they chose or why it would make any difference.

Although there are many attractive reasons to include dividends within an investment portfolio, certainly not everyone will feel that way. Take, for example, a man named Andrew who lives in Miami.

In his late 40s, after a brief discussion about an investment he was curious about, he mentioned that he couldn't figure out why he just paid so much in tax when all he had in his brokerage account were individual stocks. After all, he hadn't sold or purchased anything that year; his stocks were just left alone. A few years back, an advisor at a discount brokerage helped him set up the portfolio, but he wasn't making much headway getting any answers from them. No trading was done that could have caused him to owe taxes, but over the past year, he finally took notice that he was paying quite a bit of tax on these stocks. While the solution might have seemed obvious to some, Andrew was stumped.

One look at his statements revealed that many of the stocks were generating cash dividends. As we learned, for investors living off their portfolios, this could be a powerful way to generate income. But Andrew didn't need income from his portfolio. He was living off his earnings from his job and wisely investing a few dollars every month toward his retirement.

The solution to his problem was simple. I showed him that many of the stocks in his portfolio were paying dividends—dividends that were creating taxable events. All he needed to do was to simply realign his portfolio from growth stocks that pay dividends to growth stocks that pay no dividends.

After we carefully evaluated the portfolio, we sold off various stocks that not only were creating taxable events through the dividends they produced, but those that weren't offering much growth as well. With his portfolio realigned to stock indexes, his tax leak was fixed, he has more diversification, and his investments are still in growth mode.

Ordinary Income

Interest earned from various fixed-income investments is considered taxable at your marginal tax rate, otherwise known as ordinary income tax. This type of tax is the least desirable, by all means. While I can't see falling in love with any tax, this is generally the worst of all taxes because interest earned from various fixed-income and other investments raises your overall income, and therefore the amount of taxes you pay. Ordinary income taxes are typically generated from investing in corporate bonds, CDs, and taking withdrawals from an annuity or an IRA—events that are all taxed at any one of the highest possible rates, currently 25 percent, 28 percent, 33 percent, and 35 percent.

Many people of all ages and all stages of investing have taxable interest included in their income, when in fact they aren't using the interest for actual income. To understand the damage ordinary income tax can do to your taxes, let's use an extreme example: Suppose I didn't work this year but I had $500,000 in CDs that generated 6 percent interest, or $30,000.

Although I didn't work, the $30,000 of interest generated from my CDs will show up as *income* I earned. So, although in this situation I didn't really work this year, the IRS doesn't exactly agree. According to the IRS, because of the interest being paid from the CDs, it appears as if I *earned* $30,000, and as a result, those CDs are going cause me to pay the worst of all taxes, that of ordinary income.

Curious to know how much interest you are generating from your investments? Take a peek at page 1 of your tax return (form 1040), line 8a, "Taxable Interest." This is the total of all taxable interest you've accumulated for the year. If you're wondering where all of this interest is coming from, turn to Schedule B of the tax return, Part I, "Interest." The line items at the top of the page list the places where you are investing and the taxable interest being generated from those accounts. At the bottom of that list is the total of all taxable interest, which is then summarized on page 1, line 8a.

Eliminating or reducing taxable interest on your investments can be done in one of a few different ways, such as investing in:

- *Municipal bonds.* Interest earned from a muni bond is tax-free on the federal level. In addition, if you invest in a muni issued by the state in which you live, you won't pay state tax as well (or, if you live in an income-tax-free state such as Florida, you can invest in muni bonds issued by other states and still maintain the tax-free nature of the muni). Surprising to most people in retirement, interest on a tax-free municipal *can* increase the tax you pay on your Social Security benefits; interest from a tax-free muni is factored into something called the IRS's "Provisional Income Formula," which is used to determine how much of your Social Security is taxed. When it comes to Social Security taxation, "tax free" does not always mean "tax free."
- *IRAs and Roth IRAs.* Interest earned inside these accounts always is tax deferred.

- *Life insurance.* Interest earned on cash value inside a life insurance policy is tax deferred. If structured properly, withdrawals from the policy's cash value can also be tax-free.
- *Fixed, index, or variable annuities.* Any interest earned in annuities is tax deferred and will not show up as taxable income until you decide to withdraw money from these accounts. For retirees interested in reducing tax on their Social Security benefits, I would suggest first discussing the situation with your advisor. One *possible* way of reducing your Social Security tax is to reposition investments such as bonds and CDs that produce *taxable* interest into investments that create *tax-deferred* interest such as fixed annuities.

Capital Gains

If I had to choose to pay one type of tax, this would be it, mainly because when I have to pay this kind of tax, it can only mean one thing: I made money on the *appreciation* of an asset, and when that happens, I do appreciate it quite a bit. When it comes to capital gains tax, we are most often referring to the sale of assets that went up in value such as stocks, bonds, or real estate.

If you sell at a profit, you generate a capital gain on only the profits I earned. Suppose I invest $10,000 into a stock and later sell it for $15,000. Assuming this was an investment made with money outside an IRA, the $10,000 I originally invested is known as the cost basis and the $5,000 is known as the appreciation or the gain. When I sell this stock, I pay tax on only the gain, not on the entire amount. Currently, if you hold the investment for longer than a year and sell at a gain, you'll pay capital gains tax of 15 percent on the appreciated amount. If held for less than a year and you sell the asset at a gain, the gain will be taxed at ordinary income rates, which are often higher than 15 percent. If at all possible, it's always best to keep an investment subject to capital gains tax for longer than a year so that when you sell it you pay less tax. For maximum tax efficiency, this is exactly why rebalancing a diversified investment portfolio typically makes most sense just after one year of holding the investments.

To illustrate why, let's look at the following example.

When Is 40 Percent More Than 50 Percent?

The answer is easy: 40 percent could be more than 50 percent when you are not paying attention to *tax efficiency.*

Understanding tax ramifications when selling assets is a very important concept to keep in mind, especially when realizing that "it's not what you earn, it's what you keep." Let's look at an example:

A man in the 35 percent tax bracket invests $10,000 in a stock that goes up 50 percent. *Before* holding it for a full year, he sells it for $15,000. When tax season comes around, he'll owe $1,750 in taxes on his $5,000 gain, leaving him with a net profit of $3,250.

Let's take a look at another person who *appears* to make a *lower* return, but in reality actually earns a higher amount when paying attention to tax efficiency.

In this example, a woman invests the same $10,000 in a stock but for her, it doesn't go up 50 percent in value as it did for the man in the preceding example; it goes up only 40 percent. While it might seem as if she made *less* of a return than the man did, if she *waits* one year to sell it (as opposed to selling it *within* a year) she actually keeps more money thanks to the lower capital gains tax when holding the asset longer than a year. In this tax-efficient scenario, the sharp woman sells the stock one year later and pays 15 percent on her $4,000 gain, for a total tax of $600, leaving her with a net profit of $3,400.

Although the man in the first scenario *appeared* to have a higher rate of return, the after-tax return for the woman is actually higher thanks to the lower taxes she paid, providing a clear example of "it's not how much you earn, it's how much you keep."

Offsetting Capital Gains Tax

Capital losses and capital gains can cancel each other out dollar for dollar in the year the gains and losses are recognized (the year an investment is actually sold, thereby causing a taxable event).

To illustrate how this works, let's look at a hypothetical situation. Let's suppose a woman has only a few stocks in her portfolio, and for now, let's pay attention to her IBM and GE stocks.

Since purchasing IBM, her shares gained $10,000 in value. However, she also invested in GE, which *lost* $10,000 in value. If she sold both stocks in the same year, she would pay no taxes on these transactions. Why? The $10,000 *gain* from IBM is canceled out by the $10,000 *loss* from GE.

Many people get confused about something called the "$3,000 carryforward" concept. However, it's an important concept to understand, especially when you rebalance your diversified investment portfolio filled with your stock index children.

Let's look at the preceding scenario a different way: Suppose that when the woman sold GE, it experienced a $16,000 *loss*. The first $10,000 loss of GE cancels out the $10,000 *gain* from the sale of IBM. But now there's $6,000 of loss leftover that has not canceled out anything.

Is this $6,000 loss gone forever? Can it cancel out any future gains? It sure can. Suppose in the following year another stock in her portfolio (call it AT&T) is sold at a $6,000 gain. In this case, the *entire* $6,000 loss from last year's sale of GE can be *carried forward* to cancel out AT&T's entire $6,000 gain.

Dizzy? Stay with me. I know this is a bit confusing, but it's important. There's one last important point.

Let's go back a step. Suppose that $6,000 loss from the sale of GE still took place. In addition, suppose in the following year there was no AT&T sold at a gain. In fact, let's suppose there was *nothing* sold that year. Can one do anything with that $6,000 loss from the prior year?

You can, but you can only do it with *up to* $3,000. In this example there are no gains to cancel out, but one is allowed to carry forward up to $3,000 of prior losses. In this case, the $3,000 carry forward would reduce income by the same amount (the $3,000, which gets recorded on line 13, found on page 1 of a tax return).

You or your investment advisor should work to offset gains and losses at the end of the year to help reduce your taxes, especially when incorporating the critical need to rebalance your portfolio.

If you want to find out more about the capital gains and losses that are taking place in your investments, check out page 1, line item 13, of your 1040 tax return form. This will give you the total amount of gains and losses for the year. To find out where these gains and losses are coming from, turn to Schedule D of your 1040 tax return. In this section, the accountant doing your taxes will record short-term gains and losses. As mentioned, these short-term gains are taxed at ordinary income rates. Below this area are your long-term capital gains, which are currently taxed at 15 percent.

Remember: Gains and losses are recognized only when an investment is actually sold. If you own a stock that went up or down in value, none of those gains or losses mean anything in terms of taxes until the sale of the investment actually takes place.

Summarizing the Three Most Common Taxes

While there are other types of taxes that can be generated from investments and reported on a tax return, dividends, interest, and capital gains are the three most common ones. To recap:

1. *Dividends.* Cash paid to you from stocks that produce dividends can be used for income or reinvested to purchase additional shares. Currently, dividends are taxed at the favorable rate of 15 percent. If you are using dividends for income, the low tax rate of 15 percent is certainly quite attractive. However, if you are not using your dividends for income and are looking for ways to reduce your tax, your best bet would be to consider repositioning the portfolio to investments that pay no dividends, thereby reducing taxable events.

2. *Interest.* Taxable interest is created from investing in places such as CDs and taxable bonds, causing ordinary income tax. Withdrawals from annuities and IRAs also cause ordinary income tax, which is generally considered to be the least favorable of all investment taxes. When interest is being generated from investments outside your IRA, the IRS simply thinks you are actually earning income. When it comes to paying taxes, this is usually not a good thing.

3. *Capital gains.* Capital gains or losses take place when investments such as stocks, bonds, or real estate properties are sold. Hold the asset less than a year, sell at a gain, and you pay ordinary income tax on the appreciation. However, hold the asset for longer than a year and, based on current tax rates, you'll pay only 15 percent on the gains, which is obviously preferable. If, however, you sell something at a gain *and* sell something at a loss in the same year, you can cancel out some or all of the capital gains tax. If there are more losses than gains, then the excess loss can be carried forward to the following year and cancel out any gains for that year. However, if there are no gains to cancel out, then up to $3,000 of the prior-year loss can be carried forward to reduce your taxable income by that same amount.

Confusing, yes. Important, absolutely. If you are going to be a tax-efficient investor, then knowing some of these basics will help get you where you want to go.

Having introduced you to the most basic of concepts, I would strongly advise you to spend an extra few minutes with your qualified advisor to learn further how investments are taxed and where they are recorded on your tax returns so that you can work to retain more of your earnings.

The Mutual Fund Tax Problem

For those interested in reducing tax, the first question I usually ask is, "Are you investing in managed mutual funds outside your IRA accounts?" Because managed mutual funds are so widely used, the answer is often "yes," and that's why it's the first place I typically look to try to help reduce the tax bite.

Ironically, to some investors, the answer isn't always so obvious.

Meet Joe. While we were discussing which individual stocks in his portfolio to keep and which ones to sell, Joe rightfully wouldn't sell a single thing unless we meticulously determined precisely how much tax it would cause him.

Joe was extremely tax conscious about his individual stocks, but he also had managed mutual funds that were generating a stream of taxes that were beyond his control. On one hand, he wanted to know all about the tax consequences of selling an individual stock, yet when it came to his mutual funds, he was ignoring the tax ramifications of stock trading left in the hands of others.

Remember: When you invest your money in a mutual fund, you are typically giving it to a fund manager who sits at that roulette table every day, moving your chips from one number to another. Every time he moves your money around, you could easily wind up losing a few dollars to taxes.

While Joe and I could be highly productive and efficient in planning for gains and losses from selling his individual stocks, neither of us had *any* control over what the fund manager was doing at the roulette table.

If you look closely at your tax return, specifically at Schedule B and/or Schedule D, you will see the taxable distributions various funds are potentially creating for that given year. The distributions from dividends or capital gains in these schedules will add dollars to your income. And what do the added dollars cause? Exactly what you think it does: By increasing your income, it can easily raise you into a higher tax bracket whereby you could wind up paying even more money to Uncle Sam.

Paying Tax on a Fund That Lost Value? How Is That Possible?

Some funds generate taxes even if they lose value. In fact, the taxation of mutual funds is sometimes *higher* in years when the fund *drops* in value, and many people don't quite understand how this can happen.

When the fund is going down, what typically happens? Many investors tend to panic and take their money out of the fund. When these requests for withdrawals come in, the fund manager must sell shares to raise money for the distribution requests. Stocks are sold, and if there are many requests for withdrawals, the fund manager will likely have to start selling stocks that he or she might not otherwise want to sell, such as the stocks that are going *up* in value. Selling the winners of the fund means capital gains taxes are recognized, leaving you to pay your share even if you didn't sell out of the fund. Keeping a fund that goes down in value but having to pay income tax may seem like something out of an episode of an IRS *Twilight Zone,* but it can actually happen.

Can it get worse? It can. Imagine this: You invest in the fund in November. A month later, in December, the scenario above takes place. Guess who might have to pay taxes that year when holding the fund for only a month? You, that's who. This is precisely why buying into a fund late in the year is usually not a good idea. Many (but not all) mutual funds make their taxable distributions late in the year, and regardless of when you purchased the fund—early or late in the year—you'll be responsible to pay any taxes owed.

Bottom line: Only the fund manager controls the taxes you pay when investing in mutual funds, and that's typically not a good thing. Keeping control of your investments and the taxes you pay is much more efficient when trying to maximize the returns generated from your investments.

Solving the Mutual Fund Tax Problem

If you find that your mutual funds are causing excessive taxes and you're looking to reduce the tax, here are a few ideas that can help:

Invest in Indexes, Not Managed Mutual Funds

Of all the strategies you can use to help reduce mutual fund taxation, this is my favorite solution because:

- In terms of return on your investment, indexes have historically outperformed most mutual fund managers trying to beat the benchmark index itself.

- Indexes typically cost much less in terms of fees than most managed mutual funds.
- Indexes typically are much more tax efficient than managed mutual funds due to the passive style of investing (where few, if any, stocks within the index are traded).

As mentioned earlier, you can invest in the indexes one of two ways: index mutual funds or my favorite: index exchange-traded funds (ETFs). As previously mentioned, there are a variety of differences between an index mutual fund and an index ETF. One of the main differences is that one can sell an index ETF during the day as opposed to an index mutual fund that gets sold at the end of the day. However, if you are adding money into your index on a regular basis, consider index mutual funds over index ETFs. Adding additional money to an index mutual fund typically won't cost you anything, whereas adding money to an index ETF will often incur transaction fees.

Sticking with Mutual Funds?

If you continue investing in managed mutual funds, here are two concepts that could make the investment more tax efficient:

1. Invest in funds with low turnover.
2. Invest in tax efficient funds.

As previously mentioned, turnover refers to the number of times a fund manager changes the holdings of the portfolio. If your fund has high turnover, chances are you're paying what could be excessive tax.

If you're not sure how many times the stocks in your fund are being turned over, I would highly recommend researching the turnover of your funds by visiting various web sites, such as www.morningstar.com.

Tax-Efficient Funds

Another alternative is to look for funds that are considered tax efficient. Managers of these funds usually adopt various tax-efficient strategies such as selling winners against losers at the end of the year to cancel out as much of the capital gains tax as possible. These funds not only manage your stocks, but they also look to keep taxes to a minimum. Tax-efficient funds can also include municipal bond funds that generate tax-free interest as well.

The One Time Receiving Money from Someone Is a Terrible Thing

Here's a trivia question: When is the one time someone giving you money is a terrible thing?

Any idea what the answer is?

Think about it for a moment. . . .

A bit tricky, right?

Any ideas?

Could there ever be a time when receiving money from someone is a bad thing?

Here's a hint: For many people, this terrible event when someone gives you money typically happens around April 15. In fact, right around that date, millions of people across the country get checks in the mail. And in many cases, those checks will be for hundreds of dollars, maybe even many thousands of dollars.

How awful is that?

Will you be one of the many unlucky people in this country to get a check?

By now you might be thinking, "Is this guy nuts? Why the heck wouldn't I want to get free money?"

As crazy as it may sound, I say, "Trust me. You don't want to be one of these people."

And why is that? Why wouldn't it be a good thing to get a check in the mail with no strings attached? Is it Ed McMahon's doing? Did all those unlucky people just win Publishers Clearing House sweepstakes?

Not at all. The check I'm talking about is something called a tax refund. And although getting these checks in the mail might first sound like a great thing, this is the one time when it's really not.

And why is that?

Simply because you aren't getting a gift, and you're certainly not getting free money. You're just getting your own money back. Sadly, many people don't realize this, and it's a real shame. All a tax refund really means is that during the year, you lent the government your money, the government received interest on it, and all you got back was your own cash. That's a great deal for Uncle Sam, a bad deal for you.

Would you give me a few thousand dollars, only to get the same amount back many months later?

Would anyone volunteer to do that?

Few people would unless they also got interest, but ironically, when it comes to paying taxes, many people make that interest-free loan to Uncle Sam year after year. Getting a refund simply means you overpaid your taxes; it's as simple as that. Either you had too much money taken out of your paycheck or you overpaid your estimated taxes, and that's not a good thing. Your money went working for Uncle Sam, not for you.

So, if you're getting a refund check, don't go spending it so fast. You'll only be spending your own money. To make things more efficient for yourself, don't kill the messenger bearing the bad news here—if you received a refund, be sure to review your estimated taxes or your withholdings with a qualified tax advisor. With few exceptions, you'd be far better off keeping that money for yourself and investing it to reap the rewards, not lending it to Uncle Sam.

In any event, many people do get a tax refund. If you're one of the "unlucky" taxpayers to get one, here are a few ideas on what you can do with it:

- *Invest the money in an IRA.* An entire chapter was spent on this subject, so I will politely move on and not repeat all that has been previously said.
- *Make an extra mortgage payment.* Your mortgage will probably be the largest expenditure of your lifetime, and paying even a little bit extra toward it each year can add up to substantial savings. For example, if you buy a $150,000 home and take out a $120,000 mortgage for 30 years at an interest rate of 9 percent, at the end of those 30 years, you will have paid over $227,500 *in interest alone*—in addition to your original $120,000 mortgage. Your total expense will be more than twice the original $150,000 price of your home.

Making even one extra principal payment every year will help lower your total interest charges. If you could pay an extra $100 each month, you'll save over $82,000 in interest—and pay off your mortgage nine years and two months earlier. Can't afford $100 a month? How about an additional $50 a month? That will cut your payment time by five years and seven months and save you $52,000. An extra $25 will shave off three years and three months, saving you $30,000. Even as little as an extra $10 a month will cut your mortgage payment time by one year and save you $13,500.

* *Pay off your credit card balances.* The preceding also applies to interest on consumer loans or any other kind of debt repayment, including credit cards. The national average for credit card debt is $7,000. At an interest rate of 18 percent, it could take over 29 years to pay that debt off. That's almost as long as it takes to pay off a typical home mortgage—or the length of time it will most likely take my N.Y. Islanders to win another Stanley Cup. The interest paid on the credit card account in that time would be around $18,400—more than two and a half times the original debt. Paying the debt off, or even paying it down, will no doubt save you a lot of money.

* *Hire a financial or tax advisor.* A bigger refund isn't necessarily a good thing. As mentioned, getting a refund simply means you over-paid your taxes over the course of the tax year, which means you've essentially lent money to the government—interest free. A tax or financial advisor can help you plan so you can keep more of that money in your pocket throughout the year.

* *Give your child (or grandchild) a gift that can last a lifetime.* Each state has adopted a Uniform Gifts to Minors Act (UGMA) or a Uniform Transfers to Minors Act (UTMA). This allows individuals—such as parents, grandparents, other relatives, and even friends—to set up a custodial account for the benefit of a minor. Let's assume a parent wants to help a 10-year-old child save for college, so they start investing $200 per month or $2,400 per year until the child starts college at age 18. With a hypothetical average annual return of 8 percent, the child will have $26,541 in a college account upon reaching age 18. If the child earns his own college money or gets a scholarship and the UGMA/UTMA account is left untouched until age 65, the child will have $832,882 in the account (again, assuming the investment continues to grow at 8 percent each year for 47 years—which is about the time it will take the Islanders to win their next Stanley Cup). There are other methods to save for college—529 plans and Coverdell Education Savings Accounts, which also have some great advantages. Be sure to talk to an advisor to help sort through the options.

Conclusion

Was this section painful? I hope not. I tried keeping it short and to the point. There's no doubt that a little knowledge on some basic tax issues can help your money go a much longer way.

Given there's nothing certain in life except taxes and death, let's take a few moments to address this one last dreadful thing . . .

CHAPTER 8

The Bottom of the Ninth

So there we were, a gathering of friends sitting together on a big couch in front of the big-screen, minutes away from celebrating the New York Yankees beating the Florida Marlins in the seventh game of the 2001 World Series. There was lots of excitement, pizza, soft drinks, and fireworks ready to explode. Even Lewis the Bulldog was caught up in the action.

For those of you who don't like baseball or don't remember the game, by the time the ninth inning rolled around, it was as certain as certain can be that the Yanks were going to win, not because they were up by a bunch of runs, but simply because the greatest closing pitcher in the history of baseball was out there on the mound.

To put Mariano Rivera in perspective, a few years back a writer for a major sports magazine asked a dozen or so managers, "If you had to pick *one* pitcher in the *history* of baseball to close a game for you, who would it be?" As I recall, nearly every one of them picked Rivera, and at this World Series moment in time, Yankee manager Joe Torre was no different.

With Rivera out on the mound, the champagne was ready to fly. The Series Championship T-shirts and hats were being pulled out of boxes, the fans were going wild, and I also remember hearing that the networks had boldly moved their cameras into the Yankee locker room to get ready for the incoming celebration.

It all sounded great, except for one thing: The Yankee celebration never took place. There, in the bottom of the ninth, the unthinkable happened. After a near-perfect season record, right then and there and in the moment it really mattered most, Rivera proved that he was indeed human and wound up blowing the game.

What's the Worst That Could Happen?

When it comes to your financial bottom of the ninth, I've unfortunately seen the same thing. What good is it to follow all the steps we've covered, build wealth, get yourself a great income during retirement, and then wind up blowing it all for your heirs? What good is it to have made and accumulated so much, only to see none other than Uncle Sam enjoy too much of it? Additionally, what good would it do to prevent heirs from getting it quickly and efficiently?

Yes, I've seen some of the best "closing pitchers" out there who managed to achieve great wealth blow it in the bottom of the ninth as well. Although they never lived to see their bottom of the ninth get blown, those who were left behind certainly did.

Here are a couple of quick examples:

- Jack dies with a $10 million estate. His kids have to pay $5 million in estate taxes. To pay the tax, they have no other choice but to sell off high-quality income-producing properties they would much rather have kept.
- A parent with a fortune in a 401(k) leaves it to his kids, who when inheriting it have no other choice but to lose an astonishing 70 percent of its value to estate and income tax when cashing it out.
- Two brothers who got along just fine all their lives end up bitterly suing each other over their mom's estate. Several years into the lawsuit and as of this writing, they're still fighting like cats and dogs.
- A son-in-law assigns his deceased wife's inheritance to his new bride.
- After a prolonged legal battle, a court-appointed guardian of an estate decides how the assets are to be divided.
- Following a death, a questionable creditor comes forward and lays claim to a multimillion-dollar estate. Years later, the estate is still tied up in the courts and a decision is still pending.
- A divorced daughter is forced to divide her inheritance with her ex-husband.

The list goes on.

Needless to say, these horror stories may not be the norm, but they very well *could* happen to you. Although they are all different from one another, there is one distinct common thread: *None* of the people involved ever thought it could happen to them. When it comes to your bottom of the ninth, I strongly believe the words "couldn't happen" should be completely eliminated from the dictionary.

Instead, consider this scenario:

You and I go out for a drive one day, and no thanks to my horrific driving, we end up on a cloud somewhere. Standing there, you look down below and watch the aftermath of your movie play out.

When it comes to your assets, what happens after you're gone? Does everything happen the way you wanted, or could things develop far differently than you ever imagined? Is it possible that the kids who got along so well all those years surprisingly wind up fighting over who gets what? Maybe things between the kids go just fine, but someone named Uncle Sam unexpectedly busts down the door with his burly gang and winds up ruining everyone's day. Does the grandchild get that education you wanted to provide for? Or did your son-in-law blow it all on the new Lexus and the 100-foot plasma?

While standing on that cloud, you are somewhat relieved; you read this chapter and, as a result, you left nothing to chance: no *questions,* only *answers* and *instructions.* Why? Because before you got into that car with me you *had an estate plan.*

So, take all those question marks (?) out of your movie script and replace them with the beauty of the exclamation point (!). When it comes to estate plans, exclamation points are a terrific thing. Taking the question marks out of your life and replacing them with exclamation points doesn't require a word processor; it requires an estate planning attorney to help you write down exactly how you want your movie to play out long after you're out of the picture.

Like Joe Torre *hoped,* a good estate attorney will *make sure* your bottom of the ninth doesn't wind up getting blown. Simply put, a good estate attorney will set up an *estate plan* that will dictate, no question marks allowed, exactly what happens to your assets after you're gone.

Typically, a rock-solid estate plan such as this is done with something called a living trust. While I am not an estate planning attorney, I have been around long enough to understand how these things work, why you might want them, and why harsh, unkind events, some of which were mentioned before, would most likely *not* have transpired if there had been an estate plan in place.

Unfortunately, many people put off estate planning simply because life is just plain too busy or they don't want to think about that occasionally annoying thing called "death." Some days I do want to think about that, like the time I smashed my head on the mailbox falling off my daughter's Razor, but that's not important right now. What is important is taking the time to plan right now—while you are able to. Doing so can certainly make the transition much easier for your heirs. You can also make certain that your assets are distributed according to your wishes and not as interpreted by a court-appointed guardian. Imagine a total stranger who works for the court trying to interpret who it was that you really intended on leaving your money to when you thought the will very clearly stated, "Jake gets the Bank of America account." What kind of interpretation does that require? Unfortunately, when it comes to the courts, there's always room for misinterpretation. I've seen it happen before, and it can get really ugly.

Some people incorrectly think they have a solid estate plan because they have a will. However, relying on a will as your estate plan brings forth some serious disadvantages. Specifically, before assets are distributed, a will can easily be contested. All it takes for problems to begin is for just one person to step forward and file a claim. If a claim is filed, the will could be processed in state probate court. This can be very time-consuming and frustrating. The worst part is having to eat court commissary food for as long as it takes to get your assets out of probate and into the hands of heirs. I've had to eat probate court commissary food, and let me tell you, it's something none of your family should ever have to endure. And the prices? Please. Add a few extra dollars and we might as well feast at Nobu.

Okay, all kidding aside, probate is frustrating, time-consuming, and expensive and leaves your personal financial situation open for scrutiny by the public. I once heard an estate attorney refer to probate court as his "lifetime pension," which is certainly not the type of legacy you want your assets to leave behind.

As if having a court-appointed guardian interpret your will isn't bad enough, there's more. Before a court grants the transfer of assets to heirs, public notices have to appear in the newspapers. Have you ever seen those notices? It's scary stuff. They are published to tell the world that you died, you have assets that are about to go to a handful of people, and if anyone wants to lay claim to any of it, speak now or forever hold your peace. Years ago, before I really knew why those notices were published, I remember wondering, "Why would anyone want to publish something so personal?" If one ever wanted to get in the paper, wouldn't it have been better to have done it before they died? Thanks to the probate court, a contested will might finally give someone a final chance to get their 15 minutes of fame.

Legally, the probate courts have to publish these notices. They must give everyone a chance to come forward and lay claim to your estate before it falls into the hands of beneficiaries. So, who really looks at these notices? Do uncles and aunts, plumbers and contractors, friends and foes constantly scour these papers wondering if today was the day I finally died and they'd get their $50 back? Not quite. The people who search these notices are often those who make a small living from filing frivolous claims knowing fully well there's a chance the recipients of the estate will settle just to get rid of the claim so they can finally get the assets out of probate. Imagine that—making a business out of filing ridiculous claims. Maybe I should just give up my day job and read the daily public notices in the paper every day. As sad as it is, there are some people out there who do this.

One attorney I know was *days* away from the conclusion of a two year probate process, about to get an estate released to his client when, out of the blue, some stranger showed up in court simply saying the deceased owed him money from a gambling debt. What happened next? A few *months* of additional court investigation delayed the transfer of the estate to the client, who really needed the money.

Thankfully, arranging your will so that your assets pass through a living trust typically shelters your estate from all this potentially ugly stuff, especially from your heirs having to eat court commissary food. The only bad part is that you'll never get your 15 minutes of fame, because no court is going to print your name in the newspaper. Bad humor aside, a living trust establishes a legal entity with the power to hold title to assets. In other words, assets are owned not in your personal name, but in the name of the trust. While it may sound frightening to have your assets owned by an entity, in reality it's a relatively simple process.

Anatomy of a Living Trust

A living trust is created and governed by the terms of a trust agreement. The agreement lists the assets held in the trust and names a trustee, who is the individual with the power to manage and distribute those assets. The trust also states the beneficiaries.

Assets in a trust are still yours and, depending on state law, you typically act as trustee while you are alive and make any decisions on what happens in the trust during your lifetime. When you die, or if you become disabled, the successor trustee named in the agreement will take over the management and distribution of assets in the trust according to the terms set forth. This successor trustee can be a legal advisor, family, or friend. Sorry, no bulldogs name Lewis allowed.

While there are many advantages to having a revocable living trust, three key reasons that come to mind include:

1. *Avoiding probate.* Assets inside the trust passing to beneficiaries avoid the probate process. As a result, distributions in accordance with the terms of the trust can occur relatively quickly after your death. Typically, assets passing through a trust take place immediately without any problems or court-ordered interpretation of whom you intended to get your estate.

2. *Fewer challenges.* Any unhappy heirs will find it more difficult to challenge the provisions of the trust. While wills and estate plans such as transfer on death (TOD) designations can be contested, if the will is part of a trust, any assets being passed through that trust in accordance with the will generally *cannot* be contested.

3. *Tax efficiency.* A properly designed and funded trust could help reduce estate taxes upon death.

Think of a trust as a safe. Inside that safe are a handful of documents, such as a will, that dictate who gets what after your death. Another document typically found in that safe called the trust is a power of attorney, which grants others the power to make decisions for you in case of health problems. You will also find a variety of other important documents not mentioned here.

Along with the documents in the safe are *assets*. You fully control these assets, such as brokerage accounts, real estate, and bank accounts during your lifetime, but when you're standing on a cloud with me, these assets are controlled by the instructions outlined in the will.

Not every asset belongs inside the trust. A qualified estate attorney can help determine which assets belong as opposed to those that should reside outside the trust. Accounts such as IRAs, annuities, and life insurance policies are typically *not* placed in trust. Beneficiaries are listed on these assets and, based on federal law, they bypass probate, allowing their proceeds to be turned over directly to the beneficiaries. However, there are a few reasons as to why you may still want to consider placing those three assets in a trust; only after meeting with a qualified estate-planning attorney should you decide whether to do so.

Of the other assets that can be probated, you and your attorney will need to carefully weigh whether they belong in a trust. Although any assets owned by a trust pass to your heirs probate-free, living trusts aren't for everyone. Establishing one requires the services of an estate planning professional, since the trust agreement is a legal document and is governed by law that varies from state to state. There can also be federal and state tax consequences, depending on how the trust is structured.

There are far too many different situations and personal circumstances involved for me to have a lengthy discussion on whether or not you really need a trust and, if so, which assets belong inside it. Besides, I am not an estate-planning attorney, and only this such person should be giving you exact advice based on your specific needs.

For this reason, be sure to consult with an estate-planning attorney to determine which structure would best suit you and your heirs. Just don't think for a moment, "I don't need a trust because I don't have a big estate." That could be a very serious mistake. A trust is not at all about the *size* of your estate, and it's certainly not "only for the rich people," as I've heard many people say. There are many reasons besides money that one would consider having a trust. If you have not thoroughly considered your own circumstances or received qualified advice from an estate-planning attorney, you could be doing yourself and your family a tremendous disservice. In fact, many estate-planning attorneys offer a consultation at no charge. Take the opportunity to find out whether or not it is worth having one in your case, and please, do not base your decision on the fact that the neighbor said you don't need one. When it comes to your estate and the many years you spent accumulating it, you're selling yourself short by not investigating the possibilities of how your bottom of your ninth can potentially get blown.

Five Estate Planning Blunders to Avoid

A quality trust can help ensure that you don't end up like Rivera did in the bottom of the ninth. If you decide to create a trust, or if you already have one in place, the game isn't over yet. With a good trust in hand, there is still a couple of outs left to go in the game before you've officially won.

With your trust in hand, the bases are loaded and the tying run is at third base. You have one out left to go before you celebrate your win. The only problem is, you have one batter left to strike out. Are you going to strike him out and win the game? Or are you going to blow it by walking him, allowing the runner at third to score?

When it comes to mapping out your financial afterlife, here are a few fastballs you'll definitely want to miss:

Ball 1: Forgetting to Fund It

In many cases, the process of creating a trust begins by meeting an estate-planning attorney who asks you a lot of questions. The interview typically tells the attorney how you want the end of your movie to play out. Once your script is written into a trust, you will receive a nice big book with all of the necessary documents. After you've signed the many pages and had your signature notarized, the attorney will remind you of a few things you need to get done; it's simple stuff, but it does take a few moments of your time, and this is where the batter could get walked.

Take for example, a guy named Rick. Hypothetical he may be, but stories like his have unfortunately played out many times.

Rick gets home from his meeting with the estate-planning attorney and all is well. He knows exactly what he needs to do to finish the job, but there's one very large problem that comes up with far too many people:

When Rick walks in the door, what happens next? He sees his significant other sitting on the couch watching the latest episode of *Grey's Anatomy*. Although TiVo can easily solve the problem, he tosses the trust on the kitchen table and kicks back to enjoy the show. This is where, if Rick is like me, the next problem arises: minutes into watching the show, his head tilts back and he's snoring from a hard day of work well done.

Annoyed because she can't hear the TV, his significant other leaves the room, as well as Rick sleeping on the couch. Then, somewhere around three A.M., a rerun of *Charles in Charge* jolts Rick awake, sending him to bed for the night. Because of a poor night's sleep, he oversleeps and forgets all about the leather-bound trust on the kitchen table. A few hours later, the cleaning lady or Rick's significant other takes the trust and tosses it into the hall closet, where it remains lost behind his high school Wilson tennis racquet.

Rick did a great thing in getting that trust done. But no thanks to *Grey's Anatomy,* one really big blunder occurred: He never got around to funding the trust.

Cut to many years later when Rick and I go out for that ill-fated drive down the I-95. A car cuts us off, and next thing, Rick and I end up on a cloud together. Although upset over missing next week's *Grey's Anatomy,* Rick says to me, "It's okay. I have a trust." Rick *thinks* all is fine, but one glance down below reveals chaos. Several heirs to his estate are fighting each other over many things: his bank accounts, those stocks in his 401(k) (that he unfortunately never bothered transferring to an IRA), his brokerage account, and yes, of course, his high school Wilson tennis racquet. Why is this happening? Like far too many people, Rick spent the time to get the trust done but forgot one very important thing: to *fund* it.

What does this mean? It means that before watching *Grey's Anatomy,* he was responsible for *changing the title* of those assets belonging in the trust to the trust's name. As an example, suppose Rick had money in the bank and his estate-planning attorney told him, "That asset should be in the trust." So, along with the trust, the attorney would have very likely also provided Rick with cookie-cutter letters that required him to fill in the bank account number and mailing address, then sign and mail them to the bank, brokerage, and so on to have the title of those accounts changed to the trust. But, all because *Grey's Anatomy* was on when he brought home the trust, he never really got around to sending those letters, leaving assets such as the bank account outside the trust.

With the assets out of the trust that should have been inside it, they are now potentially exposed to claims, potential additional taxes, probate, and a few other possibilities.

These days, trusts typically have something called "pour over" provisions that help eliminate this risk, but the bottom line remains: If you get a trust, before watching the next episode of *Grey's Anatomy,* make sure you *fund* the trust. Otherwise, there may be a chance it might not be worth much more than the paper it's printed on.

Ball 2: Penny-Wise and Pound-Foolish

An estate-planning attorney told me of a woman he once met with a moderate-sized estate. After thoroughly walking her through some estate planning ideas, she asked, "How much is it going to cost?" The attorney is reasonably priced, and he and his team do great work. He is neither the most expensive nor the least expensive lawyer in town. He falls somewhere in between. As a result of being fair, honest, and very knowledgeable, he has also earned a stellar reputation.

After being informed of the cost, the woman decided to "think about it" and would get back to him, but she never quite did. Instead, a few years later, the woman's son contacted the attorney to ask for his help. The trust his recently deceased mother created with another attorney wound up having had a few serious flaws in it. Simply put, some of the legal language in the trust was incorrect and there was one significant error in it that was going to cause some excessive taxes.

The son said his mom used a different attorney for one reason: a savings of $450. Now, I'm not going to berate a $450 savings. Everyone likes $450. And if the woman had used the more expensive attorney's services, there's certainly no guarantee that everything would have gone precisely according to plan. But to save $450 on a nice-sized estate with an attorney "out of the phone book" (as the son mentioned) certainly doesn't make much sense to me. Comparison-shopping will find you the best bargain only when you compare *all* aspects of the service: the professional's track record, references, credentials, and the price of the service.

There could have been other reasons the woman didn't choose to use the more expensive attorney, but in this case, the son clearly stated that the $450 savings was the only reason she chose to use someone else. In fairness, I'm absolutely sure there are some estate-planning attorneys who charge low prices and do fantastic work for their clients. But when it comes to having a trust created, one should obviously not consider price alone. After all, this is your *estate* we're talking about, and all it takes is one simple error to potentially blow the game in your own bottom of the ninth.

Ball 3: Not Protecting the Bloodline

Karen and Pete are good people. Now in their mid-60s, they spent a lifetime accumulating an impressive nest egg. As I sat with them one day, they started talking about their son-in-law, who had recently displayed a bad attitude at a family holiday event. He wound up drinking a bit too much and said some things that offended the family. During my conversation with him, Pete mentioned he was glad their trust ensured their money went to their daughter and no one else.

Upon hearing this, I suggested that they have the trust reviewed, not because I was second-guessing their attorney, but because many living trusts do not protect what is commonly referred to as "the bloodline." Many people have never heard of this concept of protecting the bloodline, and while I'm not here to tell you that you should care about it or it *has* to get done, I am saying that if you've never heard of protecting the bloodline, it is certainly a concept you should at least be aware of.

What is the bloodline? In Karen and Pete's simplistic family tree, they have a daughter who is married and has a child who is obviously their biological grandchild. Their intention is to pass their money down the bloodline, so it goes from them to their daughter, then to the grandchild. What about their son-in-law? Forget him. When it comes to the distribution of their estate, for them, this guy definitely takes a very distant backseat. They placed various assets in trust so that when they pass away, their money passes not through probate, but around it, landing right in their daughter's lap for her use and, later in life, passing to the grandchild.

This is where the bloodline can potentially get messed up: In most cases, their assets *in trust* are passed to their daughter *by name.* When those assets pass through the trust down to their daughter, she will do as most beneficiaries do: simply put the money in the bank so she can start using it for whatever she needs. As soon as that happens, who now owns that money?

In most cases, it's typically *not* the daughter; it's very likely the *entity* of her marriage that has the legal right to Pete and Karen's money. As soon as she starts spending money that can be attributed to the marriage, the inheritance is no longer likely owned by her, but the entity of the marriage itself. This is where the problems could potentially start when the bloodline is not properly protected.

The first thing that could happen is a bad old-fashioned lawsuit. Their daughter or son-in-law is sued for whatever reason, and the winner of the lawsuit reaches into the entity of that marriage and takes money out of the family bloodline. Not a good thing.

The next circumstance that could potentially mess up the bloodline is divorce. Unfortunately, there is a high divorce rate in this country, something that Pete not so secretly wished would happen between his daughter and son-in-law. In fact, several reports recently came out stating that there are now more single people in the country than there are married people. While this is great news for Match.com and Yahoo! Personals, it's terrible news for the institution of marriage. So the chance of a divorce is certainly out there. If it happens in Pete and Karen's family, their daughter could very well wind up splitting their money with the son-in-law, and I can assure you—no way do Karen and Pete want that guy walking away with half their money.

If that's not bad enough, there is another danger and this one is typically the worst of all. Because the money was placed in a bank account that likely become a marital asset, if the daughter passes away first, the money could easily move out of the bloodline and directly into their son-in-law's pocket.

This is the part of the story where years later, the son-in-law goes out for a few groceries and, while standing in the checkout line, sees a pretty girl. He says hello, and a couple of dates later they get married. Karen and Pete's son-in-law is now with a second wife, and she brings her own child into the relationship. Nothing against the second wife, but naturally, she'll be using her new husband's inheritance during the course of their marriage.

What about Pete and Karen's grandchild? Anything can happen to that child, the worst being if the son-in-law predeceases his second wife. If that happens, there's a possibility the money will go to *her* child, not to Pete and Karen's grandchild where they *intended* their money to go to.

Not good.

Months ago, I was talking to an estate planning attorney that was busy working on a case for children that were many thousands of dollars into a lawsuit, trying to get a multi-million dollar estate back into their bloodline. The attorney told me getting it back into their bloodline was going to be difficult to do, since the bloodline was not properly protected *before* the parents passed away.

If protecting your bloodline sounds important to you, be sure to visit an estate-planning attorney who can tell you if your heirs are properly protected in your trust. If you do not have a trust, you may want to consider getting one for this very reason alone.

Ball 4: Giving It to Uncle Sam

Several times during the course of the book, I have referred to this blunder. It can easily become the biggest one of all. As if dying wasn't bad enough, the IRS wants to make it even worse for you.

I can just imagine my last scene playing out: Lying there in the casket, resting peacefully, I feel the warm presence of my friends, family, and loved ones all around me with Springsteen's greatest hits playing softly in the background. Finally, after all those years of trying to get a good night's sleep, death delivers. Suddenly, some-one named Uncle Sam comes up to my casket to pay his respects. After saying a few nice words and humming Springsteen lyrics, Sam reaches his hand into my pocket, pulls out my wallet, looks inside, and gasps. Why? Because I'm a smart guy. I've seen this happen way too many times in my life and learned from the unfortunate souls who expired long before I did. I knew this guy Sam was going to stop by one last time before they buried me forever. Knowing he was going to make this one last visit, I made sure anything in that wallet went to my family, not to him.

For many people, however, their story has a very different end-ing. They forgot that Uncle Sam stops by to pay his last respects. Yes, sad but true; when you die, Uncle Sam makes one last visit to see if you owe him anything. Here's how it generally works:

At the time of this writing, everyone has an estate tax exemption of $2 million when they die. If I died with less than $2 million, Sam gets nothing (in regard to estate tax; other taxes might apply). But anything over $2 million is typically taxed at the current estate tax rate, which can be as high as a whopping 50 percent (federal tax and other possible taxes combined). There has been a lot of talk recently about this rate changing, but so far nothing has been done to offi-cially change it. Is it possible that the estate tax will change? Absolutely. Is it likely it will be eliminated? Have you seen the federal deficit?

Do you think the government is going to get in the black anytime soon? I certainly don't think so. While the estate tax might very well change, many of us doubt there is *any* chance it's ever going away.

Let's take a quick look at how a trust can help reduce estate tax.

Suppose I die with an estate worth $3 million. Because of the $2 million estate tax exemption, the first $2 million goes to my heirs estate tax free. However, the $1 million above that can be potentially taxed at 50 percent. Within nine months following my death, in this hypothetical scenario, my kids would have to pay $500,000 in estate taxes (50 percent of the $1 million above the first $2 million exemption). This is obviously not a good thing for my heirs, especially if my assets are in real estate or another illiquid form. This is where something as simple as a life insurance policy's death benefit might be a great gift to my kids when I die. It is certainly one way of paying the estate tax, although there are other options that could very well work more efficiently due to your own personal situation.

I've been a part of a handful of cases where the lack of an estate plan has really hurt a beneficiary. As an example, suppose my wife and I never created an estate plan. We didn't bother; we saw it as a waste of time, or something we'd deal with later but never quite got around to. Or maybe we just felt the kids should just get whatever is left. "Who cares what the tax is? Let the kids get what they get. I had to fight for myself; so should they." Some people have these opinions, and I am certainly not here to judge.

But in some cases where no estate plan has been established, here is what could very well happen:

Suppose my wife and I have a $3 million estate.

I die with no estate plan in place.

The $3 million goes to my wife with no estate tax (no estate tax is owed when assets are transferred between husband and wife. Estate tax applies only when assets get transferred to the next generation or other heirs).

My wife now owns the entire $3 million estate.

Assume she dies when the estate is still worth around $3 million.

Our kids get the $3 million.

The current estate tax exemption is $2 million. Anything above that, in this case the $1 million, can be estate taxed up to 50 percent. So, on the $1 million above the $2 million, they pay 50 percent tax, or, as mentioned, $500,000 in total estate tax.

In this hypothetical case, their *after-tax* inheritance is therefore $2.5 million.

With an estate plan in place, here's where the investment of a trust could have saved the children from paying that $500,000 in tax. Let's look at how that scenario would play out with a proper living trust in place:

Suppose we have a $3 million estate.

I die *with* an estate plan in place—presumably, a living trust that splits the estate, sometimes referred to as a split trust or an A/B trust (above ground/below ground).

In this case, the entire $3 million estate does *not* go to my wife. Because of the way our estate plan was arranged, via an A/B living trust, *half* of that $3 million remains in my part of the estate. Even though I'm sitting up on a cloud somewhere, $1.5 million stays in my name. Even if it's in my name and I'm gone, my wife generally has control of it. She can make decisions on how it is invested, withdrawn, and so forth. The other half of the estate, the remaining $1.5 million, remains on her side of the estate. Simply put, even though I'm gone, the estate remains divided between us and stays that way.

Years later, she joins me up on the cloud.

But, compared to the first scenario, instead of the kids getting the $3 million from her side only, they get it from my side *and* her side. Because we split the estate between us and kept it that way, each side *retains* the (current, as of this writing) death tax exemption of $2 million. So, if each side of the estate retains its estate tax exemption of $2 million, and each side passes money that is *less than* that amount, then in this case the money each side passes to the kids is *exempt* from any estate tax.

In this scenario, the kids get the full $3 million ($1.5 million from each side) *without having to pay any estate tax*. Because of the way the living trust was designed, the kids saved $500,000 in taxes all because of one thing: We took a bit of time out to create a trust, do an estate plan, and skip *Grey's Anatomy* to ensure it got properly funded. In this case, a small amount of money invested to create a trust saved my kids $500,000 in tax, which is certainly not a bad return on our hypothetical investment.

As you can see, a little planning can really go a long way. As mentioned, some people have the philosophy of "Why bother? The kids will get whatever they wind up with." To each his own. However, having seen kids sit around a conference table writing checks out to

Uncle Sam, I can't help but cringe, because doing this is often really hard on them. Many ask, "Is there a way to reduce or avoid writing this big check?" Not really. Not if there wasn't an estate plan in place.

Personally, I'm up for supporting government. But we're talking about *family* here, or a charity, friends, a hospital, a church, or a university. *Someone* in your life I believe should get the money over the IRS, shouldn't they? So, why wouldn't you make sure a simple living trust combined with other estate planning tools helps ensure the blunders don't take place?

Ball 5: Not Protecting Your Assets

Ball 5? Okay, so there are only four balls in baseball that could wind up blowing the game by walking in the winning run, but in the game of life, there could very well be many more.

When it comes to the fifth ball, one of the blunders I've seen is the failure to protect your assets. As I'm sure you know, we unfortunately live in a highly litigious society. You didn't need to read my book to learn that. While we live in a fantastic country, the sad fact is that here anyone can sue anyone for just about anything. Somewhere, someplace, I heard that the United States accounts for around 70 percent of all lawsuits in the entire world. I can't honestly remember the exact percentage, but I know it was ridiculously high; 70 percent might even be *lower* than the actual number.

I don't need to go into details here, as we've all heard of or perhaps been part of some frivolous lawsuit. Sadly, I've seen a few people in my career lose more money due to a frivolous lawsuit than they ever did in the stock markets.

A few months ago a nice woman came up to us following a presentation to ask if I knew an attorney who could help protect her assets. She was driving in a car with her best friend and wound up getting into an accident. No one was seriously hurt, but there were some significant medical bills that needed to be paid. The woman standing in front of me was just served with a lawsuit from—you guessed it—her *best friend*.

Sad, but true.

Typically, when someone thinks about suing, they will first see an attorney. To determine the potential value of a case, some attorneys will first do an asset search to see what you have, where it is, and how much it is worth, including the amount of equity in your house. If anyone ever does a search for your assets, the best-case scenario is they find nothing. Or they find a few things that they can't get their hands on. The simple rule is: The less you have, the less likely it is that attorneys and their clients will sue you. No one wants to spend money on a lawsuit only to find out that they can't get blood from a stone. This is by no means a guarantee that you will never get sued, but it's certainly logical that the less you have, or the less you *appear* to have, the less motivation someone might have to go after you, especially if it's for a frivolous reason.

Asset protection happens in a number of ways. My personal favorite is to do it through Swiss annuities or trusts through foreign lands such as the Isle of Man; I believe both offer fantastic asset protection as well as excellent diversification for currency hedges (Swiss annuities are vastly different from American annuities—do not remotely confuse the two). Limited liability companies (LLCs) can do it as well. Other ways of protecting assets could include investing in various insurance products, encumbering a house, placing money into a spouse's name, or other various offshore trusts.

Some people assume that liability insurance policies will cover them. While these can certainly protect you, there are some cases where, (no) thanks to a loophole or two, the policy doesn't quite do the job or the settlement is higher than the insurance coverage. The bottom line here is obvious: If you have assets you want to protect, seeing an attorney to make sure they are indeed protected is yet another way to avoid a potential blunder.

Asset protection is a highly specialized area of the law that could very well make an estate-planning attorney *not* be the right person for the job. I know of and deal with several attorneys who specialize in asset protection, and, depending on your needs, perhaps you should see one to discuss this issue.

Enough about the Yankees, bad driving, and dead people. Let's liven the subject up a bit by moving on to something a bit more pleasant.

CHAPTER 9

Support and Maintenance

Ever hear of Hank Haney? Chances are you haven't. But you may have heard of his student: He's a golfer out there who goes by the name of Tiger Woods.

Yes, even the world's greatest golfer can use a few tips and someone to help watch over his game, and when it comes to investing and your overall planning, things should be no different. I hope you've learned a few things during the course of this book that will help make you a better investor for years to come. But if the greatest golfer in the world could use a coach, then when it comes to investing and planning, certainly you might consider having one as well.

Many people are already working with a financial advisor. Others have not thought of doing such a thing but for various reasons they may consider doing so in the future.

When it comes to working with or hiring a financial advisor, there are a few things you should know, and that's what this chapter is all about. First off, according to some estimates, roughly half a million people in the United States call themselves financial advisors. But not all are. By legal definition, a stockbroker is not a financial advisor. At the time of this writing, the definition of a "financial advisor" remains quite murky, and there are a lot of heated debates going on as to whether someone can use the title of "financial advisor" when, in reality, all they have is a stockbroker's license.

Qualifications

So how do you know if the person you're considering is qualified to fit the bill? Is the stockbroker qualified? What about the woman who calls herself a "CFP," or the guy across the street who has the title of "investment advisor" on his business card? What does all that stuff mean?

Navigating the financial planning waters can be pretty tricky. A strong recommendation from an entrusted friend is always ideal, but that's sometimes as difficult to find as a good blind date.

With that in mind, here are some key points to keep in mind when making your decision:

What do the acronyms following the advisor's name (if any) really mean? It's important that you understand the alphabet soup. The letters following a financial advisor's name can stand for education, experience, or registration with a trade association. But keep in mind: Having a long string of letters after their name *doesn't* mean they are fantastic financial planners. To put it bluntly, some of the worst investment blunders I have ever seen were created by advisors who had the most acronyms, validating the old adage, "Never judge a book by its cover."

Financial designations are the bunch of letters you may see after an advisor's name. While having a lot of letters after their name means they are likely well educated, in no way does it mean they are the best person for the job. As mentioned, some of the *worst* financial plans I've seen that destroyed clients' lives were from advisors with as many letters after their names as there are letters in the alphabet. So, don't consider a lot of letters or no letters after an advisor's name the end-all criterion by any means. Needless to say, having a financial designation should be just one of many criteria in hiring the person you feel is right to assist you.

Here is a list of common letters you might find following an advisor's name, and what they mean:

- *CFP—Certified Financial Planner.* CFPs have obtained three years of financial planning experience, passed several exams, and meet continuing education requirements. They can offer a broad range of advice on financial planning, investments, insurance, taxes, retirement planning, and estate planning.
- *CFA—Chartered Financial Analyst.* CFAs have earned a college degree, completed at least three years of study, been tested by the Association for Investment Management and Research, and

meet continuing education requirements. They are generally money managers and stock analysts.

- *ChFC—Chartered Financial Consultant.* ChFCs are typically life insurance agents who have completed coursework in financial planning, passed an exam, and obtained three years of financial planning experience. They generally provide all-around financial planning with an emphasis on insurance.
- *CPA—Certified Public Accountant.* CPAs are required to pass a rigorous national exam and meet continuing education requirements. They can advise you on income tax, investment, and estate planning issues.
- *PFS—Personal Financial Specialist.* PFSs are CPAs who have received accreditation from the American Institute of Certified Public Accountants (AICPA). This accreditation requires that a PFS prove financial planning experience, pass an exam, and submit references every three years.
- *RIA—Registered Investment Advisor.* RIAs are usually financial professionals, such as accountants and insurance agents, who have registered with the Securities and Exchange Commission (SEC) or individual states. The title does not constitute an endorsement by either or require an adherence to a code of behavior.
- *RR—Registered Representative.* RRs have passed a qualifying exam administered by the National Association of Securities Dealers (NASD). They are generally sales representatives for a brokerage firm. Their expertise is usually in selecting and monitoring stocks, bonds, mutual funds, and other financial products.

Is this person really a financial advisor? Know what's behind the "financial advisor" title. Many stockbrokers call themselves financial advisors when in fact they are not. According to the letter of the regulatory law, only a Registered Investment Advisor (RIA) and a Certified Financial Planner (CFP) have truly earned the title of being a financial advisor due to licensing and educational requirements.

What licenses does the financial advisor hold? The National Association of Securities Dealers (NASD) works to protect the public by requiring individuals to pass a Registered Representative exam before they can sell a securities product. The two major exams and related licenses are the Series 6 and Series 7. A financial advisor who holds a Series 6 license can sell only mutual funds, which is fine if that's all you want to ever invest in. But a financial advisor who holds a Series 7 license can sell you many types of securities (except commodities and futures), which inherently should provide you with more investment options when working with such a person.

Getting an understanding of the licenses your potential advisor holds is an important step to the decision-making process. I'll go into a bit more detail on this shortly.

Has the financial advisor explained risks and rewards? There is no such thing as the perfect investment, and a good financial advisor will explain that. If it were my money, I wouldn't work with anyone who claims to have the "perfect investment" or doesn't very clearly explain the advantages and disadvantages of what he or she is recommending. No disadvantages discussed? Then it's simple—walk away.

How is the financial advisor paid? Some financial advisors are paid by commission; that is, they earn a percentage of every transaction they make on your behalf. Some are paid a flat fee, which is often a fixed percentage of the assets they manage for you each year. Some are paid by the hour. And some are paid by a combination of commissions *and* fees. Be sure you know how the financial advisor you are considering is going to be paid and how much he or she charges. A good financial advisor will also explain any additional fees, such as those you might pay for any load funds that are purchased for you.

Generalizing which type of fee arrangement you should consider is very difficult. Everyone's situation is different. What might be right for one could be entirely wrong for another. But understanding the fee arrangement and how the advisor is getting paid is critical before any commitments are made.

Therefore, when considering how your advisor is paid or should get paid, all aspects of the relationship and investment strategies have to be considered, and certainly not just one general comment from a friend or an article in a newspaper.

Interviewing Your Potential Advisor

As you most likely found out during the course of this book, investing can be a tricky thing. As a result, I believe that many people can benefit from discussing their options with a qualified financial planner, and by financial planner I don't mean a broker whose only interest is obtaining a commission on a financial product. I'm referring to a professional who will assess every aspect of your financial life—from savings to investments to insurance—and help you develop a detailed strategy for meeting all your financial goals by using a wide variety of products, and certainly not just one thing.

It's usually not too difficult to find financial planners in your area. The same can be said for finding a date. While there might very well be a large number of single men or women out there, it's not so much the *finding* of a date that's difficult; it's finding a *good* date that can sometimes be downright impossible.

You can look through listings in the phone book, which is certainly not the best way to go. At best, recommendations from friends and colleagues can be of help. In many areas, financial advisors market themselves through public seminars, and it couldn't hurt to listen to some of these people in action. But how do you know which one to hire?

Before deciding on a financial planner, you should interview several, and you'll want to ask questions about their education and experience. But most people know this. What's more difficult is interviewing financial planners about their investment approaches and fee arrangements—two subjects that may be closely tied together.

These two topics are more difficult to discuss because financial planning services vary widely. Some planners offer only investment advice, some offer estate planning, and others even do your taxes.

The fee structure that financial planners use to charge for their services also varies widely. Some charge either a fixed or an hourly fee for the time it takes to develop your financial plan, but they don't sell investment products. Some simply receive commissions on the products they sell. And still others are paid by a combination of fees and commissions.

When hiring a financial planner, then, it's important to know in advance what services you think you'll need and what services the planner can deliver—and to ask how much those services cost, as well as how the planner gets paid. For example, if you need a comprehensive investment plan but are willing to invest your funds yourself, a financial planner who charges by the hour may be your best choice. After obtaining a clear understanding of your financial goals and risk tolerance, the financial planner will develop an asset allocation plan for you—that is, tell you how much of your money you should have invested in different asset classes such as stocks and bonds. He or she will then typically recommend specific investments to help you achieve that asset allocation, but you'll do the actual investing yourself.

However, if you already have a number of investments with different firms and you want a financial planner to manage your money on an ongoing basis, and maybe even assist with estate planning, you may want to consider a planner whose fees are asset-based. In other words, as mentioned before, you pay the planner a percentage of the assets you have invested on an annual basis, and the planner provides all the services you need. In this case, it's important to understand what you're getting. Exactly what services will the planner provide? How regularly will the planner provide those services? Will you always be working with the planner directly, or will other people be involved?

Finally, and I believe this is likely the most important of all suggestions here, you'll want to listen to how each financial planner answers your questions. Does the planner seem genuinely interested in learning more about your personal situation, such as your risk tolerance, before making any recommendations? Does he or she clearly express that there are no guarantees when it comes to most investments or does it appear that one size fits all?

Remember, you're looking for someone who will tailor a financial plan for *you* and won't over-promise more than he or she can deliver. Forget about the planners who make everything sound way too easy, such as getting you returns of 20 percent per year with little problem. Those are just accidents and train wrecks waiting to happen. If you don't feel comfortable with a planner you're interviewing, for any reason, interview someone else. This is a person you'll ideally want to be working with for a long time to come.

10 Things Some Advisors Would Rather You Didn't Know

Are you currently working with an advisor, thinking about it, or in the process of interviewing? This section can certainly be of help.

As you know, every profession has its good and bad practitioners. Many doctors save lives, but a few have wound up really hurting their patients. Financial advisors are no different. Most financial advisors I know do a stellar, honest job trying to do the best for their clients. Many have literally "saved lives."

But there are certainly others who have done harm, and that's a real shame. As a result of stories such as these, it's no doubt that some people have a hard time finding an advisor they can trust, or, in some cases, refuse to trust *anyone* at all.

Sometimes, walking into a financial advisor's office might feel like the way I used to feel when walking onto a new car lot: guarded, trusting no one, and wondering how the heck the guy with the big grin on his face and American flag on his lapel was going to royally screw me without me knowing about it.

But one thing that really helped me was a cheat sheet a friend of mine who once sold cars provided me with. Before going on the lot, this one time sales manager for a large car dealership gave me a few quick tips on things to look out for. With my cheat sheet in mind, at least I felt I had some inside information that gave me a bit of an upper hand on anyone who wasn't looking after my best interests.

As it turned out, purchasing my new car was a great experience. The guy with the big grin on his face didn't wind up screwing me at all. In fact, he helped me get the best deal for the purchase. He was completely honest and had no problem telling me where he was making his money, how the dealership was making it, and what the advantages/disadvantages were to whichever plan I was considering. It was an enjoyable experience, but there's no doubt that when I went to price out that new car, having the cheat sheet in mind made me feel a lot more confident knowing what to look out for.

So, with that, here's a little cheat sheet on things that if I were you, I'd certainly watch for. Don't think that all these things are bad or evil. Quite the contrary. Being aware of them can be very helpful to an investor's relationship with an advisor. But if any of these things come up during your relationship, at least you can go into them with eyes wide open so that there are no surprises later on.

So, in no order of priority, here goes.

#1: Anchors. A proprietary product is an investment that is offered and distributed by the same brokerage you are currently with. Only clients of that brokerage can invest in that product, which is often a mutual fund. While that may indeed be a privilege (some proprietary mutual funds have great track records), I find many have higher than average fees and their performance is lower when compared to other funds in the same category (i.e., the class of fund such as large-cap value, mid-cap, etc.).

Confused? Let me explain a bit further. I mentioned this earlier in the book, but it's worth repeating: Suppose the name of the brokerage is Alan Haft Brokerage and it offers Alan Haft Mutual Funds only to clients of the same firm. These Alan Haft Mutual Funds are therefore *proprietary* mutual funds; only clients of the Alan Haft

Brokerage can invest in that fund. Proprietary products are often mutual funds but could be other products as well.

If your advisor, or potential advisor, is recommending you invest in a fund that is proprietary, before agreeing to invest in it (as with any investment), I would recommend doing an overly careful analysis of the fund by comparing it to others in the same category. For example, ask your advisor recommending the proprietary mutual fund how it ranks when compared to others in the same category and ask him to show you the differences on a Morningstar report (as mentioned during the course of the book, Morningstar is known for its objective analysis of mutual funds).

Proprietary products have a few other potential disadvantages. One main disadvantage is that if you are not happy with the firm or your advisor and want to *transfer* the account to another firm, you will often have to sell the proprietary product before doing so. The reason for having to do this is simple: Only the firm offering the proprietary product can maintain that security in its accounts; in most cases no other firm can do so. Maybe you don't mind selling the proprietary product because of poor performance. But if you want to keep your money in the proprietary product *and* transfer the brokerage account somewhere else, this often cannot be done. In addition, having to sell the proprietary product might also incur a sales charge or taxable event, which is usually something someone doesn't want to be forced into.

Knowing this, it's certainly something to consider before investing in a proprietary product. As mentioned, the proprietary product could very well be in your best interest and something that can do a great job for you, but at least you are aware of the potential problems should you decide to make a change to a different firm.

Similarly:

#2: Extra Services. Some brokerages offer extra services such as on-line bill pay, banking, and even things such as shopping points (similar to frequent-flier miles where the brokerage gives you points that can be redeemed for various incentives). While these extra services are no doubt convenient and potentially rewarding, I typically recommend staying away from them.

Why? Well, think about it. The more extra services you take advantage of, the harder it would be to break away if you're unhappy with the advisor or firm. After all, imagine this: You switch over all your bill-paying services to a brokerage, and a few years later, after your entire life is running through the brokerage, you want out. The investments aren't doing well, or perhaps you move and want some local support. With all the excess services you've signed up for, leaving might not be as convenient as you'd like. With that, I recommend taking advantage of as few extra services as possible, and keeping these services independent of the place that manages your investments.

Or, better yet, before switching everything in your life over to these extra services, at least give the relationship ample time to mature. There's nothing wrong with waiting to make sure the relationship with the firm and your advisor is a marriage built to last.

#3: Custodian of the Account Is the Brokerage Itself. For convenience, some brokerages may offer to be what's known as the "custodian" of your investment, often in accounts such as a variable annuity. It's still yours, but the brokerage could be listed as something such as the "co-custodian." For servicing the account, having the firm listed as the custodian can be a convenience, but as with extra services such as bill pay mentioned above, should you decide to leave the firm, the brokerage serving as custodian could make transferring your account away more difficult. It's for this reason I stick with the same advice: Before allowing this to happen, make sure the relationship you are in is a marriage built to last, and just not another blind date.

#4: Selling the Account. Many brokerages offer "managed account" services. When first investing in the managed account, often the account will start with your investments in cash. From cash, the money managers will then start the investing process, which is usually on what's known as a discretionary basis, meaning they can buy and sell stocks, bonds, and other investments in the account without having to first ask your permission. These types of accounts are almost always *not* commission based, but fee based (for example, a 1 percent annual fee charged on the amount of your assets under their management).

While many of these accounts could be a good strategic choice for the investor, if things don't go well and you want out, in some cases you won't be able to transfer the account without first having to sell off all the positions, which could cause adverse things such as unwanted taxable events.

Investing in an account that would require you to sell it all before leaving should not imply "stay away from these." But knowing what *may* happen at least gives you the heads-up on what *could* take place should you decide to leave. Ask the questions, check the fine print, and at least know the facts so there are no surprises later on.

#5: Licenses. As the old saying goes, "To a carpenter with only a hammer, everything looks like a nail." This is important. Ask your advisor what licenses he or she holds. By "licenses" I refer to the two main types, insurance and securities.

Insurance: An insurance-licensed person can sell you only insurance products such as fixed or immediate annuities or life insurance products (this does not include variable life insurance that it has within it subaccounts, which are similar to mutual funds).

Securities: A securities-licensed person can enable you to invest in stocks, bonds, mutual funds, exchange-traded funds (ETFs), and many other things. But having a securities license is only the beginning, because there are two main types of securities licenses you should be aware of, and the differences are substantial:

- Series 7 licensed advisors can recommend *individual* securities such as stocks or bonds, and can offer mutual funds as well.
- Series 6 licensed individuals can recommend *only* mutual fund investments. They *cannot* offer individual securities such as a stock or bond. To simplify, a Series 6 licensed person can sell only investments that are managed by someone else, such as a mutual fund manager that does the actual buying and selling of the individual securities.

Some people believe the advisor they are dealing with should ideally have *both* a Series 7 license *and* an insurance license. Having *both* means the advisor can recommend a wide variety of different investment products, and not necessarily be a "carpenter with only a hammer."

I believe, however, there is absolutely *nothing* wrong with an advisor who has only one type of license. Some of the very best advisors I've met have only one type of license (i.e., insurance only or securities only). What makes many of these single-licensed individuals spectacular is that not only have they mastered their specialized craft and understand it thoroughly, but also they have also mastered it to the extent that they fully realize "one size does *not* fit all." When the shoe *doesn't* fit, the best advisors out there are open and perfectly willing to refer the job to someone else with the proper license that can better solve the investor's needs.

The danger typically comes in when someone with only one license tries forcing everyone into an investment simply because it's the only one they can sell. If you sense such a thing, it's probably best you get a second opinion before making the investment.

#6: Actual Fees. We've covered the basics of this in other sections of the book, but it's such an important and critical point that I feel compelled to address it again. Especially when it comes to investments such as variable annuities and mutual funds, you should be aware of *all* the fees these products contain.

When investing in a mutual fund, for example, don't just look at something such as a Morningstar report. A Morningstar report, as good as it is, typically does not report *all* the fees. When it comes to mutual funds, the best source to reveal fees is Lipper's PersonalFund (www.personalfund.com). Here, at PersonalFund, you can either search for your fund's ticker symbol, or simply enter the symbol, fill out a few details, and view a simple report that produces the results. In addition, PersonalFund usually recommends a few similar funds that have lower fees.

After a few free reports, PersonalFund requires a small monthly fee. But if you are investing in managed mutual funds, would paying a few dollars for quality research be worth the expense? If you find out from PersonalFund's research that your fees are much higher than you had believed, those few dollars spent on a good research tool will no doubt wind up saving you lots of money, especially in the long run.

And finally, I can't help but mention: You should well know by now that my simple solution to spending *any* money on looking up managed mutual fund fees is to stick with index investing only. But needless to say, many people will continue investing in managed mutual funds I'm sure for many years to come.

This point brings up something else of great importance:

#7: Read the Fine Print. When investing in a product that is sold by prospectus or other memorandum, take time to read or in the very least, browse through it. Investments such as limited partnerships, private offerings, mutual funds, annuities and a long list of other investments should always be well researched before investing.

Granted, reading through something such as a prospectus will very likely be the most boring thing you have ever done in your entire life, but the time taken to read or at least browse through the small print is usually well worth the effort. For better or worse, reading the fine print can either give you peace of mind so you don't second-guess your investments or, potentially, convince you to get rid of your advisor for not pointing out the important details.

#8: "It Won't Cost You Anything to Buy This Fund." If you ever hear that it won't cost you anything to buy a fund, be sure to ask the *next* important question, such as, "That's great, but *once I'm in it,* how much will it cost me?"

Mutual funds have several possible fee structures. Here are a few of the most common:

- *No-load funds.* The fund may truly be a no-load fund, meaning you are not paying any sales commissions to get into or out of it. This is arguably the best of all types of funds, given you can typically get in or out at any time without a sales charge.
- *"A" share funds.* An "A" share means you pay an up-front sales commission to enter the fund. Once the sales commission is paid, you are fully invested and there is typically no sales charge to leave the fund.
- *"B" share funds.* A "B" share means you don't pay any sales commission when first investing in the fund, but if you sell out of the fund before a certain number of years (typically five or six years), then you will be charged a back-end fee. The only exception to this rule is that when leaving the fund, you can usually transfer your money to another fund *within the same fund family* without incurring any sales charges.
- *"C" share funds.* A "C" share means you don't pay any sales commission when first investing in the fund. Furthermore, as long as you remain in the fund for a year, you won't get charged a back-end fee as well.

At first glance, after the ideal no-load fund structure, a "C" share *might* seem like the best bet. Or maybe a "B" share? But is it? Maybe, maybe not. One must consider a few things including, but certainly not limited to, the length of time you plan on investing in the fund, and the *internal fees* of the fund. While at first glance a "C" share might seem like the best choice, depending on how long you are planning to stay invested in the fund needs to be factored in. Why? Well, the internal fees of the "C" share might be higher than the "A" share you stayed away from because you didn't want to pay an up-front commission. But, if you were invested in the "C" share fund for a long period of time, you could have likely saved yourself signifi-cant *overall* fees by investing in the "A" fund instead.

A bit confusing? Most certainly. I completely understand and so do the regulators. If you want to evaluate which class of share would be the least costly based on your specific situation, be sure to check out the NASD's web site at www.nasd.com, the "Expense Analyzers" section, which provides some helpful tools for determining which class of mutual fund shares would be most efficient for you.

Still confused? Don't be. I'll make it really simple for you (and here I go again): With rare exceptions, I would stay away from any fund that has an "A," "B," or "C" class. The best bet, by far, is to stick with index mutual funds or index exchange-traded funds for reasons I spent enough time on already.

#9: Double Dippers. Recently, a husband and wife asked me to do an analysis of their investments. The reports that came back on their mutual funds and other products revealed some of the highest fees I've ever seen: The total costs of ownership on some of the man-aged mutual funds they were invested in were as high as a whopping 6 percent. As I recall, the lowest-cost fund they were in was some-where around 2 percent. Overall, their entire portfolio was one of the worst fee-infested accounts I have ever come across.

If that wasn't bad enough, the firm that was managing their account was charging them just under 2 percent *in addition* to the internal fees on their investments. The excessive management fees plus the internal fees on their account set an all-time record—the highest-fee portfolio I have ever seen. And to top it all off, it didn't seem as if there had been *any* changes to the portfolio over the past few years.

So, the firm was managing a portfolio that wasn't being managed at all, yet the clients were drowning in an account infested with very high fees. This is something that should obviously be quite alarming: If you're paying an advisor an excessive management fee to man-age your managed mutual funds, then that's likely a few too many management fees for anyone's liking and probably a strong sign the advisor is not working in your best interest.

#10: Independent or Dependent? Often, but certainly not always, advisors at many firms cannot offer *any* investment product, even though they are licensed to do so. Using my Bloomingdale's investment department store analogy, there may be a fifth floor of additional investment products, but for some advisors, the floor is closed off to them. The firm they work for simply won't allow them to show you the products up there, and this can leave you short.

As a result, I would recommend that, as much as you possibly can, if you consider hiring an advisor to help you out, hire one who is truly *independent.* An independent advisor typically has a large product mix to offer clients. The list of products is often more extensive than those advisors who are dependent on the brokerages they are at. Some of the most obvious opportunities I've seen people miss out on were most likely due to working with an advisor who either overlooked the obvious or, more commonly, simply could not offer the product that would have best solved the client's problem.

I quoted him before, and here I'll quote his work again. In his fantastic book *Take On the Street,* former chairman of the Securities and Exchange Commission Arthur Levitt said it perfectly when saying that in these cases, it's typically "good people caught up in a bad system." And when it comes to dependent advisors who can recommend only things such as mutual funds and little else, his statement could not be more accurate.

And a last one worth mentioning: my advisor, my best friend. My last thought certainly cannot be considered something your advisor may *not* want you to know, but it falls within a "fair warning" category. Just recently, a woman emailed me about a problem she had: Her investments weren't doing well, and she wanted a second opinion about her portfolio. Clearly, the returns weren't very good at all. In fact, even during the past few years when the market has been quite favorable, her advisor managed to lose her money due to a few bad stock picks.

While the problem was obvious, the solution wasn't, because of one key thing: The woman's financial advisor was also her brother-in-law. As a result, although she knew working with someone else would be better for her, she couldn't muster up the courage to move her accounts.

In another instance, years ago, I remember meeting someone who was pretty upset with his advisor not because the advisor *lost* money, but because the investor felt the returns weren't high enough. And similar to the woman above, this investor was having a tough time moving the account because the advisor was a close personal friend.

For the betterment of *both* sides of the relationship, I would strongly recommend *not* working with an advisor who is either a close friend or, especially, someone within the family tree. Having to leave such an advisor is obviously more difficult when there are deep personal relationships involved, and this certainly goes for other professions as well. After all, when it comes down to family and close personal friends, why potentially jeopardize the valuable relationships we all have?

Investment Clubs

There's an old adage that "no one takes better care of you than yourself." When it comes to the world of investing, another option is to simply do it all yourself.

During turbulent markets, however, such a task can sometimes be a pretty scary thing. A peaceful, restful night on a fluffy pillow can quickly take a turn for the worse when awakened by such thoughts as "Will I ever have enough to retire?" Staring at the ceiling, don't bother reaching for the Ambien or that warm glass of milk. The best medicine to calm such thoughts is perhaps to gather up a few friends and start a good old-fashioned investment club.

There are some who falsely believe an investment club is nothing but an excuse to get together and share recipes or a recap of last week's blind date. Quite the contrary. Forget leading economists, Wall Street analysts, hedge fund managers, and day traders. Some of the best investment ideas I have ever come across are from some of the investment club meetings I've been lucky enough to attend.

After all, it was the Irvine-Pacific Group that not only gave me some of the best chocolate chip cookies my belly has ever had, but, more important, some great tips on little-known food product companies. And it was the Harbor Club that turned me on to obscure energy trusts, and I'll never forget a fantastic club in Long Beach, California, that not only told me some steamy secrets about a local celebrity, but more important, a stock tip on a tiny company that turned into a blockbuster success.

Investment clubs have been around since the early 1900s, and it's estimated there are well over 100 new ones registered every month. One of the most famous investment clubs was the Beardstown Ladies of Illinois, who not only were successful investors, but they also wrote a best-selling book that sold nearly one million copies.

So, what exactly is an investment club? According to the SEC, an investment club is defined as "a group of people who pool their money to make investments. The group then decides to buy and sell shares based on the majority vote of its entire membership."

According to me, an investment club could be an exciting, enriching experience where great investment ideas often evolve. Think of an investment club as your very own private mutual fund whereby members of the fund invest money and vote on which stocks to buy. Most clubs have roughly 12 to 20 members who typically meet anywhere between once a month and once a year.

Starting an investment club is a snap. I would strongly recommend visiting the National Association of Investors Corporation (NAIC) web site at www.betterinvesting.org. It'll tell you everything you need to know about starting your own club, registering, and getting it up and running. Once the club is formed, one of the first things the crew must decide upon is how much everyone will invest and in what intervals: Single deposit? Monthly? Annually?

Next up is the investment style. Are you looking to give The Donald a run for his money, or are you committed to investing conservatively for the long haul? Going after 7 percent or 50 percent rates of return? All this and more must obviously be decided upon.

Once these decisions are made, it's time to lay down those chips and start picking some winners. While there are hundreds of different investment styles to choose from, the most successful investment clubs I've been around typically follow the most basic, prudent investment philosophies previously discussed in this book.

So, do you have a couple of friends interested in investing? Do you crave social interaction, sharing investment ideas, a good cup of coffee, and maybe a few good desserts?

By following the suggestions here, it won't be long before you and your friends are well on your way to investment success. So, watch out, Warren Buffett. I wish you and your fellow investors the very best of success, and hey, if you come across any good stock tips out there (or some fantastic chocolate chip cookies), be sure to send a couple of them my way.

CHAPTER 10

Conclusion

As a movie ends and the house lights come up, most people don't stick around for the final credits. On a number of occasions, however, some of us feel compelled to stay for humorous outtakes or a few interesting anecdotes.

With this movie about to end, I'll spare the outtakes (of which there are many) and hope you'll stick around to review a brief summary of everything we just covered. Without a doubt, we've explored many concepts, and I'm sure a quick recap of everything we discussed will help keep things fresh in your mind for the journey ahead.

With that, here are high-level highlights I believe you should take away from this book. Just like the engine powering your car, I believe *all* points are important, so be sure not to construe the first as being the most important. As the old saying goes, "A chain is only as strong as its weakest link." And when it comes to providing your financial life with a powerful engine destined for success, that old adage couldn't be any closer to the truth.

Diversification is the golden key of sustained and consistent investment success. Diversifying your money across the fundamental asset classes recognizes that with very rare exceptions, few people, if any, can accurately predict what's going to be the next hot area of the market at any given time: As the statistics prove, you have as much chance of making money with Leonard the Monkey or a handful of randomly thrown darts at the *Wall Street Journal* as you do with the individual stock pickers trying to time the market for highly attractive rates of return.

Recognizing this, the most efficient way to invest is to adapt a small handful of "children" for the long haul that represent the fundamental sectors of the market: While at any given time you might *like* some of your children more than others, you should *love them all the same* because over time, you know they will all go through various cycles of paying off quite well.

Diversification recognizes that it should *not* be complicated for it to be effective. In fact, a well-diversified investment portfolio incorporating the concepts in this book realizes that the less effort you put in, the more consistent and rewarding the results will typically be.

Minimize or eliminate the use of often costly and tax-inefficient managed mutual funds. Using stock indexes to represent each market sector of a diversified portfolio provides not only the best chances for success, but by far the lowest-cost and most tax-efficient means of investing.

If you are going to be consistently adding money into your diversified portfolio on a frequent basis, use index *mutual* funds simply because they seldom charge fees for additional investments.

For maximum control of your investments, if you are going to be occasionally adding money into your diversified portfolio, consider using index *exchange-traded* funds (ETFs) instead. ETFs allow an investor to sell the position at any time during the day. They also provide the ability to establish stop-losses, and for maximum protection, you can insure your positions by likely purchasing put options on the ETFs as well. Doing so will obligate someone to purchase your index at a future date for a price higher than it is then currently trading at.

Rebalancing a diversified portfolio once a year provides the greatest opportunity to buy low and sell high. For rebalancing to be successful, one needs to make it a *mechanical* process while keeping in mind the World's Most Difficult Investment Formula: Investing − Emotion = Success.

To satisfy a desire to try to time the market by picking individual stocks or other investments that don't belong in our diversified buy-and-hold portfolio, we should strongly consider carving out a sector of the portfolio known as the "flavors of the day." It is within this sector only that we allow the market timer in us to reside and satisfy the occasional desire to invest in anything we want at any given time.

The Most Dangerous Game takes place when someone near or in retirement relies on the speculative, possible appreciation of stocks to provide them with the income they need.

Incorporating investments into our diversified portfolio that offer reliable returns helps us avoid playing the Most Dangerous Game. These investments do not rely on the possible appreciation of stocks to provide one with the income they need. Investments that offer reliable returns for income include, but are not limited to:

- *Bonds.* For preservation of principal *and* diversification, consider bond ladders as an alternative to popular bond mutual funds: Individual bonds in a ladder generally offer a stable rate of return *and* a maturity date that gives investors the best possible chance of preserving their money. Conversely, a bond mutual fund might have a reliable rate of return, but they offer *no* maturity date.

- *Preferred stocks.* Stick with the short-term maturities, and stay away from the long-term ones. Anything other than this means you are playing the "heads I win, tails you lose" game of preferred stocks.

- *Dividend stocks.* Diversification through exchange traded-funds and/or closed-end funds that pay dividends often provides good opportunity for consistent and reliable income with possibilities for growth as well. Remember: The amount of dividends one receives is not based on the *value* of the stock, but rather on the *quantity* of stock one owns.

- *Annuities.* For investors seeking guarantees that losing money in the markets will not result in a loss of income, investing a portion of the diversified portfolio into a variable annuity with a living benefit is the only investment product that provides such a unique guarantee.

- *Certificates of deposit.* Those looking for higher rates of return on their CDs might consider structured products that include something commonly referred to as growth CDs. These CDs typically offer a minimum rate of return with the potential to earn more interest as determined by the performance of various stock market indexes.

- *Real estate investment trusts.* For those interested in real estate investments without having to purchase and manage the properties themselves, consider investing in publicly traded or privately held REITs. Most REITs provide dividends that can be used for income *and* the possibility for capital appreciation.

Treat permanent life insurance as an investment that should be considered as just another sector within a diversified buy-and-hold investment portfolio. As opposed to term life insurance that *costs* money, an investment in permanent life provides highly unique options and benefits no other sector within a diversified portfolio offers, such as:

- The critical ingredient to a Private Pension that could better than double our income at retirement and guarantee it never runs out for the rest of our life.
- The opportunity to generate tax-free income at retirement.
- The opportunity to "spend all our money" and still "leave it all behind."
- Potential long-term care benefits.
- An opportunity to potentially get our heirs or ourselves a "free" million dollars.
- Instant wealth creation through a tax-free death benefit for heirs.
- Extra money for our heirs to pay possible estate and income taxes due upon our demise.
- . . . And if later in life we determine we no longer have any need to keep the policy, investing in permanent life provides us with a potential exit strategy that could give us the opportunity to sell the policy for a profit into life insurance's secondary market.

IRAs play a highly significant role in any investment strategy due to the magic of compounding interest and tax deductions. Several important points covered include:

- How to use your IRA to purchase real estate: the self-directed IRA.
- When a bear market could be a good thing: Loss of value due to a bad market could be an opportune time to consider converting a taxable IRA to a tax-free Roth IRA.
- How to potentially sell company stock contributed to your 401(k) at a significantly lower tax rate: the little-known IRS feature known as net unrealized appreciation (NUA).
- How to leave the value of your IRA tax free to heirs: Convert the IRA to a Roth IRA or use required minimum distributions as an investment into a permanent life insurance policy that provides a tax-free death benefit to pay taxes owed upon your demise.

Tax efficiency is a critical ingredient of investing success. Paying close attention to an investment's tax ramifications could make something such as a 40 percent rate of return *greater* than one that delivers a 50 percent rate of return.

If you are looking for a risk-free way to *increase* your rate of return, one of the first places you should look to achieve this is a tax return. Quite simply, the less taxes you pay, the more you keep. Investing in managed mutual funds outside an IRA? You could be a perfect candidate to reduce your taxes by investing in stock market indexes instead.

Don't blow it in the bottom of the ninth. Incorporating estate planning documents such as a living trust into your overall financial plan will help ensure heirs receive assets quickly, efficiently, and with the least tax obligation.

Remember to properly fund your trust, and if you want the assurance that your money will remain in your family, consider protecting the bloodline through a living trust created by an estate-planning attorney.

In addition, as we unfortunately live in a highly litigious society, one might also want to consider various measures that could provide protection of our assets against lawsuits.

Lastly, if working with a financial advisor, be sure you understand important factors such as:

- What licenses does the advisor currently hold?
- Is the advisor truly independent?
- How is the advisor getting paid?
- Can the advisor recommend *any* investment product or only a few?

With the aforementioned concepts in mind, I wish you and your family the very best of luck and success during your journey ahead. May your money, health, and happiness end up with a few Oscars of their own.

For more information, visit www.alanhaft.com.

Bibliography

Anand, Shefali. "Strong Markets Had Few Losers." *Wall Street Journal,* December 29, 2006.

Bach, David. *The Automatic Millionaire.* New York: Broadway Books, 2003.

Baer, Gregory, and Gary Gensler. *The Great Mutual Fund Trap.* Reprint ed. New York: Broadway Books, 2004.

Clements, Jonathan. "Getting Actively Passive." *Wall Street Journal,* January 12, 2005.

Clements, Jonathan. "Investors Cling to Managed Funds Despite Performance of Indexing." *Wall Street Journal,* July 29, 2001.

Clements, Jonathan. "Only Fools Fall in . . . Managed Funds." *Wall Street Journal,* September 15, 2002.

Duhigg, Charles. "Late in Life, Finding a Bonanza in Life Insurance." *New York Times,* December 17, 2006.

Ellis, Charles D. *Winning the Loser's Game.* New York: McGraw-Hill, 2002.

Fabrikant, Geraldine. "Playing Hunches at Harvard." *New York Times,* March 15, 2007.

Farrell, Paul B. "'Lazy Portfolios' Win Again, Beat S&P 500!" *MarketWatch,* January 16, 2007.

Friedman, Thomas. *The World Is Flat.* New York: Farrar, Straus & Giroux, 2005.

Graham, Benjamin. *The Intelligent Investor.* Rev. ed. updated with commentary by Jason Zweig. New York: HarperCollins, 2003.

Kazanjian, Kirk. *Wizards of Wall Street.* New York: Aspen Publishers, 2000.

Levitt, Arthur, Jr. *Take On the Street.* New York: Pantheon, 2002.

Malkiel, Burton G. *A Random Walk Down Wall Street.* 9th ed. New York: W. W. Norton, 2007.

Milevsky, Moshe A. "Confessions of a VA Critic." *Research,* January 1, 2007.

Plevin, Liam, and Ian McDonald. "A Lively Market in Death Bonds." *Wall Street Journal,* February 21, 2007.

Schwed, Fred. *Where Are the Customers' Yachts?* New ed. Hoboken, NJ: John Wiley & Sons, 2006.

Town, Phil. *Rule #1.* New York: Crown, 2006.

"Investing with a Safety Net." Getting Going, *Wall Street Journal,* April 18, 2007.

Getting Going, *Wall Street Journal,* March 18, 2007.

Internet Resources

Barclays' iShares—www.ishares.com

Lipper's PersonalFund—www.personalfund.com

Morningstar—www.morningstar.com

National Association of Investors Corporation (NAIC)—www.betterinvesting.org

National Association of Securities Dealers (NASD)—www.nasd.com

PowerShares—www.powershares.com

ProFunds—www.profunds.com

StreetTracks—www.ssgafunds.com

T. Rowe Price retirement calculators—www.troweprice.com

Vanguard—www.vanguard.com

WisdomTree—www.wisdomtree.com

Yahoo! Finance—http://finance.yahoo.com

Index

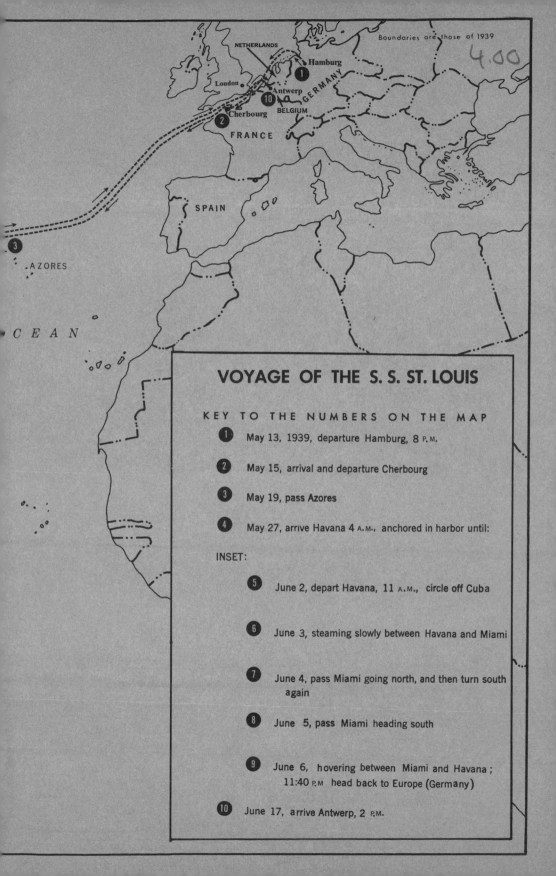

Boundaries are those of 1939

4.00

NETHERLANDS
Hamburg ①
London
Antwerp
② Cherbourg ⑩ BELGIUM
GERMANY
FRANCE
③
AZORES
SPAIN
CEAN

VOYAGE OF THE S. S. ST. LOUIS

KEY TO THE NUMBERS ON THE MAP

① May 13, 1939, departure Hamburg, 8 P.M.

② May 15, arrival and departure Cherbourg

③ May 19, pass Azores

④ May 27, arrive Havana 4 A.M., anchored in harbor until:

INSET:

⑤ June 2, depart Havana, 11 A.M., circle off Cuba

⑥ June 3, steaming slowly between Havana and Miami

⑦ June 4, pass Miami going north, and then turn south again

⑧ June 5, pass Miami heading south

⑨ June 6, hovering between Miami and Havana; 11:40 P.M head back to Europe (Germany)

⑩ June 17, arrive Antwerp, 2 P.M.